"Wayne Grudem continues to exhibit faithfulness to the biblical revelation and courage in the light of near universal opposition, as exhibited most recently in this superb volume. Sailing under the flag of feminism will take the church directly important book to read on the subject the
—PAIGE PATTERSON
President, Southwestern Bapti
Fort Worth, Texas

D1121292

"The entire Body of Christ owes an enormous debt of gratitude to Wayne Grudem for his courage in taking on what has become a Goliath within the camp of modern-day evangelicalism, and for his noncombative, gracious spirit in doing so. Those who love the truth will find here an invaluable resource in a user-friendly format that is both scholarly and accessible."
—NANCY LEIGH DEMOSS
Author, radio host, *Revive Our Hearts*

"'Wherever the battle rages, there the loyalty of the soldier is proved.' In keeping with Luther's observation, Wayne Grudem takes a vital stand and encourages us to join him. He tackles the issue firmly and fairly and with the clarity we have come to expect from his scholarly pen."
—ALISTAIR BEGG
Senior Pastor, Parkside Church, Chagrin Falls, Ohio

"The fundamental issue of biblical authority is at stake in the debate between complementarianism and egalitarianism—because if you can get egalitarianism from the Bible, you can get anything from the Bible. The weight of Grudem's cumulative argument is considerable and cannot be easily dismissed. Egalitarianism is indeed becoming a new path to defection from biblical orthodoxy."
—J. LIGON DUNCAN III
Senior Minister, First Presbyterian Church, Jackson, Mississippi
Adjunct Professor, Reformed Theological Seminary

"The egalitarian ideology is one of the most significant theological challenges in our time. Wayne Grudem presents a careful and systematic study of the cause and ramifications of this shift. In his persistent and gentle tone, Grudem challenges egalitarian thinking. While authors and scholars sympathetic to egalitarianism may be loath to consider they may in fact be wrong, Grudem pleads with his readers to reconsider their positions."
—MICHAEL EASLEY
President, Moody Bible Institute

"However fervently we hope that the answer to this book's question is a resounding no, Grudem furnishes evidence that cannot be lightly dismissed. His chapters and charges carry varying weights. But they all flow out of solid scholarship, love for the church, and zeal for the truth. All who welcome the Bible's teaching should welcome the insights of this concise and valuable study."

— ROBERT W. YARBROUGH
Editor, *Trinity Journal*
Associate Professor of New Testament,
New Testament Department Chair,
Trinity Evangelical Divinity School

"This new book is one of the most urgently needed resources for evangelical Christianity, and it represents one of the most insightful and courageous theological works of our time."

— R. ALBERT MOHLER, JR.
albertmohler.com

EVANGELICAL
FEMINISM

☦

A NEW PATH **TO** LIBERALISM?

WAYNE GRUDEM

CROSSWAY BOOKS

A PUBLISHING MINISTRY OF
GOOD NEWS PUBLISHERS
WHEATON, ILLINOIS

Evangelical Feminism: A New Path to Liberalism?

Copyright © 2006 by Wayne Grudem

Published by Crossway Books
    a publishing ministry of Good News Publishers
    1300 Crescent Street
    Wheaton, Illinois 60187

Cover design: Josh Dennis

First printing 2006

Printed in the United States of America

Library of Congress Cataloging-in-Publication Data
Grudem, Wayne A.
   Evangelical feminism : a new path to liberalism? / Wayne Grudem.
     p. cm.
   Includes bibliographical references and index.
   ISBN 13: 978-1-58134-734-0 (tpb)
   ISBN 10: 1-58134-734-0
   1. Bible and feminism. 2. Evangelicalism. I. Title.
BS680.W7G75   2006
270.8'2082—dc22   2006008159

CH		16	15	14	13	12	11	10	09	08	07
15	14	13	12	11	10	9	8	7	6	5	4	3	2

Dedicated to my
"Prayer Partners,"
with much appreciation

I testify to you this day that I am innocent of the blood of all of you, for I did not shrink from declaring to you the whole counsel of God.

ACTS 20:26-27

. . . warning everyone and teaching everyone with all wisdom, that we may present everyone mature in Christ. For this I toil, struggling with all his energy that he powerfully works within me.

COLOSSIANS 1:28-29

And the Lord's servant must not be quarrelsome but kind to everyone, able to teach, patiently enduring evil, correcting his opponents with gentleness.

2 TIMOTHY 2:24-25

CONTENTS

PREFACE

This is not a book that addresses all the questions about men's and women's roles in the home and the church today. I have already edited one such book (of 566 pages), and more recently I have written another one (of 856 pages).[1]

Nor is this a book that gives detailed, practical answers about how churches should teach on men's and women's roles in marriage and the church. I have also written extensively on that topic in my 2004 book *Evangelical Feminism and Biblical Truth*.

Nor do I attempt to explain in this book my own position on men's and women's roles in any detail, for I have already done that in *Evangelical Feminism and Biblical Truth*.[2]

Nor do I explain in this book the areas in which I think the evangelical feminist movement has brought some helpful corrections to evangelical churches and families, so that Christians today have a far greater recognition of the need for husbands to respect and honor their wives, and of the need for churches to encourage more opportunities for widespread ministries by women than they have done in the past. These areas are also covered in those earlier books.

This book is rather an expression of deep concern about a widespread undermining of the authority of Scripture in the arguments that are frequently used to support evangelical feminism. And it is also

---

[1] See John Piper and Wayne Grudem, eds., *Recovering Biblical Manhood and Womanhood: A Response to Evangelical Feminism* (Wheaton, Ill.: Crossway, 1991); and Wayne Grudem, *Evangelical Feminism and Biblical Truth: An Analysis of More Than 100 Disputed Questions* (Sisters, Ore.: Multnomah, 2004). The 1991 book was a collection of twenty-six chapters by twenty-two different authors, and it has been widely used as the standard defense of a "complementarian" position for the last fifteen years. In the 2004 book I sought to produce an exhaustive resource on all questions and topics that have been raised by evangelical authors in this controversial area in the last thirty years, and that book was the culmination of my own involvement in this controversy at the academic level for over twenty-five years.

In addition, I have also edited two other collections of significant essays on this question: see Wayne Grudem, ed., *Biblical Foundations for Manhood and Womanhood* (Wheaton, Ill.: Crossway, 2002); and Wayne Grudem and Dennis Rainey, eds., *Pastoral Leadership for Manhood and Womanhood* (Wheaton, Ill.: Crossway, 2002).

[2] I hold that men and women have equal value and importance to God and somewhat different roles in marriage and in the church, but a detailed explanation of this is found in *Evangelical Feminism and Biblical Truth* (see note 1, above).

Additional resources supporting the "complementarian" position that I hold can be found at the website of the Council on Biblical Manhood and Womanhood: www.cbmw.org.

a way of posing a question: can a movement that espouses this many ways of undermining the authority of Scripture possibly be right? If God had wanted to teach us an egalitarian position, would he have made it so hard to find in Scripture that it would require this many incorrect methods to discover and defend it?

The argument of this book first found expression in a brief chapter in *Evangelical Feminism and Biblical Truth* (500-517). Now in this present book I have added much additional material, including significant interaction with many of the essays in the recent evangelical feminist book *Discovering Biblical Equality*.[3] I have also documented several new developments in denominations and other organizations in which my argument of a "slippery slope" from evangelical feminism to liberalism has received further confirmation. Once an evangelical feminist position is adopted, the development only goes in one direction, again and again.

I wish to thank Phoenix Seminary students Ben Burdick and Chris Davis for research and editing help at various places in this book, and also Chris Cowan and Rob Lister, students at The Southern Baptist Theological Seminary in Louisville, Kentucky, for their earlier work in helping to adapt significant portions of material in *Evangelical Feminism and Biblical Truth* to the structure I used for the argument of this book. I am also grateful to my friends Ron Dickison and Trent Poling, who continue to cheerfully solve my computer problems, and to Sovereign Grace Ministries, for a grant that has provided very useful office equipment and research help.

I also wish to thank my wife, Margaret, for her constant support and encouragement as I worked to finish this manuscript.

I have dedicated this book to my "Prayer Partners," an unnamed group of friends who have quietly and regularly prayed for me for nearly ten years now, and whose specific prayers God has answered many, many times. I am thankful to God for all of you.

—Wayne Grudem
Scottsdale, Arizona
June 23, 2006

---

[3] Ronald W. Pierce and Rebecca Merrill Groothuis, eds., *Discovering Biblical Equality* (Downers Grove, Ill.: InterVarsity Press: 2004). I have also added new material interacting with the essays in *Discovering Biblical Equality* to a forthcoming book, *Countering the Claims of Evangelical Feminism* (to be published by Multnomah in October 2006). That book is a condensed version of my book *Evangelical Feminism and Biblical Truth*, and it gives an overview of the key arguments in a form suitable for church study groups, college classes, or individuals who want a shorter summary of the entire manhood-womanhood controversy.

PART I
SOME PATHS TO LIBERALISM
IN RECENT HISTORY

1

INTRODUCTION

I am concerned that evangelical feminism (also called "egalitarianism") has become a new path by which evangelicals are being drawn into theological liberalism.[1]

When I use the phrase "theological liberalism" I mean a system of thinking that denies the complete truthfulness of the Bible as the Word of God and denies the unique and absolute authority of the Bible in our lives. When I speak of "evangelical feminism" I mean a movement that claims there are no unique leadership roles for men in marriage or in the church. According to evangelical feminism, there is no leadership role in marriage that belongs to the husband simply because he is the husband, but leadership is to be shared between husband and wife according to their gifts and desires. And there are no leadership roles in the church reserved for men, but women as well as men can be pastors and elders and hold any office in the church.

In the following pages, I attempt to show several things:

(1) that liberal Protestant denominations were the pioneers of evangelical feminism, and that evangelical feminists today have adopted many of the arguments earlier used by theological liberals to advocate the ordination of women and to reject male headship in marriage

---

[1] This book is significantly adapted and extended from my article "Is Evangelical Feminism the New Path to Liberalism? Some Disturbing Warning Signs," *Journal for Biblical Manhood and Womanhood* 9/1 (Spring 2004), 35-84. That article was itself an adapted excerpt from my book *Evangelical Feminism and Biblical Truth: An Analysis of More Than 100 Disputed Questions* (Sisters, Ore.: Multnomah, 2004). All of the material in this book that overlaps with *Evangelical Feminism and Biblical Truth* is used by permission of Multnomah Publishers. (I wish to thank Chris Cowan and Rob Lister of The Southern Baptist Theological Seminary in Louisville, Kentucky, for doing much work to adapt the material in *Evangelical Feminism and Biblical Truth* for publication in the *Journal for Biblical Manhood and Womanhood* article.)

(2) that many prominent evangelical feminist writers today advocate positions that deny or undermine the authority of Scripture, and many other egalitarian leaders endorse their books and take no public stance against those who deny the authority of Scripture

(3) that recent trends now show that evangelical feminists are heading toward the denial of anything uniquely masculine, and some already endorse calling God "our Mother in heaven"

(4) that the history of others who have adopted these positions shows that the next step is the endorsement of the moral legitimacy of homosexuality

(5) that the common thread running through all of these trends is a rejection of the effective authority of Scripture in people's lives, and that this is the bedrock principle of theological liberalism

As I have taught for nearly thirty years in Christian colleges and seminaries, people have often asked me, "How do Christian colleges that were once Bible-believing, conservative colleges become so liberal, eventually denying the Bible in what is taught on campus?" Others have asked me, "How have so many denominations that used to be Bible-believing denominations now abandoned belief in the Bible? Why do liberal pastors now preach whatever is popular in the current culture rather than proclaiming the truth of the Bible as the Word of God?"

There are several different reasons, of course. But giving in to cultural pressure is often a significant factor. In every generation there are popular views in the culture that contradict what the Bible says, and it is so easy to compromise at one point or another.

In the early twentieth century it was so easy to give in to the liberal emphasis on "the Fatherhood of God and the brotherhood of man" and say that people are essentially good, and they don't need a Savior who died for their sins, and there is no such thing as hell. By following this reasoning many Christian churches followed the culture and drifted into liberalism.

Through much of the twentieth century it was easy to give in to the dominant "scientific" worldview and say that genuine miracles can't happen because they violate the "laws of nature," and so the virgin birth of Christ and other miracles in the Bible did not really happen, but that does not matter because the Bible still teaches us how to live a moral life. By following this reasoning many Christian churches followed the culture and drifted into liberalism.

Today, for scholars who work in the scientific community, it would be so easy to give in to the dominant view in the culture and say that all living things simply "evolved" from nonliving matter through random mutation and did not come about by direct design and creation by God. But those who adopt evolution as their explanation for the origin of life just follow the culture and drift into liberalism.

It can happen in any area. It happens when people grow weary of defending Jesus' words, "I am the way, and the truth, and the life. No one comes to the Father except through me" (John 14:6). Then it can be so easy to give in to the pressures of our tolerance-riddled culture and say that "all religions are different paths to the same God." And then the unique message of the gospel that alone tells us how our sins can be forgiven is lost, and Christian churches just follow the culture into liberalism.

I believe the same thing is happening today with evangelical feminism. There is tremendous pressure in present-day culture to deny male leadership in the home and the church. To prove that, just ask any pastor if he enjoys preaching and teaching about male headship in marriage and the church today. Almost nobody wants to tackle the subject! It is "too controversial," which means it will stir up objections and many people will be upset. It is not easy to stand against the culture. It is much easier to give in and say women can do whatever men can do in the church and in the home.

But what about all those Bible verses that talk about male leadership in home and church? Something has to be done with them, so for the last thirty years evangelical feminist scholars have devised thousands of pages of arguments attempting to show that those parts of the Bible don't apply to us today, or don't mean what people have always thought they mean, or aren't part of the Bible, or are contradicted by experience, or are simply wrong. And so, as I explain in the following pages, the authority of the Bible is undermined.

When that happens, little by little, step by step, colleges and churches and denominations start to slide toward liberalism. This is because the claims and arguments that evangelical feminists adopt about these specific passages in the Bible set in motion a process of interpreting Scripture that will be used increasingly to nullify the authority of Scripture in other areas as well. One by one, the teachings of Scripture that are unpopular in the culture are rejected, and, one issue at a time, the church begins to sound more and more like the secular world. This is the classic path to liberalism. And I believe that evangelical feminism is leading Christians down that path one step at a time today.

The late Francis Schaeffer, one of the wisest and most influential Christian thinkers of the twentieth century, warned of this exact trend just a few months before his death in 1984. In his book *The Great Evangelical Disaster* he included a section called "The Feminist Subversion," in which he wrote:

> There is one final area that I would mention where evangelicals have, with tragic results, accommodated to the world spirit of this age. This has to do with the whole area of marriage, family, sexual morality, feminism, homosexuality, and divorce. . . .
>
> The key to understanding extreme feminism centers around the idea of total equality, or more properly the idea of *equality without distinction.* . . . the world spirit in our day would have us aspire to autonomous absolute freedom in the area of male and female relationships—to throw off all form and boundaries in these relationships and especially those boundaries taught in the Scriptures. . . .
>
> Some evangelical leaders, in fact, have changed their views about inerrancy as a direct consequence of trying to come to terms with feminism. There is no other word for this than accommodation. It is a direct and deliberate bending of the Bible to conform to the world spirit of our age at the point where the modern spirit conflicts with what the Bible teaches.[2]

My argument in the following pages demonstrates that what Schaeffer predicted so clearly twenty-two years ago is increasingly coming true in evangelicalism today. It is a deeply troubling trend.

I am not the only one who has reached this conclusion. In the widely influential blog "Together for the Gospel," Mark Dever, senior pastor of Capitol Hill Baptist Church in Washington, D.C., recently wrote:

---

[2] Francis A. Schaeffer, *The Great Evangelical Disaster* (Westchester, Ill.: Crossway, 1984), 130, 134-135, 137, italics in original.

it is my best and most sober judgment that this position [egalitarianism] is effectively an undermining of—a breach in—the authority of Scripture. . . . it seems to me and others (many who are younger than myself) that *this issue of egalitarianism and complementarianism is increasingly acting as the watershed distinguishing those who will accommodate Scripture to culture, and those who will attempt to shape culture by Scripture.* You may disagree, but this is our honest concern before God. It is no lack of charity, nor honesty. It is no desire for power or tradition for tradition's sake. It is our sober conclusion from observing the last 50 years. . . .

Of course there are issues more central to the gospel than gender issues. However, *there may be no way the authority of Scripture is being undermined more quickly or more thoroughly in our day than through the hermeneutics of egalitarian readings of the Bible.* And when the authority of Scripture is undermined, the gospel will not long be acknowledged.[3]

On a more personal level, I want to say that I consider a number of the authors whom I name in this book to be my friends. And I consider a number of the executives at many of the colleges, seminaries, and publishing houses that I name in this book to be my friends as well. I want to say something to you at the outset.

I realize that many of you have not personally moved along the path toward liberalism that I describe in this book. You simply decided (for various reasons) that you thought the Bible does not prohibit women from being pastors or elders today, and you have changed nothing else in your theological system. You haven't moved to liberalism and you wonder why I wrote this book arguing that evangelical feminism leads to liberalism.

In fact, I agree with your strong desire to see women's gifts and ministries developed and encouraged in our churches, and I have written elsewhere about the many important ministries that I think should be open to both men and women.[4]

In addition, I realize that most of you do not think you are leading

---

[3] "Undermining Tolerance of Egalitarianism," posted May 31, 2006 by Mark Dever at http://blog.togetherforthegospel.org, accessed 6/23/06; supporting comments were later posted by Albert Mohler, Ligon Duncan, and C. J. Mahaney.
[4] See Wayne Grudem, *Evangelical Feminism and Biblical Truth*, 84-101.

churches and schools toward liberalism at all. After all, you personally love Jesus Christ and love the Bible and teach it effectively. How, you might think, could that contribute to liberalism? And furthermore, you know others who take the same approaches, and they haven't become liberal, have they?

In fact, I have a number of egalitarian friends who have not moved one inch toward liberalism in the rest of their doctrinal convictions, and who still strongly believe and defend the inerrancy of the Bible. I include among this number strong defenders of biblical inerrancy such as Stan Gundry (senior vice president and editor in chief of the Book Group at Zondervan Publishing Company); Jack Hayford (founding pastor of the Church on the Way, Van Nuys, California); Walter Kaiser (former president of Gordon-Conwell Theological Seminary); Roger Nicole (former professor at Gordon-Conwell Theological Seminary and at Reformed Theological Seminary–Orlando); and Grant Osborne (professor at Trinity Evangelical Divinity School in Deerfield, Illinois). These men are respected senior scholars and leaders in the evangelical world. If they can hold to an evangelical feminist or egalitarian position without moving toward liberalism themselves, then how can I argue in this book that evangelical feminism is a new path toward liberalism?

I do so *because of the nature of the arguments used by evangelical feminists,* arguments that I explain in some detail in the following pages. I realize that a person can adopt one of these arguments and not move any further than that single step down the path to liberalism for the rest of his life. Many of these leaders have done just that. But I think the reason they have not moved further toward liberalism is that they have not followed the implications of the kind of argument they are using and have not taken it into other areas of their convictions. However, others who follow them will do so. Francis Schaeffer warned years ago that the first generation of Christians who lead the church astray doctrinally change only one key point in their doctrinal position and change nothing else, so it can seem for a time that the change is not too harmful. But their followers and disciples in the next generation will take the logic of their arguments much further and will advocate much more extensive kinds of error. I think that is happening in a regular, predictable way in evangelical feminism, and I have sought to document that in this book.

Therefore, to all of my egalitarian friends, I ask you to consider carefully the arguments and the pattern of arguments that I discuss in this book. You may think you are doing nothing wrong, or you may think that if you adopt a doubtful or questionable interpretation here or there, it won't matter much. But I am asking you to stop and consider what is happening in the evangelical feminist movement as a whole, how the trend is to undermine the authority of Scripture again and again at this verse or in that phrase or this chapter or that context.

You may think your own role in this does not influence the larger debate, but, like the soldier in a battle line who thinks that his place is not that important, if you give way at one point you may provide a huge opening for an enemy to flood in and overrun large sections of the church.

It is easy to pick up a new article or book, skim through the argument, and think, "Well, I can't agree with his (or her) approach to this verse, or that argument, but at least the book is supporting what I know to be right: the inclusion of women in all aspects of ministry. Maybe this argument or that one is not acceptable, but I can approve the result just the same." And so, one after another, the egalitarian arguments that I list in this book accumulate and the Christian public accepts them.

But what if the assumptions made, and the interpretative principles used, actually do undermine the authority of Scripture time and again? *Does that make any difference to you?* If you allow arguments to stand that undermine Scripture again and again, just because you think the author "got the right answer for the wrong reason," isn't that eroding the foundation of your church for the future? If Scripture-eroding arguments go unchallenged in your circles, how can you protect your church or your organization in the future? While you personally may not change much else in your beliefs, your students and others who follow your leadership will take the principles you have used much further and will abandon much more than you expect.

Please consider what I say in these pages. I hope you will be persuaded, and will perhaps even change your mind on some of the arguments you have used, or even on the conclusions you have drawn. But even if at the end you are still convinced that an egalitarian position is correct, will you at least decide to challenge publicly some of the evident steps toward liberalism that other egalitarians have supported? With all of the steps toward liberalism that I detail in these pages, it surprises me to see how few egalitarian leaders publicly object to any of these arguments. I hope I can count on some of you to do so.

To other readers who are undecided on this question or who are already complementarians, I would say this: As you read this book, if you become increasingly troubled about the trends I describe, then I hope you will pray and speak up and serve in your own churches in such a way that any trends toward liberalism can be stopped, so that your church will remain faithful to God's Word for the next generation.

But I also want you to be careful not to overreact and start to become more "conservative" than the Bible! This would lead to a wrongful legalism that would restrict mature, godly, gifted women from rightful ministries, as has too often been done in the past. Such legalism can lead to a loss of God's blessing as well, and it can destroy churches as readily as liberalism (see Gal. 2:4-5; 5:1; Titus 1:10-11). I have explained elsewhere in some detail where I believe the Bible gives freedom and encouragement for women to minister in many different ways in churches today,[5] and I will not repeat that discussion here. Stated briefly, I believe that "some governing and teaching roles within the church are restricted to men,"[6] but apart from those specific governing and teaching roles all ministries are open to both men and women alike. We must obey every part of the Bible that applies to our situations today, but we also must be careful not to add to the rules of Scripture and place more restrictions on others than the Bible itself teaches (see Rom. 14:1-10; 1 Tim. 4:1-5; 2 Tim. 3:16-17; Ps. 119:1; Prov 30:5-6). It is possible to make a mistake in both directions.

"You shall not *add to* the word that I command you, nor *take from it,* that you may keep the commandments of the LORD your God that I command you" (Deut. 4:2).

---

[5] See Wayne Grudem, *Evangelical Feminism and Biblical Truth,* especially 84-100.
[6] *The Danvers Statement,* affirmation 6, from the Council on Biblical Manhood and Womanhood; see www.cbmw.org.

2

THE HISTORICAL CONNECTION BETWEEN LIBERALISM AND THE ENDORSEMENT OF WOMEN'S ORDINATION IN THE CHURCH

When we look at what happened in the last half of the twentieth century, quite a clear connection can be seen between theological liberalism and the endorsement of women's ordination. In an important sociological study published by Harvard University Press, Mark Chaves traces the history of women's ordination in various denominations in the United States.[1] From Chaves's study, we can observe a pattern among the mainstream Protestant denominations whose leadership is dominated by theological liberals (that is, by those who reject the idea that the entire Bible is the written Word of God and is truthful in all it affirms).[2] Chaves notes the dates when ordination of women was approved in each of these denominations:

Methodist Church	1956
Presbyterian Church (USA)	1956 (north), 1964 (south)
American Lutheran Church	1970

---

[1] See Mark Chaves, *Ordaining Women* (Cambridge, Mass.: Harvard University Press, 1997).
[2] A more precise statement of a clear dividing line between liberals and evangelicals is found in the statement of faith of the Evangelical Theological Society, which says, "The Bible alone, and the Bible in its entirety, is the Word of God written and is therefore inerrant in the autographs" (that is, in the original manuscripts) (available online at www.etsjets.org).

| Lutheran Church in America[3] | 1970 |
| Episcopal Church | 1976[4] |

Chaves notes an interesting example with the Southern Baptist Convention (SBC). In 1964 the SBC approved women's ordination (that is, a local congregation ordained a woman and this action was not overturned by the denomination itself). But in 1964 the denominational leadership and the control of the seminaries were in the hands of the more liberal "moderates" (the SBC term for those who did not affirm biblical inerrancy). However, in 1984, after conservatives recaptured control of the SBC, the denomination passed a resolution "that we encourage the service of women in all aspects of church life and work *other than pastoral functions and leadership roles entailing ordination.*"[5] This means that when the conservatives who held to biblical inerrancy recaptured the denomination, the denomination revoked its previous willingness to ordain women.[6]

Chaves lists dates for the approval of women's ordination for some other denominations that are not completely dominated by theological liberalism but that are broadly tolerant of liberalism and have seminary professors and denominational officials who have moved significantly in a liberal direction. (These categorizations of denominational doctrinal positions are not made by Chaves, who simply lists the denominations and the dates; they are my own assessment.) Consider the following denominations:

Mennonite Church	1973
Evangelical Covenant Church	1976
Reformed Church in America	1979

---

[3] The American Lutheran Church and the Lutheran Church in America are presently combined into a single denomination, the Evangelical Lutheran Church in America (ELCA).

[4] Chaves, *Ordaining Women*, 16-17. Chaves lists many other denominations, such as some Baptist and Pentecostal denominations, that were ordaining women much earlier and were not affected by theological liberalism. Many of these other groups placed a strong emphasis on leading and calling by the Holy Spirit (such as Pentecostal groups) or on the autonomy of the local congregation (such as many Baptist groups) and therefore they were not adopting women's ordination because of theological liberalism. My point here is that when liberalism was the dominant theological viewpoint in a denomination, from 1956 onward it became inevitable that the denomination would endorse women's ordination.

[5] Cited in Chaves, *Ordaining Women*, 35, italics added.

[6] A much stronger action than the resolution Chaves mentions was taken in June 2000, when the SBC added to "The Baptist Faith and Message" (its official statement of doctrine) the following sentence: "While both men and women are gifted for service in the church, the office of pastor is limited to men as qualified by Scripture" (added to article 6, "The Church").

Another example that occurred after Chaves finished his book was the Christian Reformed Church, which in 1995 approved the ordination of women.[7] Chaves does note, however, that the Christian Reformed Church "shifted its official position away from inerrancy only in 1972."[8]

Are there any types of denominations that are resistant to the ordination of women? Chaves indicates the following results of his study:

> Two groups of denominations are particularly resistant to women's ordination: denominations practicing sacramental ritual and *denominations endorsing biblical inerrancy.* . . . Biblically inerrant denominations are . . . resistant to formal gender equality.[9]

By "denominations practicing sacramental ritual" Chaves refers especially to Catholic, Eastern Orthodox, and Episcopalian denominations, who think of the priest as standing in the place of Christ at the Lord's Supper. Chaves thinks that explains why the Episcopal Church was rather slow in endorsing women's ordination in comparison to other denominations. But he notes that for "biblically inerrant denominations" the argument that the Bible prohibits the ordination of women is by far the most persuasive argument.[10]

I think that Chaves's observation that "denominations endorsing biblical inerrancy" are "particularly resistant to women's ordination" can be reinforced if we consider three influential evangelical denominations in the United States: the Lutheran Church–Missouri Synod (LCMS), the Presbyterian Church in America (PCA), and the Southern Baptist Convention (SBC). All three have the following characteristics in common:

(1) they have fought major battles with liberalism recently enough that such conflicts are still part of the personal memories of current leaders;

---

[7] See "CRC Reverses Decision . . . Again," *CBMW News,* August 1995, 5.

[8] Chaves, *Ordaining Women,* 86.

[9] Ibid., 84-85, italics added.

[10] Ibid., 89-91. Chaves strongly favors the ordination of women and goes on to argue that the Bible does not prohibit it.

(2) these leaders recognize that the liberal groups from which they are separate now aggressively promote women's ordination (the Evangelical Lutheran Church in America, the Presbyterian Church–USA, and the Cooperative Baptist Fellowship [CBF]);

(3) these leaders and their denominations are strongly opposed to women's ordination.

In the Southern Baptist Convention, conservatives who held to inerrancy regained control of the denomination over a ten- or fifteen-year period beginning in 1979.[11] The SBC in 2000 added a formal provision to its doctrinal statement that "The office of pastor is limited to men as qualified by Scripture" (article 6 of "The Baptist Faith and Message").

The Lutheran Church–Missouri Synod in 1974 dismissed the president of Concordia Seminary in St. Louis, a measure that soon led to the angry resignation of forty-five of the fifty faculty members of the seminary, thereby removing most of the influence of theological liberalism that denied the complete truthfulness of Scripture.[12]

Yet another example is the Presbyterian Church in America, which was formed when conservatives left the more liberal Southern Presbyterian Church in 1973.[13]

In each of these three denominations, people who currently hold positions of leadership remember their struggles with theological liberalism, and they remember that an egalitarian advocacy of women's ordination goes hand in hand with theological liberalism.

Another example of the connection between tendencies toward liberalism and the ordination of women is Fuller Theological Seminary in

---

[11] Conservatives regained control of the Southern Baptist Convention beginning with the election of Adrian Rogers as president of the denomination in 1979 (see Jerry Sutton, *The Baptist Reformation: The Conservative Resurgence in the Southern Baptist Convention* [Nashville: Broadman & Holman, 2000], 99).

[12] The Lutheran Church–Missouri Synod had been drifting toward a liberal view of Scripture for perhaps twenty or thirty years when conservatives within the denomination effectively regained control with the election of J. A. O. Preus as the denomination's president in 1969. The denominational convention in 1973 in New Orleans affirmed its clear adherence to biblical inerrancy, and with this victory the denominational leadership suspended the president of Concordia Seminary in St. Louis, John Tietjen, on January 20, 1974. In February 1974, forty-five of the fifty faculty members at Concordia Seminary left in protest, but new faculty members were appointed, and the seminary and the denomination after that remained in the control of conservatives who held to biblical inerrancy. (See Harold Lindsell, *The Bible in the Balance* [Grand Rapids, Mich.: Zondervan, 1979], 244-274, especially 259-270.)

[13] See Susan Lynn Peterson, *Timeline Charts of the Western Church* (Grand Rapids, Mich.: Zondervan, 1999), 248.

Pasadena, California. Though Fuller began as a conservative evangelical seminary, it removed the doctrine of biblical inerrancy from its statement of faith in 1971, and today there is significant influence from theological liberalism among its faculty. In addition, full-fledged advocacy of the ordination of women reigns on campus, and I doubt that Fuller would hire as a professor anyone holding another position (or if someone were hired, I doubt that he would be allowed to express his opposition to women's ordination publicly).

As long ago as 1987, the egalitarian viewpoint was so firmly entrenched at Fuller that even a responsible academic statement of a complementarian view was effectively silenced by a barrage of protests. In May 1987, I received the following letter from a New Testament professor who had been invited to teach a course at Fuller on the Pastoral Epistles:

> What reminded me to write this letter was the class on the Pastorals that I am teaching at Fuller. . . . Boy did I get in trouble. One lady walked out, incredibly irate. The Women's Concerns Committee sent a letter to all my students, claiming that I should never have been allowed to teach this and that they would try to censor any further teaching along traditional lines of interpretation. So much for academic freedom and inquiry. I wrote to the dean and will be interested to see how the actual administration will react. I find it incredibly interesting, and inconsistent, that they allow the teaching of universalism . . . but our view of the women's passage must be banned.[14]

Two months later I received a follow-up letter:

> For two and a half weeks I was slandered up and down campus. I was the major subject on the declaration board, etc. It was a real mess. . . . The vast majority of the letters were from students who were not in the class. . . . 2 1/2 weeks after the fact . . . Dean Meye finally called and we had dinner together. . . . He asked if I would be willing to retell the class what my actual intention was, and without groveling or backtracking, say that to whatever extent I was responsible for the

---

[14] Personal letter from William D. Mounce to Wayne Grudem, received May 14, 1987, quoted by permission.

misunderstanding, I apologize. . . . So I agreed and it went very well. . . . The next day Meye was deluged with letters and visits from my students who were very upset at the committee and his handling of the situation. . . . Meye never apologized, said that he or the school had behaved improperly, or that anything was mishandled except that I was allowed to teach what I thought. He accused me of such dastardly deeds as presenting my personal views with more force than the other views. . . . People need to be aware of what will happen at their schools if this situation is not dealt with properly.[15]

Endorsement of the ordination of women is not the final step in the process, however. If we look at the denominations that approved women's ordination from 1956–1976, we find that several of them, such as the United Methodist Church and the United Presbyterian Church (now called the Presbyterian Church–USA), have large contingents pressing for (a) the endorsement of homosexual conduct as morally valid and (b) the approval of homosexual ordination. In fact, the Episcopal Church on August 5, 2003, approved the appointment of an openly homosexual bishop.[16]

In more liberal denominations such as these, a predictable sequence has been seen (though so far only the Episcopal Church has followed the sequence to point 7):

1. abandoning biblical inerrancy
2. endorsing the ordination of women
3. abandoning the Bible's teaching on male headship in marriage
4. excluding clergy who are opposed to women's ordination
5. approving homosexual conduct as morally valid in some cases
6. approving homosexual ordination
7. ordaining homosexuals to high leadership positions in the denomination[17]

---

[15] Personal letter from William D. Mounce to Wayne Grudem, received July 23, 1987, quoted by permission.

[16] "Episcopal Church Elects First Openly Gay Bishop," www.foxnews.com, August 6, 2003.

[17] In the United Methodist Church, however, in April 2004, "a clergy jury in the [United Methodist Church's] Pacific Northwest regional unit voted to retain the ministerial credentials of Karen Dammann, a self-avowed lesbian who recently 'married' her partner. . . . Church members looking to their bishops for a decisive response in defense of church discipline didn't get one. In a wobbly statement, the 15-member executive committee of the UMC Council of Bishops in effect said that the bishops are committed to upholding the church's laws but what

I am not arguing that all egalitarians are liberals. Some denominations have approved women's ordination for other reasons, such as a long historical tradition and a strong emphasis on gifting by the Holy Spirit as the primary requirement for ministry (as in the Assemblies of God), or because of the dominant influence of an egalitarian leader and a high priority on relating effectively to the culture (as in the Willow Creek Association). But it is unquestionable that theological liberalism leads to the endorsement of women's ordination. While not all egalitarians are liberals, all liberals are egalitarians. There is no theologically liberal denomination or seminary in the United States today that opposes women's ordination. *Liberalism and the approval of women's ordination go hand in hand.*

Does it seem likely that all of the liberal churches who no longer believe the Bible have suddenly gotten the interpretation of the Bible regarding men's and women's roles exactly right, and that the most conservative churches who hold strongly to biblical inerrancy have gotten it exactly wrong? And does it seem likely that as soon as a denomination begins to abandon belief in inerrancy it suddenly discovers new skill and accuracy in interpreting the Bible on the roles of men and women so that it finally arrives at the correct answer?

In fact, the methods that evangelical feminists use today to interpret away the teachings of Scripture on male leadership in the home and the church are effectively undermining the authority of Scripture in their churches, and in that way they are contributing to a trend similar to step #1 above that was taken earlier by the more liberal churches.

It is to those methods of undermining the authority of Scripture that we now turn in the next several chapters.

---

regional conferences do is their own business" (Edward E. Plowman, "None of Our Business," *World* [magazine], April 17, 2004, quoted from www.worldmag.com/world/issue/04-17-04/national_5.asp). This is an indication that the United Methodist Church in one large region has reached point 6 in the seven-point sequence noted above, though the denomination's national governing body, the General Conference, took steps in May to minimize the impact of that decision. (The Methodist Church approved the ordination of women in 1956.)

EVANGELICAL FEMINIST VIEWS THAT UNDERMINE OR DENY THE AUTHORITY OF SCRIPTURE

INTRODUCTION TO
PART II

In a surprising number of evangelical feminist writings, the authors have published statements that either deny the complete *truthfulness* of Scripture or else deny the full *authority* of Scripture as the Word of God for us today. I have listed these in the following fifteen chapters (Part 2 of this book).

Then in the following section (Part 3 of the book), I list several egalitarian claims that undermine the effective authority of Scripture in a different way, by making untruthful claims about the meanings of ancient words or ancient history and thereby making people think the Bible says something other than what it really says.

SAYING THAT GENESIS IS WRONG

*Some evangelical feminists deny the authority
or truthfulness of Genesis 1–3*

Some evangelical feminists deny the authority or truthfulness of Genesis 1–3. One example of this is found in the writings of Rebecca Groothuis. Groothuis is a freelance writer and editor from the Denver, Colorado, area, and she is on the board of reference of the evangelical feminist organization Christians for Biblical Equality (CBE).

Groothuis claims that the Hebrew language of the Old Testament reflects a wrongful patriarchy. She says,

> We should note that the ancient Hebrew language was an expression of patriarchal culture. We cannot conclude, simply because the Bible was written under divine inspiration, that the languages in which the Bible was written were themselves created under divine inspiration. These languages were as male centered as the cultures they reflected and by which they were created. The fact that certain words in a language can be used to refer either to a male human or to humans in general reflects cultural concepts of gender; it says nothing about God's view of gender.[1]

Groothuis uses this statement to answer Raymond C. Ortlund's claim that male headship is hinted at when God calls the human race by the

[1] Rebecca Groothuis, *Good News for Women: A Biblical Picture of Gender Equality* (Grand Rapids, Mich.: Baker, 1997), 124.

Hebrew equivalent of our word *man*, rather than by a Hebrew word that means *woman* or a word that would mean *person*.[2] Groothuis uses this argument about the Hebrew language reflecting patriarchal culture in order to deny the meaning of some of the words of Scripture. She talks about "the languages in which the Bible was written" as if the debate were about words that occur *outside* of Scripture. But she glosses over the fact that the story of God's naming the human race *man* (Hebrew *'adam*; Gen. 1:26-27; 5:2)[3] is found in the Hebrew language *in the text of the Bible*. To say that these *words of the Bible* have a "patriarchal meaning" that God did not intend, and in fact to say that these *words of the Bible* tell us "nothing about God's view of gender," is simply to deny the authority of this part of Scripture. This is one step on the path toward liberalism.

Another example of denying the authority of Genesis 1–3 is William Webb's claim that some events in Genesis 1–3 are not historically accurate. Webb is professor of New Testament at Heritage Theological Seminary in Cambridge, Ontario, Canada. In his recent book *Slaves, Women, and Homosexuals*,[4] Webb argues that the elements of male leadership in Genesis 2 (Adam being created before Eve and receiving commands from God while alone) do not reflect the actual historical situation in the garden of Eden but were inserted there as a literary device for possibly three reasons: (1) to anticipate the fall; (2) to allow for better understanding by readers in the society and culture of Moses' time; or (3) to anticipate the agrarian society that would come into effect after the fall.

Webb agrees that "the practice of primogeniture in which the first born is granted prominence within the 'creative order' of a family unit"[5] is found in the narrative in Genesis 2, where Adam is created first, then Eve. He sees this as support for male headship within the text of Genesis 2. He also thinks this is how it is understood by Paul when he says, "For Adam was formed first, then Eve" (1 Tim. 2:13). But Webb still sees this primogeniture theme in Genesis 2 as a "cultural component" in that text.

[2] See Raymond C. Ortlund, Jr., "Male-Female Equality and Male Headship in Genesis 1–3," in *Recovering Biblical Manhood and Womanhood*, ed. John Piper and Wayne Grudem (Wheaton, Ill.: Crossway, 1991), 98.

[3] This same Hebrew word *'adam* is found twenty-five times to refer to a male human being in Genesis 1–4, as in Genesis 2:22, 23, 25; 3:8. For a full discussion see Wayne Grudem, *Evangelical Feminism and Biblical Truth* (Sisters, Ore.: Multnomah, 2004), 34-36.

[4] William Webb, *Slaves, Women, and Homosexuals: Exploring the Hermeneutics of Cultural Analysis* (Downers Grove, Ill.: InterVarsity Press, 2001).

[5] Ibid., 135.

But if there was no sin in the garden of Eden, nothing contrary to God's will, then how could there be any cultural influence in the garden of Eden—*before the fall?* Wasn't everything there perfect?

As indicated above, Webb answers this question in three ways. First, he says these indications of male headship in Genesis 1–2 may be a *literary device that anticipates the fall and God's subsequent curse*, rather than accurately recording what was in fact true in the garden:

> A second question is how cultural features could possibly be found in the garden before the influence of culture. Several explanations exist. First, the whispers of patriarchy in the garden may have been placed there *in order to anticipate the curse.*[6]

He is suggesting that the indications of male leadership in Genesis 2 are not historically accurate but were placed there "to anticipate the curse" of God on Adam and Eve, which is found in Genesis 3:16-19 and which comes after they sinned in Genesis 3:6.

In order to support this idea Webb claims that the literary construction of Genesis 2–3 includes at least one other example of "literary foreshadowing of the curse" in the pejorative description of the serpent as *"more crafty* than any other beast of the field" (Gen. 3:1). Webb then asks, "If the garden is completely pristine, how could certain creatures in the just-created animal kingdom reflect craftiness? Obviously, this Edenic material embraces *an artistic foreshadowing of events to come.*"[7]

Webb's analysis here assumes that there was no sin or evil at the time described in Genesis 3:1 *in actual fact,* but that by a literary device the author described the serpent as "crafty" (and therefore deceitful and therefore sinful), thus anticipating what he would be later, after the fall. In the same way, he thinks the elements of male headship in Genesis 2 were not there in the garden in actual fact but were inserted as "an artistic foreshadowing of events to come."

Webb then offers another explanation: he says that the "patriarchy" in Genesis 2 may have been inserted there because it was a reflection of social categories familiar to readers at the time when Moses wrote

---

[6] Ibid., 142-143, italics added.
[7] Ibid., 143, italics added.

Genesis (long after the events in the garden of Eden), and that would have kept readers in Moses' time from being confused about the main point of the story (namely, that God made everything):

> Second, Eden's quiet echoes of patriarchy may be a way of *describing the past through present categories.* The creation story may be *using the social categories that Moses' audience would have been familiar with.* God sometimes permits such accommodation in order not to confuse the main point he wants to communicate with factors that are secondary to that overall theme.[8]

Finally, Webb gives a third reason:

> Third . . . *the patriarchy of the garden may reflect God's anticipation of the social context into which Adam and Eve were about to venture.* An agrarian lifestyle . . . would naturally produce some kind of hierarchy between men and women. . . . The presentation of the male-female relationship in patriarchal forms may simply be a way of anticipating this first (and major) life setting into which humankind would enter.[9]

What shall we think of Webb's explanations of the early parts of Genesis? Even in his analysis of one specific detail, the statement that the serpent was "crafty," Webb understands Genesis 3:1 to affirm something that he thinks was not true at that time, and thus Webb denies the truthfulness of a section of historical narrative in Scripture.

But there is really no great difficulty in affirming that Genesis 3:1 is stating historical fact, and taking it at face value. Webb fails even to consider the most likely explanation: that there was sin in the angelic world sometime after the completion of the initial creation (Gen. 1:31) but prior to Genesis 3:1.[10] Because of this rebellion in the angelic world (see 2 Pet. 2:4; Jude 6), Satan himself was already evil and was somehow

---

[8] Ibid., 143, italics added. Webb explains in a footnote that the "main point" of the creation narrative "is that Yahweh created the heavens and all that is in them, and Yahweh created the earth and all that is in it—God made everything" (143n46).

[9] Ibid., 144, italics added.

[10] This is a fairly standard view among evangelical scholars, but Webb does not even consider it. See Wayne Grudem, *Systematic Theology* (Grand Rapids, Mich.: Zondervan, 1994), 412, and the relevant pages given for other systematic theologies (434-435).

speaking through the serpent.[11] So Webb's claim that the crafty serpent in Genesis 3:1 must be "artistic foreshadowing of events to come" is not persuasive. It is better to take Genesis 3:1 as historically accurate and affirm that this particular serpent, under the influence of Satan, was in fact "crafty" and therefore deceptive and sinful.

Webb also denies the historical accuracy of Genesis 2 in all three of his explanations of why the narrative indicates male leadership (what he calls "patriarchy" and "primogeniture"). In reason (1), Webb claims that "the whispers of patriarchy in the garden may have been placed there in order to anticipate the curse."[12] Webb is saying that patriarchy did not exist in the garden *in actual fact,* but the author placed hints of it in the story as a way of anticipating the situation that would come about after there was sin in the world. This, then, is also a denial of the historical accuracy of the Genesis 2 account.

In reason (2), Webb says that Moses, in the time he wrote, used "present categories" such as patriarchy to describe the past, and this was simply an "accommodation" by God "in order not to confuse the main point." That is, patriarchy did not actually exist in the garden of Eden, but Moses inserted it there in Genesis 2 so as not to confuse his audience at a later time. Thus, Moses inserted false information into Genesis 2. This is also a denial of the historical accuracy of the Genesis 2 account.

The same is true of Webb's reason (3). Webb suggests that primogeniture (Adam being created before Eve) occurs in Genesis 2, not because it reflected the actual situation in the garden of Eden but *because Adam and Eve after they sinned would enter into a situation where Adam had leadership over his wife.* This again is a denial of the historical accuracy of the headship of Adam and his prior creation in Genesis 2. It was simply "a practical and gracious *anticipation* of the agrarian setting into which Adam and Eve were headed."[13]

It is important to realize how much Webb denies as historical fact

---

[11] The serpent, the act of deception, and Satan are connected in some New Testament contexts. Paul says, "I am afraid that as the serpent deceived Eve by his cunning, your thoughts will be led astray from a sincere and pure devotion to Christ" (2 Cor. 11:3, in a context opposing false apostles whom he categorizes as servants of Satan who "disguise themselves as servants of righteousness," v. 15). Revelation 12 describes Satan as "that ancient serpent, who is called the devil and Satan, the deceiver of the whole world" (Rev. 12:9). See also John 8:44 and 1 John 3:8, with reference to the beginning stages of history.

[12] Webb, *Slaves, Women, and Homosexuals,* 142-143.

[13] Ibid., 145 (italics added); repeated 151n55.

in the Genesis narrative. He is not just denying that there was a "crafty" serpent who spoke to Eve (Gen. 3:1). He also denies the entire *theme of primogeniture* found in Genesis 2. That is, he denies the entire narrative structure that shows the man as created before the woman, for this is the basis for the primogeniture theme he sees Paul referring to when he says, in 1 Timothy 2:13, "For Adam was formed first, then Eve."

How much of Genesis 2 does that involve? In order to deny that Adam was created first, then Eve after him, how much inaccurate material has to be inserted into Genesis 2 either as a literary device foreshadowing the fall (reason 1), or as an accommodation to the situation familiar to readers at the time of Moses (reason 2), or as an anticipation of an agrarian society that would be established after the fall (reason 3)? It is no small amount:

- God placing the man alone in the garden (Gen. 2:8)
- God putting the man alone in the garden "to work it and keep it" (2:15)
- God commanding the man alone that he may eat of every tree of the garden but not of the tree of the knowledge of good and evil (2:16-17)
- God saying, "It is not good that the man should be alone; I will make him a helper fit for him" (2:18)
- God bringing the beasts of the field and the birds of the heavens to the man alone to see what he would call them (2:19)
- the man alone giving names to every living creature (2:20)
- there not being found a helper fit for the man (2:20)
- God causing a deep sleep to fall upon the man and taking one of his ribs and forming it into a woman (2:21-22)

This entire sequence, summarized by Paul in the statement "For Adam was formed first, then Eve," is merely a literary device that did not actually happen, according to Webb. And all of this then enables Webb to say that Paul's appeal to the creation of Adam prior to Eve is not proof of a transcultural ethical standard. But if a theological argument has to deny significant portions of Scripture for its support, it should surely be rejected by evangelicals who are subject to the authority of the entire Bible as the Word of God. Webb's three ways of denying the historicity of Adam's creation before Eve in Genesis 2 are three steps on the path toward liberalism.

I published a critique of Webb's treatment of the Genesis 2 narrative in June of 2004.[14] Then Webb responded to my critique in a paper read at the annual meeting of the Evangelical Theological Society, November 17-19, 2004.[15] In his response Webb objected to my saying that he denied the historicity "of the creation account" when in fact he had only denied the historical accuracy of part of it. Although I believe it was very clear from my original critique exactly what parts of Genesis 2 he said were not historically accurate,[16] I can now include here some statements from his response to me. His response simply confirms that he thinks several events reported in the Genesis 2 narrative did not actually happen. Here is what he says:

> Grudem's charge that Webb denies the historical accuracy of the creation account is yet another example of his blatant and inflammatory misrepresentation. The misrepresentation develops in two ways. On the one hand, to say that I deny the historicity of the creation account *without any qualification*, significantly misrepresents what I was doing with the two criteria in question (criteria #6 and #7). A closer reading will reveal that I am only talking about certain specific *components* of the creation account and not the creation account as a whole. . . .
>
> What I do affirm in criteria #6 and 7 on the creation narratives is that certain *components* within the creation narratives are more apt than others to be *literary* and/or *time-displaced* in nature. By saying that a component is literary and/or time-displaced is not (!) saying that the component(s) is historically inaccurate. This is nonsense. What it is

---

[14] Wayne Grudem, "Should We Move Beyond the New Testament to a Better Ethic? An Analysis of William J. Webb, *Slaves, Women and Homosexuals: Exploring the Hermeneutics of Cultural Analysis* (Downers Grove, Ill.: InterVarsity, 2001)," *Journal of the Evangelical Theological Society* 47/2 (June, 2004), 299-346.

[15] Webb's response, "A Redemptive-Movement Hermeneutic: Responding to Grudem's Concerns," is available online at www.etsjets.org.

[16] My original critique of Webb's denial of the historicity of parts of Genesis 2 is reprinted in Grudem, *Evangelical Feminism and Biblical Truth*, 610-613, where I specify exactly what parts of Genesis 2–3 Webb does not count as historically accurate. Only by lifting one of my statements out of its context can he claim that I say that Webb denies the historicity of the creation account "without qualification." My qualifications are clearly there in the context. I did not misrepresent him.

saying is that the component was (perhaps/possibly/probably) never intended by the author to make a statement that is historical in nature. In other words, the statement is *a*-historical or *non*-historical but not "historically inaccurate". (It is simply not possible to "deny the historical accuracy" within any author's words if the author never intended their words to function as a historical statement.) To say that a component within the creation narratives is literary and/or time-displaced and as such is not intended to make a historical point (a/non-historical) is not at all to say that this component is "historically inaccurate"![17]

My conclusion after reading this is that Webb in his response to me is stating even more strongly his belief that the narrative about Adam being created before Eve is not historically accurate. He explains this by claiming that the author never intended it to be representative of actual history, and therefore he does not want to say that it is historically inaccurate (!); but in saying this Webb only reaffirms the fact that he claims that Adam was not, in fact, created before Eve, but that this idea was a literary device, inserted later. In this response paper Webb also adds that he is "inclined to think the same about Adam being fashioned from clumps of ground," since other ancient near eastern creation stories had a similar theme, and modern science shows that human beings are amazingly complex.[18] So here is another aspect of Genesis 2–3 that Webb does not think is actual history containing events that actually happened. (For a summary of the reasons why we must understand Genesis 2 to be reporting actual historical facts, see Wayne Grudem, *Systematic Theology* [Grand Rapids, Mich.: Zondervan, 1994], 278-279.) Several New Testament passages understand Genesis to be actual historical fact all the way back to chapters 1–2: see Matthew 19:4-5; Luke 3:38; Acts 17:26; Romans 5:12-21; 1 Corinthians 11:8-9; 2 Corinthians 11:3; 1 Timothy 2:13-14.

The denial of the authority or truthfulness of Genesis 1–3 is a significant step on the path toward liberalism.

---

[17] Webb, "Redemptive-Movement Hermeneutic: Responding to Grudem's Concerns," 11-13.
[18] Ibid., 14.

4

SAYING THAT PAUL WAS WRONG

*Some evangelical feminists say that
Paul was wrong*

A liberal tendency to reject the authority of Scripture is also seen in the writings of Paul King Jewett, formerly a professor at Fuller Seminary in Pasadena, California; Letha Scanzoni and Nancy Hardesty, freelance writers who published an influential evangelical feminist book; Clarence Boomsma, a Christian Reformed pastor and denominational leader; and David Thompson, professor of biblical studies (with a specialty in Old Testament) at Asbury Theological Seminary, Wilmore, Kentucky.

While egalitarian positions had been advocated since the 1950s by theologically *liberal* Protestant writers, no *evangelical* books took such a position until 1974. In that year freelance writers Letha Scanzoni and Nancy Hardesty published their groundbreaking book *All We're Meant to Be.*[1] The following year, Paul Jewett, then a professor at Fuller Seminary, published *Man as Male and Female.*[2] Both books claimed that the apostle Paul's advocacy of female subordination in marriage and the church was a remnant of his rabbinic training that he had not fully resolved when he wrote his epistles, and that this particular rabbinic element was inconsistent with Paul's other emphasis on total equality for men and women in Christ. In fact, though Scanzoni and Hardesty's book

---

[1] Letha Scanzoni and Nancy Hardesty, *All We're Meant to Be: A Biblical Approach to Women's Liberation* (Waco, Tex.: Word, 1974).
[2] Paul King Jewett, *Man as Male and Female* (Grand Rapids, Mich.: Eerdmans, 1975).

was published earlier, they actually depended on Jewett's class notes from Fuller Seminary for their key argument that Paul was wrong on this issue.[3] Jewett therefore may be considered the intellectual father of the modern evangelical feminist movement.

In *Man as Male and Female* Jewett claims that Paul was wrong in his teaching in 1 Timothy 2:

> The apostle Paul was the heir of this contrast between the old and the new. . . . He was both a Jew and a Christian. . . . And his thinking about women . . . reflects both his Jewish and his Christian experience. . . . So far as he thought in terms of his Jewish background, he thought of the woman as subordinate to the man for whose sake she was created (1 Cor. 11:9). But so far as he thought in terms of the new insight he had gained through the revelation of God in Christ, he thought of the woman as equal to the man in all things. . . . Because *these two perspectives—the Jewish and the Christian—are incompatible, there is no satisfying way to harmonize the Pauline argument. . . .*
>
> Paul . . . is assuming the traditional rabbinic understanding [of Gen. 2:18-23]. . . . *Is this rabbinic understanding of Genesis 2:18f correct? We do not think that it is. . . .*
>
> The difficulty is that Paul, who was an inspired apostle, appears to teach such female subordination in certain passages. . . . To resolve this difficulty, *one must recognize the human as well as the divine quality of Scripture.*[4]

Clarence Boomsma, a pastor in the Christian Reformed Church and four-time president of synod for that denomination (and thus the former presiding officer of the denominational assembly of all of North America), holds a similar position: he says that Paul's use of Genesis 2–3 is an incorrect reading of Genesis, but it was the view common in Paul's day so he used it anyway for his audience. Both Thomas Schreiner and

---

[3] Scanzoni and Hardesty say, "The second creation narrative does say that woman was made from man, but the theological leap from this to woman's subordination is a traditional rabbinic . . . understanding that is not supported by the text" (Scanzoni and Hardesty, *All We're Meant to Be*, 28). The footnote to this sentence includes a lengthy quote from Paul Jewett's class syllabus at Fuller Seminary in 1973 in which Jewett claims that "there is no satisfying way to harmonize the Pauline argument for female subordination with the larger Christian vision of which the great apostle to the Gentiles is the primary New Testament architect" (212-213).

[4] Jewett, *Man as Male and Female*, 112-113, 119, 134, italics added.

Al Wolters point out how surprising it is to find that a Christian Reformed author thinks that Paul's use of the Old Testament is incorrect.[5] Boomsma disagrees with Paul's reasoning in 1 Timothy 2:12-14, where Paul says,

> I do not permit a woman to teach or to exercise authority over a man; rather, she is to remain quiet. For Adam was formed first, then Eve; and Adam was not deceived, but the woman was deceived and became a transgressor.

Although Paul is referring to Genesis 2 when he says, "For Adam was formed first, then Eve," Boomsma says, "there is nothing in Genesis 2 that teaches woman's subordination to man."[6] He says, "The apostle's argument from Genesis 2 is without support in the text."[7] But then he says, "This is not to say that Paul was in error when he adduces his argument from Genesis."[8] Why not? Because he used an interpretation that was currently accepted in his day, and it was useful for his argument:

> How, then, shall we account for the apostle's appeal to the Genesis data in 1 Timothy 2:13-14? We have observed that Paul's use of Genesis 2:17-24 is based upon the text as it was interpreted in his day. . . . As to his second argument, drawn from Genesis 3:1-7, 16, it was again evident that his application of the text reflected the contemporary understanding of Eve's role in the fall and its consequences for women.[9]

But Boomsma then goes on to say this was "an unacceptable argument for disallowing women full equality in the church," and adds, "Paul adopts the reading and understanding of the Genesis material that was

---

[5] Thomas Schreiner, "An Interpretation of 1 Timothy 2:9-15: A Dialogue with Scholarship," in *Women in the Church: A Fresh Analysis of 1 Timothy 2:9-15*, ed. Andreas Köstenberger, Thomas Schreiner, and H. Scott Baldwin (Grand Rapids, Mich.: Baker, 1995), 107, with reference to Clarence Boomsma, *Male and Female, One in Christ: New Testament Teaching on Women in Office* (Grand Rapids, Mich.: Baker, 1993). In a review of Boomsma's book, Al Wolters writes, "I do not believe that anyone else in the Reformed tradition has ever dared to suggest that the scriptural argumentation of an apostle is clearly mistaken and unacceptable" (Al Wolters, review of Clarence Boomsma, *Male and Female, One in Christ*, in *Calvin Theological Journal* 29 [1994]: 285).

[6] Boomsma, *Male and Female*, 60.

[7] Ibid., 58.

[8] Ibid., 59.

[9] Ibid., 81.

current in his day in order to effectively undergird his instructions to the Ephesian church." But since we now know that that is not a correct way to interpret Genesis, "It does not follow, however, that Paul's use of the Genesis data thereby endorses the quoted interpretation of the Genesis texts as divinely inspired truth to be universally applied in all circumstances and under all conditions."[10]

So both Boomsma and Jewett say that Paul was adopting incorrect Jewish understandings of Genesis 2–3 that were current in his day.

This position allows the church today to disobey the reasoning of 1 Timothy 2:11-15, saying it was a mistake. But Christians who take the entire Bible as the Word of God, and as authoritative for us today, do not have that option. The apostle Paul's interpretation of Genesis 2 as found in 1 Timothy 2 is part of the Word of God. Therefore it is "breathed out by God" and cannot contain erroneous interpretations of Genesis. To say that Paul made a mistake in writing 1 Timothy 2 is another step on the path toward liberalism.

A related claim that the apostle Paul was wrong is found in the argument of David Thompson. Thompson argues that Paul misinterprets Genesis 2, and that we can come to a better understanding of Genesis 2 than Paul did. According to Thompson, there may be unusual times when we can carefully and cautiously differ with a New Testament author's interpretation of an Old Testament text. And one of those times is when we read Paul's interpretation of Genesis 2 in 1 Timothy 2.[11]

Thompson says that 1 Timothy 2:11-15 is hard to interpret. It poses "particularly complex problems hermeneutically," and, anyway, we might be able to reexamine Genesis 2 and disagree with Paul's interpretation of it: "We should take caution in immediately assuming that Paul's reading of Genesis 2 must, without further inquiry, be ours."[12] Then he says that we should read the Genesis 2 account ourselves and understand it "on its own terms," and that our understanding of it can then be the "arbiter" of Paul's understanding: "It is entirely possible that at this point the creation account, understood on its own terms, must be the arbiter of the more specifically confined reading given by Paul."[13]

[10] Ibid.
[11] David L. Thompson, "Women, Men, Slaves, and the Bible: Hermeneutical Inquiries," *Christian Scholar's Review* 25/3 (March 1996): 326-349.
[12] Ibid., 346, 347.

Thompson's procedure also effectively denies the authority of Scripture for us today. Of course Paul's use of Genesis 2 is a problem for egalitarians because Genesis 2 shows male headship in marriage before there was any sin in the world. Therefore it shows male headship as part of the way God created us as men and women. And then (to make things worse for the egalitarian position!) Paul *quotes* from Genesis 2 to establish male headship in the church (1 Tim. 2:11-14). This means that Paul sees male headship in the church as rooted in the way God created men and women from the beginning.

But Thompson has provided egalitarians with another way to evade the force of that argument: he says that, with much caution, with careful study, with prayer, we should study Genesis 2 as twentieth-century interpreters. We should understand Genesis 2 "on its own terms." And when we understand the passage well enough, our understanding might (at times) enable us to reject Paul's interpretation. We can use Genesis 2 as the "arbiter" (or judge) of Paul's interpretation.

Note what has happened here. *We* are interpreting Genesis 2. And though Thompson may claim that *Genesis 2* is the judge of Paul's interpretation, the actual result (in the article) is that *Thompson's interpretation of Genesis 2* becomes the judge by which Paul's interpretation is pushed aside. Thompson's argument means that our interpretation can correct Paul's interpretation of Genesis 2—and, by implication, we could eventually correct Paul's interpretation of other Old Testament passages as well.

However, if the Bible is the Word of God, *then these interpretations are not just Paul's interpretations; they are also God's interpretations of his own Word.* There might be times when I cannot understand an interpretation of the Old Testament by a New Testament author, but that does not give me the right to disagree with his interpretation. If I believe the Bible to be the very words of God, then I must believe that neither Paul nor any other Scriptural author made mistakes in his interpretation of the Old Testament, or gave us interpretations of the Old Testament that we can reject in favor of better ones of our own.

The claim that Paul was wrong is another step on the path toward liberalism.

---

[13] Ibid., 347.

SAYING THAT SOME VERSES FOUND IN EVERY MANUSCRIPT ARE NOT PART OF THE BIBLE

Some evangelical feminists say that some verses that are in every ancient manuscript of 1 Corinthians are not really part of the Bible

In 1 Corinthians 14:33b-35 Paul says,

> As in all the churches of the saints, the women should keep silent in the churches. For they are not permitted to speak, but should be in submission, as the Law also says. If there is anything they desire to learn, let them ask their husbands at home. For it is shameful for a woman to speak in church.

One common interpretation of these verses, and the one I think is best, holds that Paul is saying women should "keep silent" during the judging of prophecies, which is the topic under discussion in this context (see v. 29: "Let two or three prophets speak, and let the others weigh what is said"). This would be consistent with Paul's teaching elsewhere that restricts governing authority over the entire congregation to men (see 1 Tim. 2:11-15; 3:2).[1]

---

[1] For further explanation see Wayne Grudem, *Evangelical Feminism and Biblical Truth* (Sisters, Ore.: Multnomah, 2004), 78-79, 232-242; and Wayne Grudem, *The Gift of Prophecy in the New Testament and Today,* rev. ed. (Wheaton: Crossway, 2000), 183-192.

However, a very sophisticated academic attempt to evade the Bible's authority is found in Gordon Fee's claim that 1 Corinthians 14:34-35 should not be considered part of the Bible and that these verses are "certainly not binding for Christians."[2] Fee is a highly respected New Testament scholar who taught for many years at Regent College, Vancouver, Canada, is also a member of the Committee on Bible Translation for the NIV Bible, and is now the general editor for the New International Commentary on the New Testament series (published by Eerdmans). In Fee's highly regarded commentary on 1 Corinthians (NICNT), he argues that Paul did not write 1 Corinthians 14:34-35 but that these verses were the addition of a later scribe.[3] He says,

> The case against these verses is so strong, and finding a viable solution to their meaning so difficult, that it seems best to view them as an interpolation. . . . One must assume that the words were first written as a gloss in the margin by someone who, probably in light of 1 Tim. 2:9-15, felt the need to qualify Paul's instructions even further.[4]

Fee's main reasons for this conclusion are (1) that some later Greek manuscripts move these verses so that they follow verse 40, and, (2) that the verses cannot be reconciled with 1 Corinthians 11:5, where Paul allows women to prophesy in the church. But Fee's arguments have been strongly rejected by other New Testament scholars.[5]

Is Fee's position here really an undermining of the authority of the Bible? On the one hand, some who read Fee may see his argument as merely a text-critical decision based on Fee's careful analysis of many different

---

[2] Gordon D. Fee, *The First Epistle to the Corinthians,* New International Commentary on the New Testament (Grand Rapids, Mich.: Eerdmans, 1987), 708.

[3] See ibid., 699-708. Fee makes the same claim again in "The Priority of Spirit Gifting for Church Ministry," in *Discovering Biblical Equality,* ed. Ronald W. Pierce and Rebecca Merrill Groothuis (Downers Grove, Ill.: InterVarsity, 2004), 251-252.

[4] Ibid., 705.

[5] See the discussion in Anthony C. Thiselton, *The First Epistle to the Corinthians: A Commentary on the Greek Text,* New International Greek Testament Commentary (Grand Rapids, Mich.: Eerdmans, 2000), 1148-1150, with particular reference to an article by C. Niccum, "The Voice of the Manuscripts on the Silence of Women: The External Evidence for 1 Cor 14:34-35," *New Testament Studies* 43 (1997): 242-255. Thiselton says Niccum's article "seems overwhelmingly convincing" (1149n342). See also D. A. Carson, "'Silent in the Churches': On the Role of Women in 1 Corinthians 14:33b-36," in *Recovering Biblical Manhood and Womanhood,* ed. John Piper and Wayne Grudem (Wheaton, Ill.: Crossway, 1991), 141-145.

ancient manuscripts. But, on the other hand, two factors lead me to think of it rather as a different method of rejecting the authority of these verses for the church today. (I am not speaking of Fee's intention, which I do not know, but of the actual process he followed and the result he reached.)

First, out of the thousands of ancient New Testament manuscripts that exist today, *not one manuscript has ever omitted these verses* (the Western manuscripts that move the verses to follow verse 40 are unreliable elsewhere in any case, but they still include these verses). This makes this passage significantly different from the other two examples Fee mentions where something not original has crept into the text tradition (John 5:3b-4 and 1 John 5:7).[6] In those cases the oldest and best manuscripts *lack* the added material, but in 1 Corinthians 14:34-35 *no* manuscript lacks this material. So Fee's procedure is different from every other text-critical decision made by editors of the Greek New Testament throughout history: he thinks we should exclude a passage from the New Testament that is *included* in every manuscript we have! In fact, this is not a highly doubtful text, but one that is given a "B" rating in the United Bible Societies' fourth edition of the Greek New Testament,[7] indicating that it is "almost certain" in the eyes of the editors of that text.[8]

The second thing that leads me to see this not merely as a text-critical decision but as a rejection of the authority of some verses of the Bible is the fact that the most decisive factor for Fee's conclusion is not the evidence from ancient manuscripts but rather that he thinks that these verses, which say that "the women should keep silent in the churches" (1 Cor. 14:34), are impossible to reconcile with 1 Corinthians 11. This makes me think that this is ultimately not a text-critical question but an objection he has to the content of these verses.

Fee says, "these verses stand in obvious contradiction to 11:2-16, where it is assumed without reproof that women pray and prophesy in the assembly."[9] But virtually all other interpreters in the history of the church have seen various ways to reconcile 14:34-35 and 11:5. Therefore Fee incorrectly sees those two passages as being impossible to

[6] Fee, *First Epistle to the Corinthians*, 705.
[7] *The Greek New Testament*, 4th rev. ed., ed. Barbara Aland, Kurt Aland, Johannes Karavidopoulos, Carlo M. Martini, and Bruce M. Metzger (Stuttgart: Deutsche Bibelgesellschaft and United Bible Societies, 1994) (abbreviated as UBS[4]), 601.
[8] UBS[4], 3*.
[9] Fee, *First Epistle to the Corinthians*, 702.

reconcile, and yet that is his primary argument against the authenticity of 1 Corinthians 14:34-35.

At this point Fee's procedure is different from that of all other evangelical interpreters of Scripture. There are many passages in the Bible that on first reading seem difficult to reconcile with other passages in the Bible (think, for example, of the teachings of Paul and James on justification by faith, or the astounding claim that Jesus is God and the Father is also God, when combined with the teaching that there is only one God). Historically, interpreters with a high respect for the authority and consistency of Scripture have not simply decided that one set of verses stands "in obvious contradiction" to the other set and that therefore the difficult verses should be thrown out of the Bible. (Think of what would happen if we were to follow Fee's procedure in the Gospels, where we find some manuscript evidence of scribal attempts to "fix" the difficulty in almost every parallel passage that has details that are difficult to harmonize, just as Fee finds some manuscript evidence of scribal attempts to move 1 Corinthians 14:34-35 to another context.) Rather, interpreters have returned to the difficult texts with the assumption that they have misunderstood something, and they have sought for interpretations that are fair to both texts and are not contradictory. (In fact, on pages 703-705 of his book, Fee himself lists—but then rejects—several ways interpreters have explained 1 Corinthians 14:34-35 and 1 Corinthians 11:5 so that they are not contradictory.)

Does Fee's solution to 1 Corinthians 14:34-35 then constitute evidence of a liberal tendency to reject the authority of the Bible? It should trouble evangelicals that Fee says these verses are not part of the Bible and therefore "certainly not binding for Christians." It seems to me that Fee's recommendation that we should remove some hard verses from the Bible rather than seeking to understand them in a way that does not contradict other verses establishes a dangerous precedent. When the verses that he throws out of the Bible are missing from no manuscript, and also happen to be the very verses that show Paul's insistence on male governance of the church meetings "in all the churches of the saints" (v. 33), then it seems to me to be another example of a pattern in many egalitarian writings, a pattern of using sophisticated scholarly procedures in order to evade the requirement of submitting to the authority of the Word of God. Fee's rejection of 1 Corinthians 14:34-35 as not belonging to the Bible seems to me another step on the path toward liberalism.

"LATER DEVELOPMENTS" TRUMP SCRIPTURE

Some evangelical feminists say our ultimate authority
is found not in what is written in Scripture but
in developments that came after the Bible

Another step on the path toward liberalism is found in a process of interpreting the Bible that is called "trajectory hermeneutics." The word "hermeneutics" just means "a method of interpreting the Bible" (from the Greek word *hermēneuō*, "to interpret, explain"). The phrase "trajectory hermeneutics" means a method of interpreting the Bible in which our final authority is not found in what is written in the Bible itself, but is found later, at the end of a "trajectory" along which the New Testament was progressing at the time it was being written. This view would claim that the New Testament authors did not reach the final destination of these developments, but we can sense the direction or the trajectory along which they were moving, see where they were headed, and carry their thinking further, until we reach the destination they were moving toward but did not reach in their thinking and writing. This means that our authority is the point toward which the New Testament authors were progressing in a trajectory, not what the New Testament actually taught.

One author who advocates trajectory hermeneutics is New Testament scholar R. T. France, the former principal of Wycliffe Hall, Oxford, England (an evangelical school and research center connected to Oxford University), a member of the Committee on Bible Translation for the NIV Bible, and the author of some widely respected commentaries on the Gospels. Another is David Thompson of Asbury Seminary, whose work we considered in chapter 4.

France, in his book *Women in the Church's Ministry: A Test Case for Biblical Interpretation,* argues that the Old Testament and Judaism in the time of Jesus were male-dominated and biased against women, but that Jesus began to overturn this system, and that the New Testament churches continued the process, and that we can now follow this "trajectory" to a point of full inclusion of women in all ministries. France explains:

> The gospels do not, perhaps, record a total reversal of Jewish prejudice against women and of their total exclusion from roles of leadership. But *they do contain the seeds from which such a reversal was bound to grow.* Effective revolutions are seldom completed in a year or two. In this, as in other matters, the disciples were slow learners. But the fuse, long as it might prove to be, had been ignited.[1]

France later comments on "there is no longer male and female" in Galatians 3:28 (NRSV):

> Paul here expresses *the end-point of the historical trajectory* which we have been tracing . . . from the male-dominated society of the Old Testament and of later Judaism, through the revolutionary implications and yet still limited actual outworking of Jesus' attitude to women, and on to the increasing prominence of women in the apostolic church and in its active ministry. At all points within the period of biblical history *the working out of the fundamental equality* expressed in Galatians 3:28 *remained constrained by the realities of the time,* and yet there was the basis, indeed the imperative, for the dismantling of the sexual discrimination which has prevailed since the fall. *How far along that trajectory it is appropriate and possible for the church to move* at any subsequent stage in history must remain a matter for debate, as it is today.[2]

[1] R. T. France, *Women in the Church's Ministry: A Test Case for Biblical Interpretation* (Grand Rapids, Mich.: Eerdmans, 1995), 78, italics added.
[2] Ibid., 91, italics added.

And he says that he has found his "basic position" regarding women in ministry

> not in these few texts [1 Cor 14:34-36 and 1 Tim 2:11-15] but *in a trajectory of thought and practice developing through Scripture, and arguably pointing beyond itself* to the fuller outworking of God's ultimate purpose in Christ in ways which the first-century situation did not yet allow.[3]

A similar position is argued by David Thompson in his 1996 article in *Christian Scholar's Review:*[4]

> Sensing the direction of the canonical dialogue and prayerfully struggling with it, God's people conclude that they will most faithfully honor his Word by *accepting the target already anticipated in Scripture and toward which the Scriptural trajectory was heading* rather than the last entry in the Biblical conversation. . . . The canonical conversation at this point closed without final resolution. But *the trajectory was clearly set toward egalitarian relationships.*[5]

Both France and Thompson admit that the New Testament authors did not teach the full inclusion of women in all forms of church leadership. As France says, the first-century situation "did not yet allow" this "fuller outworking of God's ultimate purpose," which he says should be our standard today.[6]

But this means that the teachings of the New Testament are no longer

---

[3] Ibid., 94-95, italics added.

[4] David L. Thompson, "Women, Men, Slaves, and the Bible: Hermeneutical Inquiries," *Christian Scholar's Review* 25/3 (March 1996): 326-349. For a more detailed response to Thompson's article, especially his hermeneutical principles and his approach to the authority of Scripture, see Wayne Grudem, "Asbury Professor Advocates Egalitarianism but Undermines Biblical Authority: A Critique of David Thompson's 'Trajectory' Hermeneutic," *CBMW News*, December 1996, 8-12 (also available online at www.cbmw.org).

[5] Thompson, ibid., 338-339, italics added.

[6] It is significant that France and Thompson basically agree with the complementarian interpretation of Bible passages that restrict some church leadership roles to men. They do not have to invent new interpretations of those passages because they simply say the passages are no longer binding on us today. This seems to be a pattern among evangelical interpreters: those who think the passages are not binding for us today agree that the passages prohibited women from teaching or governing the whole church *for the situation in which they were written.* On the other hand, those who say the verses *are* binding on us today have devised several new interpretations to argue that the verses did not prohibit women in general from governing or teaching the whole church even in the first century.

our final authority. Our authority now becomes *our own ideas of the direction the New Testament was heading* but never quite reached.

This has not been the historic position of Bible-believing Protestant churches. In fact, they have opposed such a position. In order to guard against making our authority something other than the Bible, major confessions of faith have insisted that the words of God *in Scripture* are our authority, not some position arrived at *after* the Bible was finished. This is the Reformation doctrine of *sola Scriptura*, or "the Bible alone," as our ultimate authority for doctrine and life. The *Westminster Confession of Faith* says:

> The *whole counsel of God* concerning all things necessary for his own glory, man's salvation, faith and life, is either expressly set down in Scripture, or by good and necessary consequence may be deduced from Scripture: unto which nothing at any time is to be added, whether by new revelations of the Spirit, or traditions of men.[7]

More recently, the widely acknowledged Chicago Statement on Biblical Inerrancy said:

> We affirm that God's revelation in the Holy Scriptures was progressive. We deny that later revelation, which may fulfill earlier revelation, ever corrects or contradicts it. We further deny that any normative revelation has been given since the completion of the New Testament writings.[8]

But this trajectory position would have the later standard (the supposed "goal" to which the New Testament was headed) contradict earlier revelation (which limited certain roles in the church to men).

The doctrinal statement of the Evangelical Theological Society says:

> *The Bible alone*, and the Bible in its entirety, *is the Word of God written* and is therefore inerrant in the autographs.[9]

---

[7] *Westminster Confession of Faith*, chapter 3, paragraph 6, italics added.
[8] Chicago Statement on Biblical Inerrancy, article 5, cited in *Journal of the Evangelical Theological Society* 21/4 (December 1978): 290-291.
[9] From the Evangelical Theological Society website (www.etsjets.org, italics added, accessed 2-18-06).

But this trajectory argument places authority ultimately in something beyond the New Testament writings. It thus rejects the important Reformation doctrine of *sola Scriptura* ("the Scripture alone"), the idea that the ultimate authority for our beliefs is not anything outside of Scripture but is only the words of Scripture themselves.

France supports his position by arguing (1) that we already see change from the Old Testament to the New Testament, and (2) that within the New Testament we see the apostles gradually growing in their understanding of the way Gentiles can be fully included in the church (as in the Jerusalem Council in Acts 15).[10] So why should we not allow change beyond what is in the New Testament?

The problem with France's view is that it fails to recognize the uniqueness of the New Testament. Yes, the New Testament explicitly tells us that we are no longer under the regulations of the old covenant (Heb. 8:6-13), so we have clear warrant for saying the sacrificial laws and dietary laws are no longer binding on us. And yes, we do see the apostles in a process of coming to understand the inclusion of the Gentiles in the church (Acts 15; Gal. 2:1-14; 3:28). But *that process was completed within the New Testament,* and the commands given to Christians in the New Testament say nothing about excluding Gentiles from the church. We do not have to progress on a "trajectory" beyond the New Testament to discover that.

Christians living in the time of Paul's epistles were living under the new covenant. And we Christians living today are also living under the new covenant. This is "the new covenant in my blood" (1 Cor. 11:25), which Jesus established and which we affirm every time we take the Lord's Supper. That means *we are living in the same period in God's plan for "the history of redemption" as the first-century Christians.* And that is why we can read and apply the New Testament directly to ourselves today. To attempt to go beyond the New Testament documents and derive our authority from "where the New Testament was heading" is to reject the very documents God gave us to govern our life under the new covenant until Christ returns.

I agree, of course, that the church later formulated doctrines, such as the Trinity, that are not spelled out explicitly in the New Testament.

---

[10] France, *Women in the Church's Ministry,* 17-19.

But that is far different from what France and Thompson advocate, because Trinitarian doctrine was always *based on the actual teachings of the New Testament,* and its defenders always took the New Testament writings as their final authority. By contrast, France and Thompson do not take the New Testament statements as their final authority but "go beyond" the New Testament to a "target" that *contradicts or nullifies* the restrictions on women's ministry given by Paul. No Trinitarian doctrine was ever built by saying we need a view that contradicts and nullifies what Paul wrote in the New Testament itself.

This is also the problem with another "trajectory hermeneutic" approach, adopted by I. Howard Marshall, honorary research professor of New Testament at the University of Aberdeen, Scotland, when he discusses Paul's teachings on marriage in a chapter in the egalitarian book *Discovering Biblical Equality.* Marshall acknowledges that Paul told wives to submit to their husbands in the first century, but he says that those commands need not be followed by Christian wives today:

> Paul wrote as he did about marriage because in his world he did not know any other form than the patriarchal. As he did with other relationships, he worked within the structures of his time and gave directions for Christian behavior within them. The danger is to think that this validates the setup for all time.[11]

Marshall also writes:

> The concept of marriage between equal partners is just beginning to be perceived in the New Testament, and Paul should not be expected to step outside his time and see the consequences of his teaching. . . . in the first-century context submission can be seen as appropriate, but the element of authority is not inherent for all time. . . . A recognition of the fully egalitarian implications of scriptural teaching thus takes place at the level of the application of Scripture to the contemporary reader, rather than solely at the level of what individual texts were saying specifically to the original readers.[12]

---

[11] I. Howard Marshall, "Mutual Love and Submission in Marriage: Colossians 3:18-19 and Ephesians 5:21-33," in *Discovering Biblical Equality,* ed. Ronald W. Pierce and Rebecca Merrill Groothuis (Downers Grove, Ill.: InterVarsity, 2004), 204.

[12] Ibid., 195, 199, 203.

Thus Marshall's argument applies to the marriage texts the same procedure that France applies to the church: The passages taught that wives should be subject to their husbands *for that day,* but today other moral standards apply.

Then how do we know what the new standards are that should replace the New Testament commands? Just as France finds his controlling principle in the "fundamental equality" of Galatians 3:28, so Marshall takes his preferred New Testament principle, that of "mutual love," and finds that this principle eventually should override Paul's teaching on the submission of wives to their husbands. He says, "Mutual love transcends submission."[13]

What Marshall fails to recognize is that his argument for nullifying Paul's commands to wives is completely unlike other later doctrinal developments such as the doctrine of the Trinity or of Christology (which he mentions as parallels),[14] for Marshall is saying the New Testament commands on "mutual love" *nullify* the commands for wives to be subject to husbands, but no Trinitarian doctrine had to nullify and contradict the explicit teaching of any New Testament passages. If we take the entire New Testament as the very words of God for us in the new covenant today, then any claim that the "mutual love" commands should overrule other texts, such as Ephesians 5:22-24 and Colossians 3:18, should be seen as a claim that Paul the apostle contradicts himself, and therefore that the Word of God contradicts itself.

This "trajectory hermeneutic" argument of France, Thompson, and Marshall, and now featured so prominently in the major egalitarian work *Discovering Biblical Equality,* is a striking example of the way that arguments adopted forty years ago by theological liberals are now being endorsed by evangelical feminists. Krister Stendahl, the former academic dean at Harvard Divinity School, wrote something remarkably similar to Marshall's argument in a 1966 book arguing for women's ordination:

---

[13] Ibid., 194. It seems to me that several places in his chapter Marshall also fails sufficiently to recognize that the moral standard Christians are to obey (whether in the first century or today) is not the *practice of current culture* regarding marriage or anything else, but *what Paul commands* as he writes the Word of God for believers. Regarding Marshall's other argument, the claim that we have to move beyond the New Testament to advocate the abolition of slavery, see my discussion in the next chapter (pages 76-79); and in Grudem, *Evangelical Feminism and Biblical Truth* (Sisters, Ore.: Multnomah, 2004), 339-345.

[14] Ibid., 203.

If the actual stage of implementation in the first-century becomes the standard for what is authoritative, then those elements which point toward future implementation become neutralized and absorbed in a static "biblical view." . . . The correct description of first-century Christianity is not automatically the authoritative and intended standard for the church throughout the ages. It has no means by which it can account for the ensuing centuries of church history as God's history. It becomes a nostalgic attempt to play "First-Century."[15]

This 1966 book by Stendahl is the precursor of much modern egalitarian thinking. But Stendahl was not an evangelical in his view of the Bible. In fact, as academic dean of Harvard Divinity School, he was one of the most visible liberal theologians in the United States in 1966. Stendahl's approach to Scripture (which I could briefly paraphrase as "Yes, this is what the New Testament commanded for its time, but we don't have to obey that today") is essentially the same as the approach to Scripture taken by France, Thompson, and Marshall in their "trajectory hermeneutic." Evangelicals are just adopting liberal arguments thirty years later.

Another approach similar to Stendahl's is that of Peter Davids's essay on 1 Peter 3:1-7 in this same egalitarian collection of essays, *Discovering Biblical Equality.* (Davids is professor of biblical theology at St. Stephen's University in St. Stephen, New Brunswick, Canada, and formerly taught at Regent College, Vancouver, Canada.) However, Davids does not argue for a "trajectory" of development beyond the New Testament but argues that when Peter told wives, "be subject to your own husbands" (1 Pet. 3:1), his main purpose was to tell them not to give offense to the culture. Davids writes,

However, unless we assume that first-century Greco-Roman society is the only form of society upholding virtues approved by God (an unlikely assumption), we may find that a direct application of Peter's teaching in modern and postmodern societies would subvert his original intentions. . . . Ironically, interpretations that focus on the uni-

[15] Krister Stendahl, *The Bible and the Role of Women: A Case Study in Hermeneutics*, trans. Emilie T. Sanders (Philadelphia: Fortress, 1966; first published in Swedish in 1958), 35-36. I am grateful to David W. Jones for pointing out how much of current egalitarian argumentation was first stated by Stendahl in his 1966 book. For a further response to Stendahl, see Grudem, *Evangelical Feminism and Biblical Truth*, 358-361.

lateral obedience or submission of wives to husbands, regardless of cultural context, achieve the opposite of Peter's intention. Rather than promoting harmony with culture, they set Christian marriage partners at odds with culture and thus heighten the tension, and Christianity is perceived as undermining culture in a retrogressive way. This is precisely what Peter is seeking to minimize.[16]

Davids then gives a paraphrase of 1 Peter 3:1-6 in which he says that Peter's words today do not mean "Wives, be subject to your own husbands," but "Wives, *embrace your marital relationship.*" Verse 6, which says, "as Sarah obeyed Abraham, calling him lord," can be paraphrased, "Sarah was committed to Abraham and behaved accordingly *within her culture.*"[17]

But if the Bible simply means, "Follow what you perceive to be good in the culture around you," then why do we need the Bible? Davids, like liberal Protestants before him, has simply decided that obeying cultural expectations about marriage should be our standard, rather than obeying what the Bible commands. This is a clear and significant step toward liberalism.

To return to the "trajectory hermeneutic" argument of France, Thompson, and Marshall, however, we should recognize that they all think the trajectory found in the New Testament was heading toward egalitarianism. But the process of determining a "trajectory" is so subjective that the same argument could be used in just the other way. Someone could take France's view of Galatians 3:28 and argue that the trajectory looks like this:

FROM PAUL'S EARLY WRITINGS	TO PAUL'S LAST, MORE MATURE WRITINGS	TO THE FINAL TARGET FOR THIS TRAJECTORY	APPLICATION TODAY
Galatians 3:28: women in all positions of leadership	1 Timothy 2–3; Titus 1: only men can teach or be elders	women cannot participate in any ministry in the church	all ministry of all kinds must be done by men

---

[16] Peter Davids, "A Silent Witness in Marriage: 1 Peter 3:1-7," in Pierce and Groothuis, eds., *Discovering Biblical Equality*, 224-238.

[17] Ibid., 236, italics added. For a response to Davids's argument that this is similar to what we do regarding women's clothing in church and braided hair (236), see Grudem, *Evangelical Feminism and Biblical Truth*, 330-339, 397-402.

This is a ridiculous conclusion, but if we accept the "trajectory" principle of France and Thompson, it would be hard to say it was wrong.

Or we could take a "trajectory" argument on divorce:

FROM JESUS' TEACHINGS	TO PAUL'S TEACHINGS	TO THE FINAL TARGET FOR THIS TRAJECTORY	APPLICATION TODAY
Only one ground for divorce: adultery (Matt. 19:9)	Two grounds for divorce: adultery or desertion (1 Cor. 7:15)	Divorce for any hardship	God approves divorce for any hardship in marriage

We may think these trajectories are foolish, but they use the same process as France and Thompson use in moving from earlier to later biblical writings. And these trajectories all have one thing in common: *we no longer have to obey what the New Testament teaches.* We can devise our own ideas about the direction things were heading at the end of the New Testament, even ideas that contradict direct New Testament commands. This method has no controls on it. It is subjective, and the final authority is not the Bible but anyone's guess as to where the trajectory was heading.

One of the distinctive differences between historic, orthodox Protestants and the Roman Catholic Church has been that Protestants base doctrine on "Scripture alone" (once again, the Latin phrase commonly used for this is *sola Scriptura*), while Roman Catholics base doctrine on Scripture *plus* the authoritative teaching of the church through history.[18]

This "trajectory" argument of France, Thompson, and Marshall is disturbingly similar to Roman Catholicism in this regard, because they place final authority not in the New Testament writings but in their own ideas of where that teaching was leading. Yet Roman Catholics could argue that more reliable than egalitarian *speculation* on where New Testament teaching was leading are the *historical facts* of where the teaching did lead. So the trajectory (which actually was fulfilled in church history) would look like this:

---

[18] The book *Catechism of the Catholic Church* (San Francisco: Ignatius Press, 1994), which Pope John Paul II approved as "a sure and authentic reference text for teaching catholic doctrine" (5), says, "Both Scripture and Tradition must be accepted and honored with equal sentiments of devotion and reverence" (paragraph 82, page 26).

FROM JESUS' TEACHINGS	TO PAUL'S TEACHINGS	TO THE FINAL TARGET FOR THIS TRAJECTORY	APPLICATION TODAY
No local church officers or governing structure mentioned	Increased authority given to elders and deacons	Worldwide authority given to the pope, cardinals, and bishops	We should submit to the authority of the pope and the Roman Catholic Church

It is difficult to say how the approach of France, Thompson, and Marshall could *in principle* guard against this conclusion. But the Reformation principle *sola Scriptura* was formulated to guard against the kind of procedure France, Thompson, and Marshall advocate, because the Reformers knew that once our authority becomes "Scripture plus some later developments" rather than "Scripture alone," the unique governing authority of Scripture in our lives is lost. On several grounds, then, this trajectory argument must be rejected as inconsistent with the view that "all Scripture is breathed out by God" (2 Tim. 3:16), and as inconsistent with the command,

> Every word of God proves true. . . .
> Do not add to his words,
>   lest he rebuke you and you be found a liar (Prov. 30:5-6).

By undermining the authority of what Scripture actually teaches, and by substituting imagined later developments for the teaching of Scripture, the trajectory hermeneutic viewpoints of R. T. France, David Thompson, and I. Howard Marshall are another step on the path toward liberalism.

"REDEMPTIVE MOVEMENT" TRUMPS SCRIPTURE

Some evangelical feminists adopt William Webb's "redemptive-movement" approach and cast all the ethical commands of the New Testament into doubt

A variation of the "trajectory hermeneutic" discussed in the previous chapter is found in the "redemptive-movement hermeneutic" of William Webb, author of *Slaves, Women, and Homosexuals: Exploring the Hermeneutics of Cultural Analysis,*[1] whom we considered in another context in chapter 3.

Webb's book is similar to the "trajectory hermeneutic" approach of R. T. France and David Thompson discussed in the previous chapter, but I think it is even more harmful because it proposes an entirely new, highly complex process for evaluating all New Testament ethical commands; and, for Christians today, Webb's principles cast all of the New Testament's ethical commands into doubt. Because Webb's system is so complex and wide-ranging, I have given it a chapter of its own.

Webb says that the New Testament teachings on male headship in marriage and male leadership in the church were simply points along the path toward an ethic superior to that of the New Testament, an "ultimate ethic" toward which the New Testament was heading. Webb proposes a system that he calls a "redemptive-movement hermeneutic" to

---

[1] William Webb, *Slaves, Women, and Homosexuals: Exploring the Hermeneutics of Cultural Analysis* (Downers Grove, Ill.: InterVarsity Press, 2001).

defend his position. Through his use of this system, Webb argues that the New Testament texts about male headship in marriage and male church leadership are culturally relative.

Webb's view of what the New Testament taught for its own time is interesting. In contrast to many evangelical feminists who argue that the New Testament does *not* teach that wives should be subject to their husbands, and that it does *not* teach that only men should be elders, Webb believes that the New Testament *does* teach these things *for the culture in which the New Testament was written,* but he claims that in today's culture the treatment of women is an area in which "a better ethic than the one expressed in the isolated words of the text is possible."[2]

THE X→Y→Z PRINCIPLE

At the heart of Webb's system is his "redemptive-movement hermeneutic." (He notes that some may prefer calling his approach a "progressive" or "developmental" or "trajectory" hermeneutic, and says that that's fine with him.)[3] Webb explains his hermeneutic by what he calls "the X→Y→Z Principle." The letter X represents "the perspective of the *original culture.*" The letter Y indicates what the Bible says about a topic. Webb says, "The *central position* (Y) stands for where the isolated words of the Bible are in their development of a subject." The letter Z represents "an *ultimate ethic,*" that is, God's final ideal that the Bible is moving toward.[4]

Therefore, what evangelicals have ordinarily understood to be the teaching of the Bible on particular subjects is in fact *only a point along the way* (indicated by letter Y) toward the development of a final or ultimate ethic (Z). Webb says,

> The X→Y→Z Principle illustrates how numerous aspects of the biblical text were *not* written to establish a utopian society with complete justice and equity. They were written within a cultural framework with limited moves toward an ultimate ethic.[5]

---

[2] Ibid., 36, italics added.
[3] Ibid., 31.
[4] Ibid.
[5] Ibid.

Therefore, Webb discovers a number of points where "our con-temporary culture" has a *better* ethic than what is found in the Bible. Our culture has a better ethic today "where it happens to reflect a bet-ter social ethic—one closer to an *ultimate ethic* (Z) than to the ethic revealed in the isolated words of the biblical text."

With regard to the Bible's teachings about women, therefore, Webb admits that the Old and New Testaments improved the treat-ment of women when compared with their surrounding cultures, but he says,

> If one adopts a redemptive-movement hermeneutic, the softening of patriarchy (which Scripture itself initiates) can be taken a consider-able distance further. Carrying the redemptive movement within Scripture to a more improved expression for gender relationships . . . [today] ends in either ultra-soft patriarchy or complementary egalitarianism.[6]

So what is Webb's position on women's roles in marriage and the church? Later in the book, Webb defines "ultra-soft patriarchy" as a position in which there are no unique leadership roles for men in marriage or in the church, but men are given "a certain level of *symbolic* honor."[7] He defines "complementary egalitarianism" as a sys-tem in which there are full interdependence and "mutual submission" within marriage, and the only differences in roles are "based upon biological differences between men and women," so that, for instance, Webb would favor "a greater participation of women in the early stages of child rearing."[8] Thus, Webb's "ultra-soft patriarchy" differs from his "complementary egalitarianism" only in the slight bit of "symbolic honor" that ultra-soft patriarchy would still give to men. For all practical purposes, Webb is an evan-gelical feminist, and that explains why his book has been so eagerly welcomed and promoted by the evangelical feminist organization Christians for Biblical Equality.

---

[6] Ibid., 39.
[7] Ibid., 243.
[8] Ibid., 241.

I have written a far more detailed analysis of Webb's book else-where,[9] but I can summarize several points in this chapter.

WEBB'S SYSTEM NULLIFIES IN PRINCIPLE THE MORAL COMMANDS OF THE NEW TESTAMENT

What gives Webb's system some plausibility at first glance is that he agrees that homosexual conduct is morally wrong, and that the New Testament condemnations of homosexual conduct are transcultural.[10] He also affirms that the New Testament admonitions for children to be subject to their parents are transcultural.[11] So evangelicals may think his system has no dangers for Christians today. But that is an analysis simply based on looking at his *conclusions* on homosexuality and on children, not at the basis he used to reach those conclusions.

The important point to realize is that the *basis* on which Webb affirms that these commands are transcultural is not the teaching of the New Testament itself but Webb's own system, which has filtered those teachings and given them approval. There is a monumental difference in how Webb reaches his conclusions about Scripture and how traditional evangelicals would reach their conclusions.

Most evangelicals read a text such as, "Children, obey your parents in the Lord, for this is right" (Eph. 6:1), and conclude that children *today* are to obey their parents because the New Testament was written for Christians in the new covenant age (the time between Christ's death and his return). The teaching is there in the New Testament and therefore it applies to us. Most evangelicals reason the same way about the New Testament texts concerning homosexual conduct (see, for example, Rom. 1:26-27; 1 Cor. 6:9), concluding that these texts are morally binding on us today because we are part of the new covenant age and these texts were written to new covenant Christians.

---

[9] For a more detailed critique of Webb's book, see Wayne Grudem, "Should We Move Beyond the New Testament to a Better Ethic? An Analysis of William J. Webb, *Slaves, Women and Homosexuals: Exploring the Hermeneutics of Cultural Analysis*," *Journal of the Evangelical Theological Society* 47/2 (June 2004): 299-347; also reprinted as an appendix in Wayne Grudem, *Evangelical Feminism and Biblical Truth* (Sisters, Ore.: Multnomah, 2004), 600-645. For another analysis of Webb, see Thomas R. Schreiner, "Review of *Slaves, Women, and Homosexuals*," *Journal for Biblical Manhood and Womanhood* 7/1 (Spring 2002): 41-51. (His review was originally published in *The Southern Baptist Journal of Theology* 6/1 [2002]: 46-64.)

[10] Webb, *Slaves, Woman, and Homosexuals*, 39-41, 250-252, and many other places in the book.

[11] Ibid., 212.

But for Webb, the process is entirely different, and the basis of authority is different. The commands concerning children and homosexuals are binding on us today not because we are part of the new covenant age, for which the New Testament was written (I could not find such a consideration anywhere in Webb's book), but rather *because these commands have passed through the filtering system of Webb's eighteen criteria and have survived.* (I have further discussion of those eighteen criteria below.)[12]

In essence, therefore, *Webb's system invalidates the moral authority of the entire New Testament,* at least in the sense that we today should be obedient to the moral commands that were written to new covenant Christians. Instead, only those commands that have passed through Webb's eighteen-part filter are binding on us today.

According to Webb's system, then, Christians can no longer go to the New Testament, read the moral commands in one of Paul's epistles, and just obey them, as Christians have done throughout history. Webb thinks that would be to use a "static hermeneutic" that just reads the "isolated words of the text" and fails to understand "the spirit-movement component of meaning which significantly transforms the application of texts for subsequent generations."[13] Rather, we must realize that the New Testament teachings simply represent one stage in a trajectory of movement toward an ultimate ethic.

WEBB'S SYSTEM MAKES IT IMPOSSIBLE FOR ORDINARY CHRISTIANS TO DISCOVER WHAT PARTS OF THE BIBLE TO OBEY TODAY

So how can we know what biblical teachings to obey today? How can Christians discover this "ultimate ethic"? If we use Webb's system, the

---

[12] Actually, the command for children to obey their parents has not entirely survived Webb's filtering process, because Webb believes the command means that *adult* children in New Testament times were to continue to be obedient to their parents throughout their adult lives, but this aspect of the command was culturally relative and need not be followed by us today. That was just what the New Testament taught for its own time (point Y in Webb's X→Y→Z system). Today we have a better ethic than that (point Z, the ultimate ethic) and so today adult children do not have to be subject to their parents, even though that is what the New Testament command means when interpreted according to its original context and original author's intent.

Webb does not consider the far simpler possibility that first-century readers themselves would have understood the word "children" (Greek *tekna*) to apply only to people who were not adults, and so we today can say that Ephesians 6:1 applies to modern believers in just the same way that it applied to first-century believers, and no "cultural filters" need to be applied to that command.

[13] Ibid., 34.

answer is incredibly complicated. Webb takes the rest of his book to explain eighteen fairly complex criteria (to which he gives names such as "preliminary movement," "seed ideas," "breakouts," and "competing options") by which he thinks Christians today should evaluate the commands of the Bible and thereby discover the more just, more equitable ethical system the Bible was heading toward. Once that ultimate ethic has been discovered, then it becomes the moral standard we should follow and obey.

Just to give some idea of the criteria that Webb says we must use to determine if a biblical command is culturally relative, I will quote his explanation of how to use the first criterion, the one he calls "preliminary movement":

> Assessing redemptive-movement has its complications. Without going into an elaborate explanation, I will simply suggest a number of guidelines: (1) the ANE/GR [ancient Near Eastern/Graeco-Roman][14] *real* world must be examined along with its *legal* world, (2) the biblical subject on the *whole* must be examined along with its *parts*, (3) the biblical text must be compared to a number of other ANE/GR cultures which themselves must be compared with each other and (4) any portrait of movement must be composed of broad input from all three streams of assessment—foreign, domestic, and canonical.[15]

And this is just his procedure for the first of eighteen criteria! Who will be able to do this? Who knows the history of ancient cultures well enough to make these assessments?

Speaking from the perspective of more than thirty years in the academic world, I will not say that only one percent of the *Christians* in the world will be able to use Webb's system and tell us what moral standards we should follow today. I will not even say that one percent of the *seminary-trained pastors* in the world will be able to follow Webb's system and tell us what moral standards we should obey today. I will not even

---

[14] What Webb means by the "ancient Near Eastern/Graeco-Roman" world is the cultures of ancient Greece and Rome, and also the rest of the nations and cultures in the ancient Near East at the time when each part of the Bible was written.

[15] Ibid., 82. I added the explanatory words in square brackets, which he writes out in full elsewhere.

say that one percent of the *seminary professors* will have the requisite expertise in ancient cultures to use Webb's system and tell us what moral standards we should follow today. That is because the evaluation and assessment of any one ancient culture, to say nothing of all the ancient cultures surrounding the Bible, is a massive undertaking, even for one narrow subject such as laws concerning marriage and divorce, or property rights, or education and training of children. It is time-consuming and requires much specialized knowledge and an excellent research library. Therefore I will not even say that one percent of the *seminary professors who have academic doctorates in Old Testament or New Testament* will be able to use Webb's system and tell us what moral standards we should follow today. No, *in the end Webb's system as he describes it above can only be used by far less than one percent of the professors of New Testament and Old Testament in the Christian world today,* those few scholars who have the time and the specialized knowledge of rabbinic studies, of Graeco-Roman culture, and of ancient Egyptian and Babylonian and Assyrian and Persian cultures, and who have access to a major research library—only this very select group will be able to use Webb's "redemptive-movement hermeneutic" in the way he describes in the paragraph just quoted. This tiny group of experts will have to tell us what moral standards God wants us to follow today.

And that is only for Criterion 1 in his list of eighteen criteria!

If the evangelical world begins to adopt Webb's system, it is not hard to imagine that we will soon require a new class of "priests," erudite scholars with expertise in the ancient world who will be able to give us reliable conclusions about what kind of "ultimate ethic" we should follow today.

But this will create another problem, one I have observed often as I have lived and taught in the academic world: *scholars with such specialized knowledge often disagree.* Anyone familiar with the debates over rabbinic views of justification in the last two decades will realize how difficult it can be to understand exactly what was believed in an ancient culture on even one narrow topic, to say nothing of the whole range of ethical commands that we find in the New Testament.

Where then will Webb's system lead us? *It will lead us to massive inability to know with confidence anything that God requires of us.* The more scholars who become involved with telling us "how the Bible was moving" with respect to this or that aspect of ancient culture, the more opinions we will have, and the more despair people will feel about ever being able to know what God requires of us, what his "ultimate ethic" is.

How different from Webb's system is the simple, direct teaching of the New Testament! We read, "Therefore, having put away falsehood, let each one of you speak the truth with his neighbor, for we are members one of another" (Eph. 4:25), and we know we have to tell the truth and not lie. We read, "Children, obey your parents in the Lord, for this is right" (Eph. 6:1), and we read, "Fathers, do not provoke your children to anger, but bring them up in the discipline and instruction of the Lord" (Eph. 6:4), and we know those are God's commands for us today! We don't have to use Webb's eighteen criteria and study them through the filters of ancient Near Eastern/Graeco-Roman culture to know whether they apply to us! Nor do we need any specialist scholars to decide that for us. That is not the system God intended. His words are for his people to understand and obey.

THE SERIOUS DANGERS FOR CHRISTIAN MORALITY

But my larger concern about Webb's system is not even that it is so difficult for anyone to follow. My larger concern is that in actual practice, Webb's system means that *the moral authority of the New Testament is completely nullified, at least in principle.* There may be some New Testament commands that Webb concludes actually do represent an ultimate ethic, but even then we should obey them *not because they are taught in the New Testament* but because Webb's system has found that they meet the criteria of his "ultimate ethic."

The implications of this for Christian morality are extremely serious. It means that our ultimate authority is no longer the Bible but Webb's system. Of course, he claims that the "redemptive spirit" that drives his hermeneutic is *derived* from the biblical text, but by his own admission this "redemptive spirit" is not the same as the teachings of the Bible. It is derived from Webb's analysis of the interaction between the ancient culture and the biblical text.

Someone may object at this point, "Doesn't everyone have to use some kind of cultural filter like this? Doesn't everyone have to test the

New Testament commands to see if they are culturally relative or trans-cultural, before deciding whether to obey them?"

No, we do not at all have to use Webb's kind of test. There is a significant difference between Webb's approach and that of traditional evangelicals. Most evangelicals (including me) believe we are under the moral authority of the New Testament and are obligated to obey its commands *when we are in the same situation as that addressed in the New Testament command* (such as being a parent, a child, a person contemplating a divorce, a church selecting elders or deacons, a church preparing to celebrate the Lord's Supper, a husband, a wife, and so forth). When there is no exact modern equivalent to some aspect of a command (such as "honor the emperor" in 1 Pet. 2:17), we are still obligated to obey the command, but we do so by *applying* it to situations that are essentially similar. Therefore, "honor the emperor" is applied to honoring the president or the prime minister. In fact, in several such cases the immediate context contains pointers to broader applications (such as 1 Pet. 2:13-14, which mentions being subject to "every human institution" including the "emperor" and "governors" as specific examples).

But with Webb the situation is entirely different. He does not consider the moral commands of the New Testament to represent a perfect or final moral system for Christians. They are rather a *pointer* that "provides the direction toward the divine destination, but its literal, isolated words are not always the destination itself. Sometimes God's instructions are simply designed to get his flock moving."[16] In this way Webb's system undermines the moral authority of the Bible. Once people adopt Webb's system, all sorts of new "redemptive movements" will be discovered whenever someone wants to justify disobedience to some other part of Scripture. The moral authority is no longer the teaching of the Bible itself but some standard that people imagine as coming after the Bible. In this way, Webb's redemptive-movement hermeneutic is a major step down the path toward liberalism.

Webb responded to my earlier critique of his position[17] in a paper read at the annual meeting of the Evangelical Theological Society,

---

[16] Ibid., 60.
[17] See Grudem, *Evangelical Feminism and Biblical Truth*, 600-645.

November 17-19, 2004.[18] He denied that his system nullifies in principle the moral authority of the New Testament, because it is grounded in the New Testament. Here is the heart of his response:

> There is a *solid link* in meaning between the underlying redemptive spirit (movement meaning) and an *ultimate ethic* that is *hardly foreign* to what the Bible says. The *better social ethic* is not "Webb's better ethic" (contra Grudem) but an expression of an ethic that is deeply rooted within the Bible. It is the Bible's ethic, not mine![19]

But this response only confirms my concerns. He says his ethic is "the Bible's ethic" because he uses the Bible to see the direction of progress that can be made beyond the Bible! Therefore he uses the Bible as an authority to prove that we should move beyond the moral standards taught in the Bible. This is exactly what I mean by undermining in principle the moral authority of the New Testament.

The fact remains that Webb claims that the moral standards of his "better social ethic" (his point Z in his X→Y→Z system) are an improvement on the moral commands stated in the New Testament. Of course he says there is a "solid link" and his new moral standards are "hardly foreign" to what the Bible says, because he can always trace some similarities between these different standards, but they are still new standards, "better" standards that he says improve on the moral standards of the Bible. And so we can never know, without Webb's system, which commands of the New Testament we should obey and which we should improve on. This is what I call nullifying in principle the moral authority of all the New Testament commands.

To give one specific example, the New Testament says, in 1 Timothy 2:12:

> I do not permit a woman to teach or to exercise authority over a man . . .

But Webb's system concludes that

---

[18] Webb's response, "A Redemptive-Movement Hermeneutic: Responding to Grudem's Concerns," is available online at www.etsjets.org.
[19] Ibid., 25, italics added.

We should permit a woman to teach and to exercise authority over a man.

Webb tells us that this is "a better social ethic" than what is written in the New Testament. So how can he still say that this "is the Bible's ethic"? Only by giving a different sense to "is," making the word "is" mean *is a system that results from projecting development beyond the* Bible's ethic." This is hardly the normal sense of the word "is."

Webb then restated his system for the 2004 release of the egalitarian book *Discovering Biblical Equality,* in his chapter, "A Redemptive-Movement Hermeneutic."[20] Here he more clearly stated the question:

> All agree that the New Testament moves beyond the Old Testament in its development or realization of ethic; that is, it takes the Old Testament redemptive spirit further. However, the New Testament is still *like* the Old Testament in expressing the unfolding of an ethic at certain points in an incremental (not absolute) fashion. In the end, therefore, the issue is not the New Testament's status as final revelation but *the degree to which the New Testament is similar or dissimilar to the Old Testament with respect to its realization of ethic.* Do contemporary Christians need to move *with* the redemptive spirit of the New Testament toward a realization of that movement beyond certain concrete, frozen-in-time particulars?[21]

Here Webb reinforces his idea that, just as New Testament Christians had different moral standards than those in the Old Testament, and no longer had to follow all the Old Testament laws, so we need to explore how we can "move with the redemptive spirit of the New Testament" and go *beyond* the New Testament's moral commands when our culture "happens to reflect a better ethic."[22]

How then is Webb's system "based on" the Bible and "subject to" the Bible's authority? Not in the normal way that people have understood those expressions, but only in the sense that he uses the moral

---

[20] William Webb, "A Redemptive-Movement Hermeneutic: The Slavery Analogy," in *Discovering Biblical Equality*, ed. Ronald W. Pierce and Rebecca Merrill Groothuis (Downers Grove, Ill.: InterVarsity, 2004), 382-400.
[21] Ibid., 393.
[22] Ibid., 383.

standards of the Bible *to show him the direction he should move away from the standards of the Bible* and move toward better standards, toward a "better ethic," than that found in the Bible.[23]

Webb still seems unaware of, or unable to represent fairly, any responsible interpretative process that has been used by evangelicals before he proposed his system. The only alternative to his position that he mentions is a "static" approach that "understands the words of the text in isolation from their ancient historical-cultural context and with minimal—or no—emphasis on their underlying spirit"[24] or that understands the meaning of the words "isolated from historical and canonical contexts."[25] But what responsible evangelical interpreter says we should understand New Testament commands "isolated from their historical and canonical contexts"? Webb simply ignores the dominant view of the Protestant (not Roman Catholic) churches for centuries: that commands should be understood in light of their literary, historical, and canonical contexts, but without seeking to go beyond the New Testament commands to find a "better ethic."

Before concluding this chapter, I need to respond to two arguments Webb has put forth to defend his system. First, he argues that his system is needed in order to show that the Bible does not endorse slavery. Second, he argues that Christians have always used some kind of "redemptive-movement" hermeneutic like his.

BUT DOES THE BIBLE ENDORSE SLAVERY?

With respect to the first question, whether we need Webb's system to show that the Bible does not endorse slavery, Webb does not seem to be sufficiently aware of how Christians in the past have used the teachings of the Bible itself (item Y in Webb's system) to oppose and defeat slavery. They have not used Webb's "redemptive-movement hermeneutic" and found their moral standards in some development beyond the New Testament.

Most evangelical interpreters say that the Bible does not command

---

[23] I should also note that while Webb earlier commended Thomas Schreiner for understanding him correctly (see Webb, "Responding to Grudem's Concerns," 2), Schreiner now agrees with my critique of Webb's system: see Thomas Schreiner, "An Interpretation of 1 Timothy 2:9-15: A Dialogue with Scholarship," in *Women in the Church*, 2nd ed., ed. Andreas Köstenberger and Thomas Schreiner (Grand Rapids, Mich.: Baker, 2005), 223n177.

[24] Webb, "Redemptive-Movement Hermeneutic," 382.

[25] Ibid., 383.

or encourage or endorse slavery, but rather tells Christians who were slaves how they should conduct themselves, and also gives principles that would modify and ultimately lead to the abolition of slavery (1 Cor. 7:21-22; Gal. 3:28; Philem. 16, 21; and note the condemnation of "enslavers" at 1 Tim. 1:10, ESV, a verse that was previously overlooked in this regard because it was often translated "kidnappers"). By contrast, Webb *believes that the Bible actually endorses slavery,* even though it is a kind of slavery with "better conditions and fewer abuses" than the kind of slavery practiced in the surrounding culture.[26]

In claiming that the Bible endorses slavery, Webb shows no awareness of biblical anti-slavery arguments such as those of Theodore Weld in *The Bible Against Slavery,*[27] a book that was widely distributed and frequently reprinted by anti-slavery abolitionists in nineteenth-century America. Weld argued strongly against American slavery from Exodus 21:16, "he that stealeth a man and selleth him, or if he be found in his hand, he shall surely be put to death" (KJV) (13-15), as well as from the fact that people are in the image of God and therefore it is morally wrong to treat any human being as property (8-9, 15-17). He argued that ownership of another person breaks the eighth commandment, "Thou shalt not steal," as follows:

> The eighth commandment forbids the taking of *any* part of that which belongs to another. Slavery takes the *whole.* Does the same Bible which prohibits the taking of *any* thing from him, sanction the taking of *every* thing? Does it thunder wrath against the man who robs his neighbor of a *cent,* yet commission him to rob his neighbor of *himself?* Slaveholding is the highest possible violation of the eighth commandment" (10-11).

In the rest of the book Weld answered detailed objections about various verses used by slavery proponents. The whole basis of Weld's anti-slavery book is that *the moral standards taught in the Bible are right,*

---

26 Webb, *Slaves, Women, and Homosexuals,* 37.

27 Theodore Weld, *The Bible Against Slavery* (4th ed., New York: American Anti-Slavery Society, 1838). The book was first published in Boston in 1837; my citations are from the 1838 edition. See also several essays in Mason Lowance, ed., *Against Slavery: An Abolitionist Reader* (New York: Penguin, 2000).

and there is no hint that we have to move beyond the Bible's ethics to oppose slavery, as Webb would have us do.

In Webb's 2004 restatement of his position in *Discovering Biblical Equality*,[28] he insists even more strongly that only his "redemptive-movement hermeneutic" can keep Christians from endorsing slavery today. He says, "Unless one embraces the redemptive spirit of Scripture, there is no biblically based rationale for championing an abolitionist perspective," and says "a redemptive-movement hermeneutic applied to the New Testament" is "the only valid way to arrive at the abolition of slavery."[29] In these statements Webb reveals a surprising ignorance of nineteenth-century anti-slavery movements that had no "redemptive-movement hermeneutic" and still argued against slavery from the moral standards found in the Bible itself. Webb's system never abolished slavery, but courageous Christians who relied on the New Testament as a perfect and final moral standard did abolish it.

In addition, Webb shows no knowledge of the differences between the horrible institution of slavery as it was practiced in America before the mid-nineteenth century and the first-century institution described by the Greek term *doulos* (the Greek word which is usually translated "slave" or "servant" in the New Testament, but which the NASB and NKJV often better translate as "bond-servant" or "bondservant," showing that it was a different institution). I have discussed the institution of being a "bondservant" (Greek *doulos*) in detail elsewhere,[30] but it may be briefly said here that this was the most common employment situation in the Roman Empire in the time of the New Testament. A bondservant could not quit his job or seek another employer until he obtained his freedom, but there were extensive laws that regulated the treatment of such bondservants and gave them considerable protection. Bondservants could own their own property and often purchased their freedom by about age 30, and they often held positions of significant responsibility such as teachers, physicians, nurses, managers of estates, retail merchants, and business executives.

For example, note Jesus' parable where some "bondservants" were entrusted with huge sums of money:

---

[28] William Webb, "Redemptive-Movement Hermeneutic: The Slavery Analogy," 382-400.
[29] Ibid., 395.
[30] See Grudem, *Evangelical Feminism and Biblical Truth*, 339-345.

> For it will be like a man going on a journey, who called his *servants*
> [plural of Greek *doulos*] and entrusted to them his property. To one
> he gave five talents, to another two, to another one, to each accord-
> ing to his ability. Then he went away (Matt. 25:14-15).

A "talent" was a monetary unit worth about twenty years' wages for a
laborer. To put this in contemporary (2006) terms, a laborer working at
$10 per hour would earn about $20,000 a year, so a "talent" would be
20 X $20,000 or $400,000. Five talents would be $2,000,000. Jesus tells
this parable as if that were the kind of thing that "masters" did with their
bondservants, entrusting them with much responsibility and considerable freedom.

This first-century institution of "bondservants" is far different from the
picture that comes to mind when modern readers hear the word "slavery."
This helps us understand why the New Testament did not immediately prohibit the institution of "bondservants," while at the same time giving principles that led to its eventual abolition. And it helps explain why the
Christians in England and the United States who campaigned for the abolition of slavery based on the moral teachings of the Bible saw it as a far worse
institution, one that was not at all supported by the Bible but was so cruel
and dehumanizing that it had to be abolished completely and forever.

Webb is wrong in thinking that his system is needed to show that
the Bible opposes slavery. Yes, some slave owners tried to use the Bible
to support slavery in nineteenth-century America, *but opponents of slavery used the Bible too*, and they were far more persuasive, *and they won
the argument*. They did this all without needing to go beyond the moral
standards of the Bible as Webb would have us do.

HAVE CHRISTIANS ALWAYS USED A SYSTEM LIKE WEBB'S?

When Webb claims that "A redemptive-movement hermeneutic has always
been a major part of the historic church, apostolic and beyond,"[31] and
therefore that all Christians believe in some kind of "redemptive-movement" hermeneutic, he is not representing the history of the church accurately, because he fails to make one important distinction: evangelicals have
always held that *the redemptive movement within Scripture ends with the*

---

[31] Ibid., 35.

New Testament! Webb carries it beyond the New Testament. To attempt to go *beyond* the New Testament documents and derive our authority from "where the New Testament was heading" is to reject the very documents God gave us to govern our life under the new covenant until Christ returns.

Like many egalitarian books, Webb's book is published by InterVarsity Press.[32] Because Webb provides a new argument for abolishing any significant male leadership roles in the home and the church, it is not surprising that Webb's book is promoted by the evangelical feminist organization Christians for Biblical Equality and is sold on their website (www.cbeinternational.org).

But it is somewhat surprising to me that Webb's book has endorsements on the back cover by such recognized evangelicals as Darrell Bock, New Testament professor at Dallas Seminary (who wrote the foreword to Webb's book), Stephen Spencer (formerly a theology professor at Dallas Seminary but now teaching at Wheaton College), Craig Keener (of Palmer Seminary, formerly Eastern Baptist Seminary), and Craig Evans (of Trinity Western University). In addition to this, Sarah Sumner, a theology professor at Azusa Pacific University, says that Webb's book is "the most helpful book I know" on discerning which passages are culturally bound and which are transcultural.[33]

William Webb's book has become a major influence supporting evangelical feminism. But Webb's "redemptive-movement hermeneutic" undermines Scripture's authority just as do the trajectory hermeneutic positions of France and Thompson critiqued in the previous chapter. And Webb's system is more harmful because he applies it more systematically to the whole of the New Testament. Webb's redemptive-movement hermeneutic nullifies in principle the moral authority of the entire New Testament. And in that way it undermines the authority of the Bible.

Therefore, William Webb's attempt to support evangelical feminism with his "redemptive-movement hermeneutic" is a huge step down the path toward liberalism.

---

[32] InterVarsity Press–USA has a policy of promoting evangelical feminist books: see Jeff Robinson, "IVP Casts Egalitarian Vision Within Publishing Mission" at gender-news.com (www.gender-news.com/article.php?id=72, accessed 4-19-05). InterVarsity Press–UK is a separate company, and several egalitarian books that have been published by IVP-USA have not been published by IVP-UK, due to a different set of criteria used in publishing decisions.

[33] Sarah Sumner, *Men and Women in the Church* (Downers Grove, Ill.: InterVarsity Press, 2003), 213.

8

IS IT JUST A MATTER OF CHOOSING OUR FAVORITE VERSES?

Some evangelical feminists claim that our position on gender roles just depends on which Bible passages we choose to prioritize

A different kind of movement toward liberalism is found when scholars such as R. T. France, Stanley Grenz, and Sarah Sumner assert that our position on the roles of men and women simply depends on which Bible verses we choose to emphasize. As I mentioned in an earlier chapter, R. T. France is the former principal of Wycliffe Hall, Oxford, and a member of the Committee on Bible Translation for the NIV Bible. Sarah Sumner is a theology professor at Azusa Pacific University. Stanley Grenz, prior to his untimely death in 2005, was professor of theology at Carey Theological College, Vancouver, Canada, and had previously taught for many years at Regent College, Vancouver.

One example of this approach is found when R. T. France says,

> We have seen that fundamental to this issue has been the question of which among differing biblical texts or themes is considered to be basic. . . . Once we choose to begin at a given point, everything else will be viewed and interpreted in the light of that starting point. . . . There is no rule of thumb—that is precisely our problem. A judgment has to be made, and not all will make it in the same way. Probably we all have our "canon within the canon" (by which we mean those parts of Scripture with which we feel comfortable, and which say

what we would like them to say) which we regard as "basic." But those instinctive preferences are normally derived from the tradition within which we have been brought up, rather than from an informed and principled choice made on the basis of the texts themselves.[1]

In his book *Women in the Church: A Biblical Theology of Women in Ministry,* Stanley Grenz adopts a similar view in a section titled "The Question of Hermeneutical Priority":

> Yet one question remains: Which Pauline text(s) carry hermeneutical priority in our attempt to understand Paul's teaching about women in the church? Are we to look to the egalitarian principle the apostle set forth in Galatians 3:28 as the foundation for our understanding of the apostle's own position? Or do we begin with those passages which seem to place limitations on the service of women (1 Cor 11:3-16; 14:34-35; 1 Tim 2:11-15) and understand the Galatians text in the light of such restrictions?
>
> Egalitarians often claim that Galatians 3:28 deserves hermeneutical priority. . . . At this point, egalitarians, and not complementarians, are on the right track. . . . The seemingly restrictive texts complementarians cite . . . cannot be universal rules but Paul's attempts to counter the abuses of specific situations.[2]

Sarah Sumner says we have to decide "which verse(s) should take priority over the others," or "which verse stands in charge as the boss" (which she then calls the "boss verse").[3] Elsewhere she claims that we disagree because "we bring so many assumptions to the text," and if we bring egalitarian assumptions we will find egalitarian teaching in the text, but if we bring complementarian assumptions we will find complementarian teaching in the text.[4]

---

[1] R. T. France, *Women in the Church's Ministry: A Test Case for Biblical Interpretation* (Grand Rapids, Mich.: Eerdmans, 1995), 93-94.

[2] Stanley Grenz, *Women in the Church: A Biblical Theology of Women in Ministry* (Downers Grove, Ill.: InterVarsity Press, 1995), 106-107. A similar approach is found in the egalitarian compendium *Discovering Biblical Equality,* in I. Howard Marshall's argument that the texts on mutual love in the New Testament eventually override the texts on a wife's submission to her husband: see the discussion in chapter 6 above, pages 58-59.

[3] Sarah Sumner, *Men and Women in the Church* (Downers Grove, Ill.: InterVarsity Press, 2003), 128; see also 256-257.

[4] Ibid., 249. She also says that our viewpoints are often the result of traditional assumptions inherited from church history (see 275, 285, 292-293).

But this is not an approach toward Scripture that evangelicals should accept. This approach essentially claims that various parts of the Bible teach different, self-contradictory positions, so people can just decide what position they want to find in Scripture and then go there and find it! In the end, rather than Scripture having authority over our lives, this process allows us to have authority over the Bible, because we can just go there and find what we want to find and decide that these verses will have "hermeneutical priority." If other verses appear to contradict our view, we just say that we have chosen not to make those verses a priority, and therefore they are overridden by the verses that we have chosen.

Someone might object, "Doesn't everybody have to do something like this? When there are verses that seem to conflict, don't we all have to decide which ones we will favor and emphasize?"

No, I do not think so. I think that when we rightly understand all the relevant Bible verses on any topic, they will be seen to be not contradictory but complementary. And I believe that is the underlying conviction of all current complementarian writers (those who, like myself, hold that men and women are equal in value but have different roles in marriage and the church).

Of course, I cannot examine all complementarian writings here to demonstrate this point. But I can use my own writings on this subject as one example, probably a representative example. Nowhere in my writings have I claimed that we must minimize or ignore so-called "egalitarian texts" (like Gal. 3:28) on the basis of some kind of "hermeneutical priority" of other texts. I do not believe we should treat Scripture that way, because *all* of it is God's Word, and *all* of it is "profitable for teaching, for reproof, for correction, and for training in righteousness" (2 Tim. 3:16). We must not minimize these texts but rather treat them fairly and remain subject to their authority. This certainly includes such "egalitarian texts" as Galatians 3:28, and the passages about Deborah, Huldah, Phoebe, Priscilla, and Junia(s). Even if we studied all of these texts *first* and drew conclusions from them before we looked at any "complementarian texts" such as 1 Timothy 2:12, these "egalitarian texts" would not lead us to affirm that women could have governing and teaching roles over New Testament churches. The texts would not lead us to *affirm* that, because they do not *teach* that. They surely honor the ministries of women and their equality in value and dignity, but they do not tell us that women could govern or teach a New Testament church.

But it is difficult to imagine that an egalitarian advocate could do the same with passages such as 1 Corinthians 14:33-36, 1 Timothy 2:11-15, the passages about male elders in 1 Timothy 3 and Titus 1, and the passages about the twelve male apostles. It would be difficult to believe that an egalitarian could begin with those texts and reach the conclusion that all roles in the church are open to women as well as men, because these texts set a pattern that so clearly affirms the opposite.

I am not saying that we all should *emphasize* every verse of the Bible equally. There will always be passages that a pastor will emphasize more than others in his preaching and teaching. He will probably spend more time teaching from Romans or 1 Corinthians than from Leviticus, for example. But that is not because this pastor thinks that Romans is part of a "canon within the canon" or that it has more authority than Leviticus. It is rather because Leviticus was written to a situation we no longer find ourselves in—the situation of God's old covenant people, who had to follow ceremonial rules and regulations. But the New Testament epistles are written to people in the same situation we are in today—members of the New Testament church who live after Jesus' resurrection and before his second coming. Preaching from Leviticus is worthwhile and is "profitable for teaching, for reproof, for correction, and for training in righteousness" (2 Tim. 3:16), but its application to our situation is less direct and more difficult to understand, and it is not wrong to give it less emphasis in preaching than many of the New Testament books. This question of emphasis, however, is different from an evangelical feminist claim that implies we can decide to be subject to some parts of Scripture and not to others.

I am troubled by the evangelical feminist claim that it all depends on what texts we choose as basic, because that suggests there are other texts we can decide do *not* apply to us today and do *not* have authority over us today. Once again, that position weakens the authority of Scripture in our lives.

The egalitarian and the complementarian positions are not the same in how they treat the texts they emphasize. Egalitarians *wrongly limit* the application of male leadership texts by saying they *don't apply today to the very same kinds of situations* they applied to when originally written (namely, conduct in the assembled church and the office of elder with governing authority over the church). And then egalitarians *wrongly expand* the application of equality texts far beyond the kinds of situations they were originally written to address (as mentioned above, the "egalitarian texts" were not written to address situations of governing or teaching over the church).

By contrast, the complementarian position *rightly applies* the texts on male leadership to exactly *the same kind of situations* they applied to when originally written (governing and teaching God's people in the church). And the complementarian position *rightly applies* the "equality texts" to exactly *the same kinds of situations* they applied to when originally written (affirming all sorts of ministries for women except governing or teaching over the assembled church, and affirming the full dignity and value of women in God's sight and in the ministry of the church).

The complementarian position does not "limit the application" of the so-called "equality texts" in Scripture (such as Gal. 3:28) but understands them to be limited by their own contexts and subject matter and wording.[5] This is not wrongly understanding these texts; it is understanding them according to the principles by which we should understand all texts. And we understand these texts in a way that does not require them to nullify or contradict other texts about male leadership in the church.

Thus, the two positions clearly differ in the way they interpret and apply biblical texts, not just in which texts they "choose as basic."

In fact, this egalitarian claim that first derives a principle of "equality" from Galatians 3:28 and then uses that *general principle* to override the *specific teaching* of texts that talk about church leadership, looks dangerously similar to a procedure that has been used numerous times in the past to deny the authority of Scripture and allow all sorts of false doctrine into the church. For example, in the early part of the twentieth century, liberals routinely appealed to a *vague general principle* of the "love of God" (which surely can be found in many passages) in order to deny that God had any wrath against sin. And once they denied God's

---

[5] See, for example, Richard Hove, *Equality in Christ? Galatians 3:28 and the Gender Dispute* (Wheaton, Ill.: Crossway, 1999).

wrath, then it was easy to believe that all people everywhere would be saved (for God is a "God of love" and not of wrath). After that, it was also easy to believe that Jesus' death was not a substitutionary sacrifice for our sins—that is, he did not bear the wrath of God against our sins— but rather that his death was somehow merely an example for us. In this way a vague biblical principle ("God's love") was used to deny many specific passages of Scripture on the wrath of God and on Christ's death, and to deny a major doctrine such as substitutionary atonement.

This is similar to the egalitarian claim that the *vague general principles* of equality and fairness (as derived from Galatians 3:28) require that women have access to the same governing and teaching roles in the church that men do. Vague general principles (equality, fairness) are also used to weaken or nullify specific passages of Scripture.

Therefore the positions of R. T. France, Stanley Grenz, and Sarah Sumner, all of whom claim that our decision in the question of men's and women's roles in home and church just depends on which verses we choose to give priority to, ultimately assume that there are contradictory positions taught in different parts of Scripture. They assume that we should be free to choose verses that support one of those contradictory positions, and that choice then allows us to decide that the verses that support the other position are not morally binding on us. We have given other verses "priority" and therefore we are free to disregard or disobey these "lower priority" verses.

In this way, the views of France, Grenz, and Sumner, who claim that our position just depends on which verses we choose to prioritize, undermine the authority of Scripture in our lives. And thus they are another step on the path toward liberalism.

CAN WE JUST IGNORE THE "DISPUTED" PASSAGES?

Some evangelical feminists silence the most relevant
Bible passages on men and women by saying
they are "disputed"

Another evangelical feminist method of effectively denying the authority of Scripture is one taken by authors Cindy Jacobs, Sarah Sumner, and Rich Nathan, and also by the position paper of the Assemblies of God on "The Role of Women in Ministry."

Cindy Jacobs is a widely known speaker and writer whose writings on prayer have been greatly appreciated, especially in charismatic circles. Her book *Women of Destiny*[1] identifies her on the dust jacket as "founder and president of Generals of Intercession, an international prayer ministry" and also as a member of the international board of Aglow International. Her book is published by Regal Books. Sarah Sumner is a theology professor at Azusa Pacific University, and her book *Men and Women in the Church*[2] is published by InterVarsity Press. Rich Nathan has had a very successful ministry as senior pastor of Vineyard Church of Columbus, Ohio, and is on the National Executive Board of the Association of Vineyard Churches. Nathan's book *Who Is My Enemy?*[3]

---

[1] Cindy Jacobs, *Women of Destiny* (Ventura, Calif.: Regal, 1998).
[2] Sarah Sumner, *Men and Women in the Church* (Downers Grove, Ill.: InterVarsity Press, 2003).
[3] Rich Nathan, *Who Is My Enemy?* (Grand Rapids, Mich.: Zondervan, 2002).

is published by Zondervan. The Assemblies of God is a major Pentecostal denomination (over 2 million members) that was founded in 1914.

These authors claim in their writings that *they cannot figure out what the Bible teaches on this issue,* so our decision must be made on the basis of observing what kinds of ministries are effective today. But as I will explain below, this procedure *effectively silences the ability of Scripture to speak to a matter where every church must make decisions every day.* It is a different kind of rejection of the authority of Scripture, and a different kind of step down the path toward liberalism.

Cindy Jacobs writes,

> As I've studied the so-called "difficult passages" about women, I have concluded that the differing interpretations are rather like that of teaching on end-time eschatology. Throughout the years I've heard excellent sermons on just about every position, all using Scripture, and all sounding as if they had merit![4]

A few pages later she affirms this principle regarding controversial passages of Scripture:

> Controversial passages lacking consensus from godly people of different persuasions usually mean that the passages are not clear enough to resolve with certainty. Therefore we must be tolerant on [sic] different views on those passages.[5]

A similar approach is taken by the Assemblies of God position paper on "The Role of Women in Ministry":

> We all agree that Scripture must be our final authority in settling questions of faith and practice. But when born-again, Spirit-filled Christians, following proper hermeneutical principles, come to reasonable but differing interpretations, we do well not to become dogmatic in support of one position.[6]

---

[4] Jacobs, *Women of Destiny,* 175. Later she compares arguing about 1 Timothy 2:11-15 and 1 Corinthians 14:34-35 to arguing about "other obscure passages" such as "the verse that deals with baptism for the dead (see 1 Cor 15:29)" (234).

[5] Ibid., 178 (Jacobs says she got this principle from Robert Clinton of Fuller Seminary).

[6] From http://ag.org/top/beliefs/position_papers/, accessed 2-28-06 (under "Women, The Role of . . . in Ministry," paragraph 2). However, in the body of the Assemblies of God paper

Sarah Sumner says,

> We don't know how to translate 1 Timothy 2, much less interpret it
> correctly or apply it appropriately today. That's why this passage is
> so humbling; to some extent it has stumped us all, scholars and prac-
> titioners alike.[7]

Rich Nathan writes,

> It is not at all plain what Paul meant to communicate to his original
> readers, plus it is even less plain how Paul's words should be applied
> today. . . . My files include at least fifteen very different interpreta-
> tions of 1 Timothy 2. . . . To summarize, there is no common agree-
> ment on what these individual words mean in 1 Timothy 2:9-15.[8]

The heart of this approach is that sincere Christians like Cindy
Jacobs, the leaders of the Assemblies of God, Sarah Sumner, and Rich
Nathan are saying they cannot reach a decision on the meaning of
1 Corinthians 14, 1 Timothy 2, and the passages in 1 Timothy 3 and
Titus 1 that say elders are to be the husband of one wife.[9] When anyone
tries to reason from these verses, their response is, essentially, "I'm not
going to base my decision on these verses—nobody knows what they
mean."

It is important to recognize what this kind of response does in this
debate on the role of women in the church. It effectively prevents
1 Corinthians 14, 1 Timothy 2, 1 Timothy 3, and Titus 1 from speaking to this question. If someone says, "I'm not going to base my decision on these verses because nobody can figure out what they mean
anyway," then he has essentially said that *those passages cannot play a
role in his decision about this question.* And that means that the passages

---

they do affirm a position on the decisive passages (such as those in 1 Corinthians 14;
1 Timothy 2; 1 Timothy 3; Gal. 3:28; and other passages), in each case adopting egalitarian
interpretations as the most likely. Near the end they say, "we conclude that we cannot find
convincing evidence that the ministry of women is restricted according to some sacred or
immutable principle" (fourth paragraph from end).

[7] Sumner, *Men and Women in the Church*, 248.

[8] Rich Nathan, *Who Is My Enemy?* 142-144.

[9] However, it is interesting that both Sumner and Nathan elsewhere say that they have decided
that 1 Timothy 2:12 means that women who are teaching false doctrine in the church at
Ephesus should be silent.

that *most directly* speak to the question of women teaching and governing in the church are silenced and excluded from discussion on that very question. In essence, this approach guarantees that a decision about women teaching and governing in the church will be made without reference to the passages in the Bible that speak most directly to the topic. *It is hard to think of an approach more likely to lead to a wrong decision.*

A. WHY IS THE ISSUE OF WOMEN'S ROLES IN CHURCH AND HOME DIFFERENT FROM QUESTIONS ABOUT THE END TIMES OR BAPTISM OR PREDESTINATION?

At this point someone may object as follows: "But we all do this with hard questions! Many people decide they can't figure out the differences between premillennial, postmillennial, and amillennial views of Christ's return, or between pre-tribulation and post-tribulation views of the end times. And many people can't figure out how to reconcile predestination and our individual choices, or how to understand the doctrine of the Trinity. In addition, many Christian organizations have said they simply will not take a stand regarding different views of baptism or Calvinism and Arminianism. None of these decisions is a concession to liberalism! How is this issue different?"

My response is that *this issue is different from those questions* in several important ways. Here are the factors to consider:

(1) **Hidden things.** I agree that *there are some things that God has not told us* in Scripture. He has not told us how he can be three persons and yet one God. He has not told us exactly how predestination fits together with the reality of our individual choices.[10] Regarding mysteries like these, we have to remember Deuteronomy 29:29: "The *secret things* belong to the LORD our God, but the *things that are revealed* belong to us and to our children forever, that we may do all the words of this law."

But the role of women in the church is not like this. It is not a "secret

---

[10] However, God has told us quite a lot about those topics, while still not answering all our questions. See Wayne Grudem, *Systematic Theology* (Grand Rapids, Mich.: Zondervan, 1994), chapters 14 (on the Trinity), 16 (on providence), and 32 (on predestination).

thing" on which God has told us nothing. There are specific passages that speak to the issue.

(2) *Predictions of the future.* I also agree that *the Bible makes predictions about the future whose application to future events are uncertain.* It is hard for anyone to be sure exactly what kind of age is meant when the Bible says that people "came to life and reigned with Christ for a thousand years" (Rev. 20:4).[11] It seems reasonable for broadly based Christian organizations to allow some freedom of interpretation regarding Scriptures that speak of these future events. That is the nature of the case when dealing with prophecies about the future.

For example, the Jewish people had many uncertainties about the Old Testament predictions of a coming Messiah (see 1 Pet. 1:10-12), and Jesus had to explain to his disciples how the prophecies applied to him (see Luke 24:27). He had to explain how he came the *first* time to earn our salvation (and fulfilled certain Old Testament prophecies about the Messiah) and would come the *second* time to bring judgment and to reign over the earth (and would fulfill other Old Testament prophecies about the Messiah). Understanding predictions of the future is, in the nature of the subject matter, a difficult issue for us. Some of these controversies will continue to be impossible to resolve with certainty until the future arrives! It should not surprise us that God has left us with some aspects of mystery concerning the end times.

But the role of women in the church is not a "prediction of end times events" as these prophecies are. It concerns the here-and-now, everyday, ordinary conduct of every church.

(3) *Practices with no direct commands.* I agree that *there are some disputed practices in churches today, concerning which the Bible does not give explicit commands.* On baptism: should infants be baptized or not? On church government: should local churches be independent or should they be subject to the authority of bishops and archbishops or "district superintendents"?

These are disputed primarily because there is no direct command settling the exact point of dispute. There is no verse that says, "Parents

---

[11] I have given my best understanding of the passages on the millennium in Grudem, *Systematic Theology*, chapter 55. But there is still considerable uncertainty in the details of anybody's position on the millennium.

should baptize their infant children," and there is no verse saying, "Parents should not baptize their children until the children are old enough to make a personal decision to trust in Christ."[12] There is no verse saying, "Regional bishops should govern all the churches in a region," and there is no verse saying, "Local churches should be independent of any control by people outside each local church."[13] The different positions that people hold are argued from the implications of various verses that tell us other things about baptism and church government. Since there are no specific, direct commands about the precise matters in dispute, it is not surprising that churches and denominations have different conclusions on these matters.

But the role of women in the church is not like those matters, because we have direct Scriptural commands saying (in the context of a passage that speaks about the assembled church) that Paul does "not permit a woman to teach or to exercise authority over a man" (1 Tim. 2:12). We have specific commands saying that an elder should be the "husband of one wife" (1 Tim. 3:2; Titus 1:6). These commands speak directly to the issues in question. So this issue is not really like the baptism and church government issues.

(4) *We cannot "not decide" this issue.* On some issues, we don't have to come to a decision. We don't have to figure out how God can be three persons and one God—in fact, we probably will never be able to understand this fully, not even in heaven! And regarding the end times, many Christians can go about living their Christian lives for decades and never decide what they think about the future millennium or the timing of the future great tribulation. There is nothing about those issues that forces us to make a decision now.

But the role of women in the church is a different matter. There are really only two options: *either a church has women pastors and elders, or it doesn't.* Or, to put it another way, either a church reserves some governing and teaching roles for men (a complementarian position), or it doesn't (an egalitarian position). Even those churches and groups who say, "We are still studying this issue" still have some current practices

---

[12] However, I have argued that one particular view of baptism seems to be more consistent with Scripture (*Systematic Theology*, chapter 49).

[13] However, I have argued that a particular system of church government seems to be favored by Scripture (*Systematic Theology*, chapter 47).

that they have decided to follow, and that commits them (for the present time at least) to either a complementarian or an egalitarian position.

So this issue is different from questions about the end times, because *every church and every organization has to make some decision or another on this issue.* Leaders on both sides of this issue seem to agree that no real "middle ground" is possible. In fact, the editors of the recent egalitarian collection of essays *Discovering Biblical Equality* wrote:

> Though we speak strongly in favor of unity, points of agreement and dialogue, it must be noted at the start that *we see no middle ground on this question.* . . . two essential questions remain. Are all avenues of ministry and leadership open to women as well as men, or are women restricted from certain roles and subordinated to male authority on the basis of gender alone? Likewise, do wives share equally with husbands in leadership and decision making in marriage, or does the husband have a unique responsibility and privilege to make final decisions, based on his gender alone? The answers to these questions will continue to distinguish clearly between the male leadership and gender equality positions.[14]

Actually, the role of women in the church is in one way similar to the question of baptism, in that *churches* have to make *some* decision. Either they will baptize infants or they will not. They have to make a decision as soon as the first baby is born in a church.[15]

And churches on both sides of the baptism question have *explanations* for why they think their view is consistent with Scripture. The leaders among the Lutherans and the Episcopalians and the Presbyterians don't say, "The Bible verses about baptism are too hard for us to decide, but we baptize infants because it makes parents happy" (or some other such non–Bible based answer). And the leaders among the Baptists don't say, "We can't decide the disputed verses about baptism in the Bible because there are godly scholars on both sides, but we have decided to

---

[14] Ronald W. Pierce and Rebecca Merrill Groothuis, "Introduction," in *Discovering Biblical Equality,* ed. Ronald W. Pierce and Rebecca Merrill Groothuis (Downers Grove, Ill.: InterVarsity Press, 2004), 17, emphasis added.

[15] Even the Evangelical Free Church of America, which allows parents to decide for themselves whether they want their infants baptized, has made a decision: it has decided it will allow the validity of infant baptism when the parents want it.

baptize only those who make a personal profession of faith because that is the tradition we were brought up in" (or some other such non–Bible based answer). Leaders on both sides give arguments from the Bible and base their convictions on what they think the Bible says.

However, the case is different for parachurch organizations regarding baptism. Many parachurch organizations do not baptize people at all, but leave it to the local churches. Therefore they do not have to come to any decision on baptism. For groups that don't baptize anyone, it is easy to say, "As an organization we won't decide what we think the Bible teaches about baptism." They have no need to do so.

By contrast, regarding women's roles in governing and teaching men, every parachurch organization that carries out Bible teaching ministries has to make some kind of decision on this: are we going to have women doing Bible teaching to groups of both men and women, or not? Either they will or they will not. The same is true of reaching a decision of what kind of leadership roles are open to women in the parachurch organization: all roles, or only some?[16] *Some* decision has to be made. We cannot "not decide."

(5) *Do we really think God has left his Word unclear on something about which every church must decide?* This consideration follows on the previous one. Since the role of women in the church is an issue that every church and every Christian organization has to decide in some way, do we really think that God has left his Word unclear on it?[17]

Of course I agree that we have to decide on some things that the Bible does not speak to. For example, I don't think it specifies what "order of worship" we should have when we come together each week (whether we start with a hymn or a prayer or a Scripture reading, for example). God has given us freedom on it because his Word does not specify any particular "order of worship."

But the matter of the role of women in the church is not something

---

[16] I have discussed the question of women's roles in various categories of leadership of parachurch organizations in *Evangelical Feminism and Biblical Truth* (Sisters, Ore.: Multnomah, 2004), 384-392.

[17] We could make a similar argument regarding marriage if anyone argued that "we can't decide what the passages on male headship mean": the question of whether God has established a husband's leadership role in the family is an issue that every married couple will have to decide in some way. Do we really think that God has left his Word unclear on it? The authors I quote in this chapter do not make this argument about marriage, however, as far as I know.

on which the Bible is silent. Rather, it is something on which God has given specific instructions:

> **1 Timothy 2:12:** I do not permit a woman to teach or to exercise authority over a man; rather, she is to remain quiet.

> **1 Timothy 3:2:** Therefore an overseer must be above reproach, the husband of one wife . . .

> **Titus 1:6:** if anyone is above reproach, the husband of one wife . . .

Where God has spoken so specifically, we need to be careful that the claim "We don't know what these commands mean" does not become just an excuse for disobeying God's commands. All of us who have been parents know that children can sometimes cloak their disobedience in the claim "I didn't understand you!" when in fact what we told them was perfectly clear. So in this case, I want to raise a question about whether that may be happening with some branches of evangelical feminism. Is it really true that God's words on gender roles cannot be understood?

Think again about what is happening when people say, "I don't know what these verses mean." It is something like this:

> **God's Word:** "I do not permit a woman to teach or to exercise authority over a man" [when Christians assemble to worship and to hear the Bible taught, as the context indicates].

> **Evangelical feminists:** "We're sorry, God, we can't understand what you mean. Incidentally, we have women teaching and exercising authority over men in our services. That is because we can't understand what you mean when you say not to have a woman teach or exercise authority over a man."

> **God's Word:** "Therefore an overseer must be above reproach, the husband of one wife . . ."

> **Evangelical feminists:** "We're sorry, God, we can't understand what you mean. Incidentally, we have women who are overseers and elders

and pastors. That is because we can't understand what you mean when you say elders should be the husband of one wife."

By contrast, the response of complementarians to these verses is simple. It looks like this:

God's Word: "I do not permit a woman to teach or to exercise authority over a man" [when Christians assemble to worship and to hear the Bible taught].

Complementarians: "Okay, God, we won't have a woman teaching or exercising authority over men when we assemble as a group of Christians for worship and Bible teaching."

God's Word: "Therefore an overseer must be above reproach, the husband of one wife . . ."

Complementarians: "Okay, God, we will only have men as overseers, elders, and pastors."[18]

Now I realize that people can raise hundreds of questions about specific situations and how these commands *apply* to one situation or another. But those are questions of wisdom in application. We are not saying, "We can't understand what it means." We are saying (as all Christians have to do with all of God's commands), "We need godly wisdom to *apply* this command rightly in this or that specific situation." But we are seeking to *apply it* from a position of understanding what it means and being willing to obey it.[19]

Do we think this topic is something that God cares about? Do we think it is something that he counts as a matter of obedience to him? Or

---

[18] People differ on the exact sense of "husband of one wife," but they all obey it in the sense they think it has. Some think "husband of one wife" means "not having multiple wives, not being a polygamist," and they obey the verse in that way. Some think it means "never being divorced or widowed and then remarried," and they obey the verse in that way. Some (very few) think it means an elder must be married (not a bachelor) and they obey it in that way. I hold the first view and have argued for it in *Systematic Theology*, 916-917.

[19] I discuss the application of these verses to dozens of specific situations in *Evangelical Feminism and Biblical Truth*, 84-101.

do we think that God does not really care what we do about this question and therefore he has not spoken clearly about it?

This is no minor issue. The issue of roles of men and women in the church affects, to some degree, every Christian in the world, for it affects whom we choose as leaders in our churches, and it has a significant effect on what kinds of ministries the men and women in our churches carry out. If we say, "It is impossible to decide what the Bible teaches on this," *we imply that God did not think this to be an important enough issue to give us clear guidance in his Word.* We imply that God has left us instructions that are unclear or confusing on this issue.

Do we really want to say this about God and his Word, on a topic that affects *every* church in the world *every* week of the year, for the *entire church age* until Christ returns? Is it really true that God has left us unclear instructions on this topic?

(6) *The role of women in the church is not an issue on which the church has been divided for centuries.* If we look back at the history of the church, there have been controversies about the end times since the very early centuries of the church's history. There have also been controversies for centuries about the millennium, about Calvinism and Arminianism, and about baptism, for example. *But there have not been controversies about whether the roles of pastor and elder are reserved for men.*

Apart from a few sectarian movements, the entire Christian church from the first century until the 1850s agreed that only men could be pastors and elders, and the vast majority agreed that only men could do public Bible teaching of both men and women.[20] From the 1850s until the 1950s in the United States, women pastors were a tiny minority, but over 98 percent of evangelical churches (over 99 percent of the broader Christian church if Roman Catholic and Orthodox groups are included) had only men as pastors.[21] Allowing women to be ordained in significant numbers began with some liberal Protestant denominations in the 1950s and spread to a number of evangelical groups under the influence of evangelical feminism in the 1970s and 1980s. *Before the advent of*

---

[20] See the historical evidence for this paragraph in *Evangelical Feminism and Biblical Truth*, 457-469.

[21] Even among those evangelical denominations that had women pastors, such as the Assemblies of God, the International Church of the Foursquare Gospel, and the Church of the Nazarene, women pastors constituted a small minority.

evangelical feminist writings in the 1970s, today's "disputed passages" on women in ministry were not thought to be unclear. Therefore this matter is much different from disputes over the end times or baptism or Calvinism and Arminianism.

B. AVOIDING DISPUTED PASSAGES WILL LEAVE THE CHURCH VULNERABLE TO MANY FALSE TEACHINGS

There is another serious problem with an approach that says we will not make decisions based on any "disputed" passages. If people really adopted this principle, they wouldn't be able to take a stand against any major heresy in the church. In the fourth-century controversy over the deity of Christ, the Arians (who denied the full deity of Christ) were apparently godly people *who disputed every major verse used by those who argued for the full deity of Christ.* That meant that all the passages on the deity of Christ were "disputed passages," with godly, praying scholars on both sides of the question.

In the debate over biblical inerrancy in the 1970s and 1980s, many genuinely godly people vigorously debated the key verses used to support inerrancy. In another example, the "Oneness Pentecostals" (who deny the Trinity) hotly dispute all the verses brought to support the Trinity.[22] If we are going to avoid making a decision on disputed passages, we cannot defend the deity of Christ, or inerrancy, or the Trinity.

To take another example, I wonder how many who take this "avoid disputed passages" approach have ever tried to discuss justification by faith alone with a born-again Roman Catholic. Within the Roman Catholic church are "godly people" *who make every verse on justification by faith alone a point of controversy.* If one is committed to avoiding disputed passages, one could never decide whether Protestants or Catholics are right about justification by faith alone.

Two final examples: If the principle of "avoiding disputed passages" were followed consistently, no Christian could ever come to any conclusion about whether to baptize infants, because "godly people" differ on whether infants should be baptized, and every verse is in dispute! And

---

[22] See my *Systematic Theology*, 242-243. I am not speaking of Pentecostals generally, who clearly affirm the Trinity, but only of one splinter group, the United Pentecostal Church, who were forced out of the Assemblies of God in 1916 over this issue.

on the matter of spiritual gifts, all the key passages about miraculous gifts are "disputed" by sincere Christians. Must we say about all those passages, "These are disputed passages, and evangelical scholars will never reach agreement; therefore, we cannot use these passages to decide what we think about miraculous gifts today"?

Once we begin to use the "avoid disputed passages" approach, we lose the ability to appeal to hundreds of passages in God's Word that he gave us to understand, to believe, and to obey. When that happens, our churches will be "tossed to and fro by the waves and carried about by every wind of doctrine" (Eph. 4:14).

A better approach is to say that God has given us his Word so that it can be understood. Therefore we must study these "controversial texts" and follow the arguments on both sides until we come to a satisfactory answer on what they mean.

C. THE IMPORTANCE OF MAKING DECISIONS BASED ON SEEING THE EVIDENCE, NOT ON THE MERE CLAIM OF SOME EVANGELICAL SCHOLAR

In disputed areas like this, another important principle must be kept in mind. If a position is true to God's Word, it should not be based on "just trust me" arguments from scholars who appeal to evidence that lay people cannot examine and evaluate, or who just quote the opinions of other authors to "prove" their points. Even when it involves arguments about Greek and Hebrew words, or ancient history, the evidence should be laid out in clear English, the examples of word usages should be given in English translation, and interested lay persons should be able to look at the evidence and evaluate it for themselves, so that people can come to their own conclusions about what the Bible says.[23]

I say this because much of the dispute on the question of men's and women's roles in home and church does not come about because the Scripture passages are difficult to understand. The "controversy" and "lack of consensus" over the key passages on women in ministry is in

---

[23] For an example of laying out the evidence in this way, see appendices 3 and 7 in Grudem, *Evangelical Feminism and Biblical Truth*, where I give in English translation with context over fifty examples of the Greek word *kephalē* ("head") used to mean "person in authority over" (544-551) and all eighty-two extant examples of the verb *authenteō* ("to exercise authority") (675-702). Even readers with no technical training in Greek can read these examples and decide whether they think certain egalitarian claims or complementarian claims are supported by the relevant evidence.

many cases *caused by lack of information or by untrue statements being repeated again and again in egalitarian literature* (see Part 3 of this book for several examples).

With regard to most of the crucial questions, the supporting evidence is not something that is restricted to the realm of specialist scholars with technical knowledge. Even in those cases where the argument depends on the meaning of a Greek or Hebrew word, the relevant evidence from ancient literature can usually be presented in a clear and forthright way (in English translation) so that interested lay people have an opportunity to make an informed decision.

Sadly, again and again I find that Christians accept evangelical feminist arguments *not* because people have *actually seen* hard evidence proving these views to be valid but rather *because they have read the interpretation of the evidence (not the actual evidence itself) in some evangelical writer whom they trust.* What readers don't realize is that often these writers are depending on the statements of other writers, and those writers on yet other writers, with only speculation but no proof behind the original statement that started it all. In a number of cases, the egalitarian scholar is advocating an extremely doubtful theory about the evidence that no one has ever before advocated. But seldom is the actual evidence itself provided. In many cases, that is because such evidence simply does not exist. In other cases, the egalitarian scholar who is trusted has promoted an unusual understanding of the ancient world or a novel interpretation held by no other expert in the field before or since, yet the lay person believes and trusts the egalitarian scholar while having no idea how strange that scholar's views actually are, or how widely what the egalitarian author claims wanders from the actual truth about the ancient world.[24]

D. CONCLUSION: SILENCING THE MOST RELEVANT VERSES BY SAYING THEY ARE DISPUTED IS ANOTHER STEP TOWARD LIBERALISM

I realize that the evangelical feminist authors who say the verses on women in the church are "too hard to decide" do not think they are

---

[24] For one example, see my discussion of Cindy Jacobs's uncritical acceptance of a highly dubious argument from Richard Kroeger and Catherine Kroeger about the history of ancient Ephesus (see chapter 24, pages 190-191 below).

moving their churches toward liberalism. They may just be over-whelmed with all the literature written on these topics and so they conclude, "I can't decide this." But then they *do* decide it. They decide to adopt an evangelical feminist view, contrary to the sense of those passages that has been plain to millions of readers for centuries. In doing so, they take their churches toward liberalism.

The position that says, "We can't decide these disputed passages, so we will make decisions based on factors other than these passages," is guaranteed to silence the most important and most relevant passages of Scripture on roles for men and women. When evangelical feminists claim, "Nobody knows what these passages mean," no further reasoning or argument from these verses can influence their decisions. Their position is: "The verses are too hard to decide. They are confusing. We can't figure them out. Therefore we won't consider these verses anymore. They cannot speak to us on this issue."

But to say this on an issue where God has given direct instruction, and where churches have to make decisions every day, and where the whole Christian church has had widespread agreement until the advent of modern feminism, results in silencing the most relevant verses, and thus it is ultimately another way to undermine the authority of the Bible. Saying that such passages are too hard to decide is another dangerous step on the path to liberalism.

DOES A PASTOR'S AUTHORITY TRUMP SCRIPTURE?

Some evangelical feminists say that women can teach if they are "under the authority" of the pastors or elders

Another liberal tendency among evangelical egalitarians is the claim that a woman may teach Scripture to men if she does so "under the authority of the pastor or elders." I say this is indicative of a liberal tendency because on no other area of conduct would we be willing to say that someone can do what the Bible says not to do as long as the pastor and elders give their approval.

This position is found fairly often in evangelical churches. What makes this position different from others we have treated up to this point in the book is that many who take this view say they genuinely want to uphold male leadership in the church, and they say they *are* upholding male leadership when a woman teaches "under the authority of the elders" who are men (or of the pastor, who is a man).

On the other hand, this is not a commonly held view among the main egalitarian authors or those who support Christians for Biblical Equality, for example.[1] These writers do not think only men should be

---

[1] In fact, egalitarian author J. Lee Grady rejects this idea. He writes, in the context of talking about women who have public preaching ministries: "And in many cases, leaders have innocently twisted various Bible verses to suggest that a woman's public ministry can be valid only if she is properly 'covered' by a male who is present" (J. Lee Grady, *Ten Lies the Church Tells Women* [Lake Mary, Fla.: Creation House, 2000], 89).

elders, so they surely don't think that women need any approval from male elders to teach the Bible!

But this view comes up fairly often in phone calls or e-mails to the Council on Biblical Manhood and Womanhood (CBMW) office, and I often hear it in personal conversations and discussions of church policies.

Is it really true that a woman is obeying the Bible if she preaches a sermon "under the authority of the pastor and elders"?

The question here is, *what does the Bible say?* It does not merely say, "Preserve some kind of male authority in the congregation." It does not say, "A woman may not teach men *unless she is under the authority of the elders.*" Rather, it says, "I do not permit a woman to teach or to exercise authority over a man" (1 Tim. 2:12).

Can a pastor or the elders of a church give a woman permission to disobey this statement of Scripture? Certainly not! Can a woman do what the Bible says *not* to do and excuse it by saying, "I'm under the authority of the elders"? Would we say that the elders of a church could tell people "under their authority" that they have permission to disobey *other* passages of Scripture?

What would we think of someone who said, "I'm going to rob a bank today because I need money and my pastor has given me permission, and I'm under his authority"? Or of a person who said, "I'm committing adultery because I'm unhappy in my marriage and my elders have given me permission, so I'm still under the authority of my elders"? Or of someone who said, "I'm committing perjury because I don't want to go to jail and my pastor has given me permission, and I'm under his authority"? We would dismiss those statements as ridiculous, but they highlight the general principle that *no pastor or church elder or bishop or any other church officer has the authority to give people permission to disobey God's Word.*

Someone may answer, "But we are respecting the Bible's *general principle* of male headship in the church." But Paul did not say, "*Respect the general principle of male headship* in your church." He said, "*I do not permit a woman to teach or to exercise authority over a man*" (1 Tim. 2:12). We do not have the right to change what the Bible says and then obey some new "general principle of the Bible" that we have made up.

Nor do we have the right to take a specific teaching of Scripture and abstract some general principle from it (such as a principle of "male headship") and then say that principle gives us the right *to disobey the specific commands of Scripture* that fall under that principle. We are not free to abstract general principles from the Bible however we wish, and then invent opinions about how those principles will apply in our situations. Such a procedure would allow people to evade any command of Scripture they were uncomfortable with. We would become a law unto ourselves, no longer subject to the authority of God's Word.

We could try this same procedure with some other passages. Would we think it right to say that the Bible teaches that men should pray "without anger or quarreling, *unless they quarrel under the authority of the elders*" (see 1 Tim. 2:8)? Or that women should adorn themselves "with modesty and self-control, *unless the elders give them permission to dress immodestly*" (see 1 Tim. 2:9)? Or would we say that those who are "rich in this present age" should "be generous and ready to share, *unless the elders give them permission to be stingy and miserly*" (see 1 Tim. 6:17-19)? But if we would not add "unless the elders give permission to do otherwise under their authority" to any of the other commands in Scripture, neither should we add that evasion to 1 Timothy 2:12.

If a woman says, "I will teach the Bible to men only when I am under the authority of the elders," she has become no different from men who teach the Bible. No man in any church should teach the Bible publicly unless he also is under the authority of the elders (or pastor, or other church officers) in that church. The general principle is that anyone who does Bible teaching in a church should be subject to the established governing authority in that church, whether it is a board of elders, a board of deacons, a church governing council, or the church board. Both men and women alike are subject to that requirement. Therefore, upon reflection, it turns out that this "under the authority of the elders" position *essentially says there is no difference between what men can do and what women can do in teaching the Bible to men.*

Do we really think that is what Paul meant? Do we really think that Paul did not mean to say anything that applied only to women when he said, "I do not permit a woman to teach or to exercise authority over a man" (1 Tim. 2:12)?

Allowing a woman to disobey 1 Timothy 2:12 by saying she is doing so "under the authority of the elders" is setting a dangerous precedent by saying, in effect, that church leaders can give people permission to disobey Scripture. It is thus another step on the path toward liberalism.

11

TEACHING IN THE PARACHURCH?

Some evangelical feminists evade New Testament commands by saying, "We are not a church"

Yet another liberal tendency is the claim that if an organization is not a church, it does not have to follow the New Testament commands regarding such activities as women teaching the Bible to men. The reason I say this is indicative of a liberal tendency to avoid the authority of Scripture is that, while we may agree that parachurch organizations are not required to do *everything* that the New Testament commands for churches, nevertheless, when a parachurch organization *does those same things* that the New Testament talks about for churches, *it is required to follow the same rules* that the New Testament lays down for churches. It is not as if we can set up a separate organization next door to a church and then say that the rules no longer apply to us.

This is another argument that is not usually made by thoroughgoing egalitarian writers, because to make this argument someone has to assume that the New Testament restrictions on women in ministry *do* apply to a *church* situation. That is an assumption egalitarians are not willing to make.

But this argument is frequently made by people who *claim* to be complementarian and say they support male headship in the home and the church. Yet they say that *because they are part of a parachurch organization* (such as a seminary, a mission board, or a campus ministry), the New Testament instructions on women not teaching or having authority over men do not apply to their organization. I have listed this argument here as an "egalitarian claim" because it often functions in practice to advance egalitarian goals and to encourage women to function in ways contrary to New Testament teachings. It is thus a kind of "closet egalitarian" argument.

To respond to this argument it is necessary to point out, first, that there is some truth in the argument, but it is not the whole truth. There is some truth regarding *some kinds* of New Testament commands, but it is not the whole truth regarding the commands relating to women's roles in ministry situations.

The *truth* in this argument is that parachurch organizations *do not function in every way as churches do.* Take, for example, some of the parachurch organizations I have been involved with. As far as I know, Phoenix Seminary, where I teach, has never

- baptized anyone
- ordained anyone to the ministry
- conducted a wedding or a funeral for anyone
- held morning Sunday school classes for children
- held Sunday morning worship services

Nor does Christian Heritage Academy of Northbrook, Illinois, a Christian school that my children attended, do such things. Nor does Crossway Books, the publisher of this book. Nor does the Evangelical Theological Society, a professional academic society I have been a member of for many years. As a general practice, I do not think these activities are carried out by Campus Crusade for Christ or Focus on the Family or Promise Keepers or the Council on Biblical Manhood and Womanhood. These are all "parachurch" organizations in that they serve special purposes alongside the work of the church, and *there are some "church" activities they do not do.* If asked why they do not do these things, they will probably answer, "Because we are not a church."

But that is not the whole story. In another sense, *there is only one church,* the worldwide body of Christ, and these organizations are all part of it. They are just not part of any one local church or any one denomination.

In addition, these organizations seek to obey *many commands* that were first written to churches. They don't say, "First Corinthians was written to a church, and we are not a church, so we don't have to obey First Corinthians." These organizations obey many instructions that are in parts of the Bible that were written to churches. For example, all of these organizations would probably think it important to follow the procedures of Matthew 18:15-17 in dealing with cases where one person sins against another. But these instructions assume they will be carried out by a church: "If he refuses to listen to them, *tell it to the church*" (Matt. 18:17).

The same is true of mission boards. If their missionaries baptize new converts, they will think it important for the missionaries to obey the New Testament teachings on baptism (and not baptize people indiscriminately whether they profess faith or not, for example).[1] They do not say, "We are not a church, so we don't have to follow the New Testament teachings about baptism, which were written to a church."

All of the New Testament epistles were written to churches (or to individuals such as Timothy and Titus and Philemon who were involved in local churches). Therefore the argument that "we are not a church, so we don't need to follow the instructions written to churches," taken to its logical conclusion, would mean that parachurch organizations do not have to obey anything written in the entire New Testament! Surely that conclusion is wrong.

How then can we know when "we are not a church" is a valid reason not to follow a New Testament command and when it is not?

The principle that allows us to distinguish between commands that parachurch organizations should obey and those they do not need to obey is a simple one. It is a general principle that Christians often use, sometimes even instinctively, in the application of Scripture to all of life. The principle, which we have already touched on in previous chapters, is that *we should obey the command when we are doing the same activity as, or an activity very similar to, what the command is talking about.*

Therefore, Crossway Books *should not* "appoint elders in every

---

[1] Missionaries who hold to believer's baptism would baptize only those who make a profession of faith, while those who hold to infant baptism would also baptize the infant children of those who make a profession of faith. In both cases they are seeking to follow what they think the New Testament teaches. Neither is saying, "We are not a church, so what the New Testament teaches about baptism does not apply to us."

town" (Titus 1:5) where it sells books because it is not planting churches in those places, as Paul and Titus were. On the other hand, if a mission organization is planting churches in a region, it *should* make plans for how it could "appoint elders in every town" by raising up indigenous Christian leaders. Similarly, the Evangelical Theological Society might never celebrate the Lord's Supper at one of its meetings. But if it did decide to celebrate the Lord's Supper, then it should follow Paul's directions in 1 Corinthians 11.

The principle then is simple: *parachurch organizations should follow New Testament commands written to churches when those organizations are engaged in the activities that the command is talking about.*

How does that conclusion apply to women's roles in parachurch ministries?

With all of the thousands of parachurch organizations in the world today, and the hundreds of thousands of activities carried out by those organizations, situations will vary widely. Before any decisions are made, leaders in each organization will need to ask for God's wisdom, according to James 1:5-8, in order to understand how their situations are *similar to* or *different from* the situations and activities found in the New Testament. Although in some cases it will be difficult at first to say how much the situation is similar and how much it is different, I believe in most cases the application of this principle will be quite clear.

Teaching the Bible to an assembled group of men and women is so much like the situation Paul had in mind when he said, "I do not permit a woman to teach or to exercise authority over a man" (1 Tim. 2:12), that only men should do this. I believe that such a principle should apply not only to meetings in local churches but also to Bible conferences, weekend retreats, and annual meetings held by parachurch organizations or denominations. For similar reasons, I do not think it appropriate for women to hold Bible teaching positions in Christian colleges and seminaries. Teaching the Bible to a mixed group of both men and women in a college or seminary classroom is sufficiently similar to teaching the Bible to men and women in a local church setting, and thus the same restrictions apply. Another reason is that teaching Bible in a college or seminary carries a responsibility that is very similar to the Bible teaching role of elders in the New Testament, or even to the role of a mature, senior elder training younger elders.

The activities and responsibilities that a military chaplain carries out are not significantly different from the activities and responsibilities carried out by a pastor/elder in a local church. Therefore, just as ordination to the pastorate is restricted to men, so appointment to the military chaplaincy, to be consistent, should also be restricted to men.[2] However, if there are military chaplaincy roles that do not involve Bible teaching or governing authority over groups of Christian men, then such roles are appropriate for women as well as men.

What about other positions of leadership and authority in parachurch organizations? A member of an elder board in a church has great responsibility for the lives, conduct, and spiritual well-being of members of the church. Christians are to "be subject" to the elders (1 Pet. 5:5), and the author of Hebrews says, "Obey your leaders and submit to them, for they are keeping watch over your souls, as those who will have to give an account" (Heb. 13:17). But the member of a parachurch governing board has authority over an *organization*, and over certain *activities* that people carry out within that organization, not over the entire lives of the members. So, for example, I consider myself to be subject to the authority of my pastor and the elders at Scottsdale Bible Church (of which I am a member), but I don't think of my life as subject to the authority of the governing board of the Council on Biblical Manhood and Womanhood (of which I am also a member). In like manner, the members of the board of a Christian school have authority over the school and its activities, but they do not have elder-like authority over the lives of the parents who make up the association that owns that school.[3]

---

[2] I realize that the military chaplaincy includes chaplains from many denominations, including those that ordain women. The military should accept such women chaplains if denominations send them, I think, because the decision to ordain and endorse them for the chaplaincy does not belong to the military but to the various denominations. Freedom of religion in a country includes freedom to hold different views on whether women should be ordained. What I am advocating here is that denominations that wish to be faithful to Scripture should not ordain or endorse women as chaplains, in my judgment.

[3] Theological seminaries have reached different decisions on this question. Both Trinity Evangelical Divinity School, where I taught for twenty years, and Phoenix Seminary, where I now teach, have women on their governing boards. I have not objected to this, since governing the activities of a seminary is sufficiently different from governing a church. The boards meet rather infrequently and make decisions regarding broad policies and budgets. They have exercised almost no direct authority over me or over my conduct in the seminary, nor have I thought of them as having the kind of pastoral responsibility for my life that I think my pastor and elders have. Some board members have even attended an adult Sunday school class that I taught and where I was in charge. One board member was also a student in one of my classes, and neither of us ever thought there was any kind of elder-like authority functioning

In fact, if an employee of a parachurch organization is involved in conduct that brings reproach on the organization (for example, if a Christian school teacher were discovered in sexual immorality), the organization would dismiss the employee, but the elder board at the person's church, not the school board, would pursue church discipline for that person. Therefore when Paul says, "I do not permit a woman to teach or to exercise authority over a man," the kind of authority he has in mind is *sufficiently different* from the kind of authority a governing board member generally has in parachurch organizations, and the argument "We are not a church" is a helpful distinction in this situation.

To take a somewhat different example, the person serving as an academic dean in a theological seminary is supervising a number of men (the male faculty members) in their Bible teaching ministry. He does "exercise authority" over these men with respect to what they teach and their conduct as they teach and relate to students and to each other. His role is very much like that of a pastor or elder to these faculty members, and therefore it is appropriate for only men to have this role.

To take another example, the campus director of a parachurch ministry on a college campus has a supervisory authority over the other staff members on that campus that is very similar to the role of a pastor or elder in a church. Therefore, in my judgment, it is not appropriate for a woman to have the role of campus director in such a ministry and to "exercise authority" in such a direct way over the men in that ministry. That would be doing what Paul said not to do.

On the other hand, supervisory positions in other types of organizations may be different. Are these roles mostly like the role of a pastor or elder, overseeing and supervising people's *whole lives* as they minister to others? Or are they more like the role of a supervisor in a secular work-

---

in that situation (except perhaps in a reverse sense, in that I as a teacher felt some responsibility for the spiritual lives of my students). On the other hand, Westminster Theological Seminary in Philadelphia decided that the role of a board member was similar in many respects to the role of an elder in the church, and it decided to require that its board consist only of people who had previously been ordained as elders in Presbyterian or Reformed churches, subject to the qualifications in 1 Timothy 3 and Titus 1. Within the conservative Reformed circles that Westminster serves, this rule effectively meant that all board members would be men. (The seminary at one point was threatened with loss of accreditation by the Middle States Accrediting Association unless it added women to its board. The seminary decided to fight this in court on First Amendment freedom of religion grounds, but before the matter could go to court, the accrediting agency, under pressure from the U.S. Department of Education, backed down.)

place, overseeing only specific kinds of on-the-job activities? It will require godly wisdom to decide in each situation.

The commands in the New Testament do not say that Christians should follow them "only in church settings." This is a crucial point. The reason some New Testament commands don't apply to parachurch organizations is *not* that they are not churches, but that *they are not performing the activity mentioned in those commands.* The Council on Biblical Manhood and Womanhood may never observe the Lord's Supper together, and therefore they will not have to follow the New Testament directions for the Lord's Supper. But *if they ever do observe the Lord's Supper,* then they will have to follow those commands. Whether CBMW is a church is not the crucial point. The crucial point is whether that organization is carrying out an activity for which the New Testament gives commands.

We must continue to insist strongly that the New Testament applies to *all* Christians in *all* societies and *all* cultures and *all* situations. *Its commands are valid whenever Christians carry out the activities included in those commands.* I cannot imagine the apostle Paul writing to the Corinthians, "Follow these instructions if you are doing this as part of the church in Corinth, but if you are doing this same activity as part of a Christian organization outside the church, then you do not have to obey my commands." The New Testament never speaks that way, or hints at any such way to "escape" from being accountable to obey it. This should make us reject any claims that allow us to ignore New Testament commands that speak to the same kind of situations we are in. Otherwise, the "we are not a church" argument will function as a "closet egalitarian" argument that will effectively nullify the authority of Scripture to govern those areas of our lives.

For these reasons, therefore, the argument "We are not a church; therefore we have women teaching the Bible to men" is another step on the path toward liberalism.

12

TRADITION TRUMPS SCRIPTURE

Some evangelical feminists put church tradition above the Bible

A different kind of rejection of the Bible's ultimate authority is found in the claim of Kevin Giles that theological differences cannot be settled by appealing to the Bible, so the historical tradition of the church must be the basis for our decisions. Giles is vicar of St. Michael's Church (Anglican) in North Carlton, Australia, and his writings have been published by InterVarsity Press in the United States. In his book *The Trinity and Subordinationism*,[1] Giles explicitly tells readers that he will not argue his case from Scripture:

> In seeking to make a response to my fellow evangelicals who subordinate the Son to the Father, I do not appeal directly to particular scriptural passages to establish who is right or wrong. . . . I seek rather to prove that orthodoxy rejects this way of reading the Scriptures.[2]

First, some background: Why does Giles write about the Trinity in connection with the debate over men's and women's roles in the church? It is because many complementarians, including myself, have claimed a

---

[1] Kevin Giles, *The Trinity and Subordinationism: The Doctrine of God and the Contemporary Gender Debate* (Downers Grove, Ill.: InterVarsity Press, 2002). Giles is also scheduled to be one of the main speakers at the 2007 conference of the egalitarian organization Christians for Biblical Equality (www.cbeinternational.org, accessed 5-4-06).
[2] Ibid., 25.

parallel between the Trinity and marriage. Just as the Father and Son in the Trinity are equal in deity and equal in importance but different in roles, so the husband and wife in marriage are equal in human personhood and equal in importance but different in roles. This is based in part on 1 Corinthians 11:3:

> But I want you to understand that the head of every man is Christ, *the head of a wife is her husband,* and *the head of Christ is God.*

Here Paul says that just as in the Trinity the Father is the leader and has authority over the Son, so in marriage the husband is the leader and has authority over his wife.[3] The remarkable thing is that the parallel with the Trinity proves that it is possible to have *equality in being but differences in roles.* This then disproves the evangelical feminist argument that, "If you have different roles in marriage, then men and women are not equal in value." It also disproves the corresponding argument that, "If men and women are equal in value, then you can't have different roles in marriage." In response to those arguments, the doctrine of the Trinity proves that you can have both equality and differences.

Evangelical feminists have responded to that argument by saying that there have not been different roles in the Trinity for all eternity, but that the Son's subordination to the Father's authority was only a voluntary submission for a limited time (his time on earth) and for a specific purpose (his work of redemption). They have argued that there is no eternal subordination of the Son to the Father in the Trinity. I have responded to that claim elsewhere with an abundance of Scriptural evidences and testimonies from church history.[4]

Giles disagrees with my position and the position of other complementarians. His book argues that there is no eternal submission of the Son to the authority of the Father, no eternal leadership of the Father in the Trinity, no eternal subordination of the Son to the authority of the Father. But in making this argument, Giles decides not to appeal to Scripture.

Giles has a reason for not appealing to Scripture: *he does not think*

---

[3] See chapter 25 below for a discussion of the meaning of the word "head" in this verse.
[4] See Wayne Grudem, *Evangelical Feminism and Biblical Truth* (Sisters, Ore.: Multnomah, 2004), 405-443.

that citing verses from the Bible can resolve theological questions in general. He thinks that the Bible can be read in different ways, and even though "given texts cannot mean just anything," he says that "more than one interpretation is possible."[5]

Giles even admits that it is possible to find evidence for the eternal subordination of the Son in Scripture: "I concede immediately that the New Testament *can* be read to teach that the Son is *eternally* subordinated to the Father."[6] But for him that is not decisive, because, as he tells us at the outset, "This book is predicated on the view that the Bible can often be read in more than one way, even on important matters."[7]

Giles's fundamental approach should disturb evangelicals, for it means that, in his system, appeals to Scripture can have no effect. He can just reply, "Yes, the Bible can be read that way, but other readings are possible." And thus the voice of God's Word is effectively silenced in the church. (Giles's argument in this respect is similar to the argument considered in chapter 9, where evangelical feminists claimed that the verses on women's roles in the church were too difficult to decide.)

How then does Giles think we should determine which view is right? The answer, he says, is found in church history: "In relation to the doctrine of the Trinity my argument is that the tradition should prescribe the correct reading."[8] For Giles, then, the tradition of the church becomes the supreme authority. His approach is similar to Roman Catholicism but contradictory to the Reformation doctrine of *sola Scriptura* ("Scripture alone") and contrary to beliefs of evangelical Protestants. In fact, I find it somewhat surprising that InterVarsity Press would decide to publish this book. I am not surprised at this because of the conclusion Giles holds (egalitarianism) but because of the underlying view of authority on which he bases his argument (the superiority of church tradition, not Scripture, because Scripture can be read in different ways).[9]

---

[5] Giles, *Trinity and Subordinationism*, 10.
[6] Ibid., 25.
[7] Ibid., 9.
[8] Ibid. He argues that what he claims to be the traditional view of the Trinity was right and should be followed, but the traditional view of male headship was wrong and should not be followed, since on that matter no other reading was open to people in earlier centuries (9-10).
[9] Though it was published by IVP in the United States, Giles's book was not published by IVP-UK, which is a separate company.

Finally, it should be noted that Giles's understanding of the historic view of the church on the Trinity is deeply flawed. He continually blurs the distinction between the heresy of *subordinationism* (the view that the Son is a lesser being than the Father) and the orthodox view that the Son has a *subordinate role* but is equal in his being (this he also calls subordinationism, making the book simply a contribution to confusion on this topic) (see his pages 16-17, 60-69).[10] He even equates modern complementarians with ancient Arians, who denied the deity of the Son (page 66). An extensive and insightful review of Giles's book by Peter Schemm also points out several significant inaccuracies in Giles's reporting of the views of others, so his book should be read with much caution.[11]

In his claim that we cannot decide the doctrine of the Trinity and its relationship to marriage from the Bible, but must make our decision based on the historical positions of the church, Kevin Giles and those who promote his book take a major step down the path toward liberalism.

---

[10] Giles continues this confusing use of terminology, and continues his inaccurate representation of the doctrine of the Trinity in church history, in "The Subordination of Christ and the Subordination of Women," in *Discovering Biblical Equality*, ed. Ronald W. Pierce and Rebecca Merrill Groothuis (Downers Grove, Ill.: InterVarsity, 2004), 334-352. For further response to Giles, see chapter 27 below; and Grudem, *Evangelical Feminism and Biblical Truth*, 405-429, especially 426-429.

[11] Peter Schemm, "Kevin Giles's *The Trinity and Subordinationism*: A Review Article," *Journal for Biblical Manhood and Womanhood* 7/2 (Fall 2002): 67-78; for Giles's inaccuracies, see page 74 (also available online at www.cbmw.org). For further discussion of the historic view of the church regarding the subordination of the Son to the Father (in role, not in being), see chapter 27, below.

13

EXPERIENCE TRUMPS SCRIPTURE

*Some evangelical feminists put experience
above the Bible*

Another procedure egalitarians use to avoid obedience to the New Testament concerning the differing roles of men and women is to place such a strong emphasis on *experience* that the teachings of Scripture no longer are the highest authority. This occurs when egalitarians such as Sarah Sumner, whom we have encountered in previous chapters, argue that "Every generation produces gifted women who minister effectively to women and men," and then use this as one of their primary arguments why women should be allowed to be pastors.[1] Sumner several times uses herself as one example of such gifted women.[2]

Cindy Jacobs says that God's blessing on the ministries of women pastors shows that what they are doing is right, and therefore objections based on what Scripture teaches are discarded. Jacobs argues,

> Women in numerous different ministries teach both men and women and are producing godly, lasting fruit for the Kingdom. Would that be happening if their work wasn't sanctioned by God? Wouldn't their ministries simply be dead and lifeless if God weren't anointing them?[3]

[1] Sarah Sumner, *Men and Women in the Church* (Downers Grove, Ill.: InterVarsity Press, 2003), 49.
[2] Ibid., pages 15, 17-19, 20-21, 49, 51-53, 73-74, 95-96, 104, 187, 195-197, 226, 308-309, 315.
[3] Cindy Jacobs, *Women of Destiny* (Ventura, Calif.: Regal, 1998), 176.

In personal conversation, people will sometimes say, "I heard Anne Graham Lotz preach, and it changed my mind about women preaching." Or they will hear Beth Moore preach to both men and women at a conference and think, "This is such good Bible teaching. How can it be wrong?" But is this reasoning true? Does the evident blessing of God on some women pastors prove that what they are doing is right?

A. HOW CAN GOD BLESS THE MINISTRIES OF SOME WOMEN?

It is not surprising to me that there is some measure of blessing when women act as pastors and teach the Word of God, whether in a local congregation, at a Bible conference, or before a television audience. This is because God's Word is powerful, and God brings blessing through his Word to those who hear it. But the fact that God blesses the preaching of his Word does not make it right for a woman to be the preacher. God is a God of grace, and there are many times when he blesses his people even when they disobey him.

One example where God brought blessing in spite of disobedience is the story of Samson in Judges 13–16. Even though Samson broke God's laws by taking a Philistine wife (Judges 14), sleeping with a prostitute at Gaza (16:1-3), and living with Delilah, a foreign woman he had not married (16:4-22), God still empowered him mightily to defeat the Philistines again and again. This does not mean that Samson's sin was right in God's sight, but only that God in his grace empowered Samson *in spite of his disobedience.* Eventually God's protection and power were withdrawn, "but he did not know that the LORD had left him" (16:20), and the Philistines captured and imprisoned him (v. 21).

If God waited until Christians were perfect before he brought blessing to their ministries, there would be no blessing on any ministry in this life! God's grace is given to us in spite of our failings. But that does not mean that it is right to disobey Scripture, or that God will always give such blessing.

On the other hand, there are many successful ministries by women that are fully consistent with obedience to Scripture. For example, nothing in the Bible prevents women from doing evangelism locally or in other countries, whether speaking privately or to large groups of people. Thus, I have no objection to women serving as missionaries and planting churches, but then encouraging indigenous male leaders to assume governing and teaching roles in those churches.[4] And I certainly have no objection to women teaching the Bible to large groups of other women. What the Bible does not allow is women serving as elders or pastors over a church or teaching the Bible to an assembled group of men and women, but many other ministries are open to women and God does bless those ministries.[5]

B. THE DANGER OF LOSS OF GOD'S PROTECTION AND BLESSING

If a woman goes on serving as an elder or pastor, I believe she is doing so outside the will of God, and she has no guarantee of God's protection on her life. By continuing to act in ways contrary to Scripture, she puts herself spiritually in a dangerous position. I expect that eventually even the measure of blessing God has allowed on her ministry will be withdrawn (though I cannot presume that this will be true in every case).

One example of this is the tragic story of Aimee Semple McPherson (1890–1944) at the end of her ministry. Ruth Tucker recounts the story as follows:

> Aimee Semple McPherson, one of the most celebrated evangelists in the early decades of the twentieth century . . . was a crowd-pleaser who played up to her audiences with a dramatic flair, never seeming too concerned that her eccentricities might demean the cause of Christ. Nor was she particularly careful about her personal life: she left her first husband to go on the road as an itinerant evangelist, later remarried, and finally claimed to have been kidnapped—a story challenged by reporters, who insisted that she was hiding out with another man. . . . She cannot be excused for apparent moral lapses . . . but her ministry does demonstrate the power of God that often prevails despite sin and failure.[6]

---

[4] See Grudem, *Evangelical Feminism and Biblical Truth* (Sisters, Ore.: Multnomah, 2004), 84-101, for a long list of ministries that should be open to both men and women, and see 77-78 for a detailed example of a local male leader naturally assuming the teaching role in a church planted by a woman missionary.
[5] See Wayne Grudem, *Evangelical Feminism and Biblical Truth,* 84-101, for a longer discussion of many ministries in the church that are open to women.
[6] Ruth A. Tucker, *Women in the Maze* (Downers Grove, Ill.: InterVarsity Press, 1992), 187.

There is no doubt that God accomplished much good through Aimee Semple McPherson, including the founding of the International Church of the Foursquare Gospel and of the 5,300-seat Angeles Temple in Los Angeles. C. M. Robeck says, "She was undoubtedly the most prominent woman leader Pentecostalism has produced to date."[7] She was perhaps the most prominent woman leader in the entire history of Christianity in America.

But there was much personal tragedy after she began preaching widely around 1915, including her divorce in 1921; the scandal of her disappearance while swimming off Venice Beach in 1926, followed by her subsequent discovery in Mexico a month later; a nervous breakdown in 1930; another failed marriage in 1931; and death from "an apparently accidental overdose of a medical prescription" in 1944.[8]

Another tragic example is found more recently in the life of Judy Brown. Brown was a popular Bible teacher at Central Bible College (Assemblies of God) in Springfield, Missouri. She wrote a book, *Women Ministers According to Scripture*,[9] in which she argued extensively for an evangelical feminist position. She later moved to Salem, Virginia, and became pastor of the Salem Worship Center church. But on March 26, 2004, Brown was sentenced to thirty years in prison when she was found guilty of "malicious wounding and burglary with the intent to commit murder."[10] She had begun a lesbian relationship with the wife of another pastor, Ted Smart, and then attempted to murder Pastor Smart to get him out of the way. According to the report in *World* magazine,

> Then, on Aug. 25, 2003, when Mrs. Smart was out of town and after their son left for school, Ms. Brown broke into the family's basement. She threw the switches on the fusebox, shutting off power in the

[7] C. M. Robeck, Jr., "Aimee Semple McPherson," in *International Dictionary of Pentecostal and Charismatic Movements*, rev. and expanded ed., ed. Stanley M. Burgess and Eduard van der Maas (Grand Rapids, Mich.: Zondervan, 2002), 858.
[8] Ibid., 856-859.
[9] Judy L. Brown, *Women Ministers According to Scripture* (Springfield, Ill.: Judy L. Brown, 1996).
[10] Gene Edward Veith, "Murder, She Wrote: The Strange and Sad Case of Felon/Theologian Judy Brown," *World*, April 30, 2005, 29.

house. Mr. Smart went downstairs to investigate. Whereupon the theologian hit him on the back of the head with a crowbar.

Though she hit him two more times, Mr. Smart, bleeding, fought her off, made his way upstairs, and called the police. When they arrived, they found Ms. Brown on the front lawn. In the basement, they found a Wal-Mart bag containing a large trash bag, three pairs of latex gloves, a washcloth, and a butcher knife.

Investigators determined that Ms. Brown had planned to kill her lover's husband, dismember his body, and dispose of it, so that she could have Mrs. Smart all to herself.[11]

What happened to Judy Brown? I expect that she probably had a deep love for God and a strong spiritual gift of Bible teaching. If she had continued to use this gift within the bounds of Scripture and decided she would teach the Bible only to women, she likely would have had a remarkably fruitful ministry with much blessing from God throughout her life. But she stepped outside the bounds of appropriate women's ministry as described in Scripture. And then she became a leader in the evangelical feminist movement, forcefully advocating her position through her speaking and writing. She became the pastor of a church, a role that Scripture reserves for men. And then it appears that God simply withdrew his blessing and withdrew his hand of protection from her life. She tragically lost the ability to make wise judgments, and disastrous consequences followed.

Someone may object to my bringing up the examples of these women, and say, "But what about the hundreds of male pastors who have committed great sins, bringing reproach on themselves and their churches? Why pick on these two women when many more men have sinned just as badly?"

I agree that many male pastors have also fallen into very serious sin. And I do not doubt that in many of those cases God also withdrew his protection and blessing from them. But in their cases the reason cannot be that the Bible forbids men to become pastors! Surely nobody would

---

[11] Ibid. Veith also points out that Judy Brown had contributed a chapter called "God, Gender, and Biblical Metaphor" to the egalitarian book, *Discovering Biblical Equality*, ed. Ronald W. Pierce and Rebecca Merrill Groothuis (Downers Grove, Ill.: InterVarsity Press, 2004), but when IVP heard about Judy Brown's prison sentence they withdrew the book from publication and reissued it without her chapter.

argue that. Often the sins of pride and a refusal to be accountable to any-one are mentioned in reports of a male pastor committing ministry-destroying and life-destroying sins. Surely those are serious sins as well, and they are also violations of the Bible's standards.

But with these women pastors, the most obvious, evident sin is that of disobeying God's directions that a woman should not "teach or . . . exercise authority over a man" in the context of an assembled church (1 Tim. 2:12). And that is why I believe there is a connection between women being ordained and exercising leadership as pastors and tragic results in their personal lives.

Why then have such tragic events not happened to all women who have become pastors or elders? We cannot know the full answer in this life, but part of the answer is the same thing we must say regarding God's apparent continued blessing on those who are disobedient to Scripture with respect to other areas of life. In his great patience and grace, God does not always withdraw his blessing and bring discipline to our lives immediately when we disobey him: he is "slow to anger" (see Ex. 34:6; Ps. 103:8-9).

And what shall we say about the "experience" of blessing on a woman's ministry? We seldom see the full story. But if a woman goes on serving as an elder or pastor, I believe she is dangerously straying out-side the will of God, and outside of his protection.

C. WHAT DOES HISTORICAL "EXPERIENCE" REALLY DEMONSTRATE ABOUT WOMEN'S MINISTRIES?

Arguments based on experience are seldom conclusive. Even today, in the strongly egalitarian popular culture of the United States, by far the largest and most successful ministries (by any measure), the ministries that seem to have been most blessed by God, have men as senior pas-tors. Even those few large evangelical churches that have women as part of their pastoral team (such as Willow Creek Community Church) usu-ally have a man (such as Bill Hybels) as the senior pastor, and men do most of the preaching. Evangelical churches with women pastors are few in comparison to the large number of churches that have only men as pastors and elders.

This fact should not be lightly dismissed. If it really were God's ideal for men and women to share equally in eldership and pastoral leadership roles, then at some point in the last two thousand years, and especially today, would we not expect to see a remarkable blessing of God on some churches that have an equal number of men and women as elders and that share the main Bible teaching responsibilities equally between men and women pastors? If this is God's ideal, then why have we not seen a pattern of God's evident blessing on such churches, among the millions of churches that have existed in the last two thousand years?

Liberal denominations that ordain women pastors have continually declined in membership and income. Historian Ruth Tucker summarizes this trend:

> The role of women in the church in the twentieth century will perplex future historians. . . . Those historians who dig deeper will discover that the mainline churches that were offering women the greatest opportunities were simultaneously declining in membership and influence. Some of these churches, which once had stood firm on the historic orthodox faith, were becoming too sophisticated to take the Bible at face value. The gains that have been made, then, are mixed at best.[12]

Tucker's assessment can be supported by observing the membership trends in the large liberal denominations that have been the strongest proponents of women's ordination:[13]

---

[12] Tucker, *Women in the Maze,* 184. Additional information on the decline of liberal Protestant churches and the rapid increase of conservative, Bible-believing churches is found in Dave Shiflett, *Exodus: Why Americans Are Fleeing Liberal Churches for Conservative Christianity* (New York: Sentinel, 2005) (his summary statistics on denominations are on xiii–xiv). Among conservative denominations that do not ordain women, Shiflett documents some remarkable growth in the last ten years: for example, the Southern Baptist Convention grew 5 percent, the Presbyterian Church in America grew 42.4 percent, the Christian and Missionary Alliance grew 21.8 percent, and the Evangelical Free Church grew 57.2 percent (xiv; however, Shiflett also notes an 18.5 percent increase in the Assemblies of God, which does ordain women).

[13] The information in this chart was compiled for me by my teaching assistants Travis Buchanan and Steve Eriksson from Martin B. Bradley et al., *Churches and Church Membership in the United States, 1990* (Atlanta: Glenmary Research Center, 1992); and Dale E. Jones et al., *Religious Congregations and Membership in the United States, 2000* (Nashville: Glenmary Research Center, 2002); and from reference material compiled by Justin Taylor of Bethlehem Baptist Church, Minneapolis (now of Good News Publishers, Crossway Books and Bibles, Wheaton, Illinois). Numbers for the Evangelical Lutheran Church in America use the combined totals for the American Lutheran Church and the Lutheran Church of America for 1971 and 1980.

Denomination	1971	1980	1990	2000
American Baptist Church	1,693,423	1,922,467	1,873,731	1,767,462
Evangelical Lutheran Church in America	5,500,687	5,273,662	5,226,798	5,113,418
Episcopal Church	3,024,724	2,823,399	2,445,286	2,314,756
Presbyterian Church–USA	4,649,440	4,012,825	3,553,335	3,141,566
United Methodist Church	11,535,986	11,552,111	11,091,032	10,350,629

Not all the churches in those denominations have women pastors, of course. And not all of the individual congregations within those denominations have adopted a liberal view of the Bible. Therefore this information must be used with caution. Anecdotal evidence that people have told me about over the years suggests that a detailed study of those denominations would show that within those denominations the congregations that have grown the most also have the most conservative views of the Bible and have resisted the trend toward women pastors, but I do not have actual data to prove this (and I am sure that people could point to individual exceptions).[14] In any case, the argument that churches must ordain women pastors in order to do effective evangelism and grow in modern society simply is not supported by the evidence.

D. WE CANNOT IMMEDIATELY SEE ALL THE CONSEQUENCES OF WOMEN BEING PASTORS

When people say there is "much blessing" from the ministries of women pastors, I do not think they are able to see all the consequences. Once a woman pastor and women elders are installed in a church, several other consequences will follow:

> (1) Many of the most conservative, faithful, Bible-believing members of the church will leave, convinced that the church is disobeying Scripture and that they cannot in good conscience support it any longer.[15]

---

[14] Others could object that such statistics are not conclusive because some Pentecostal and charismatic groups have seen rapid growth even though they ordain women. I agree that groups such as the Assemblies of God and the International Church of the Foursquare Gospel have experienced remarkable growth, but pastors within those groups also tell me that the larger and more rapidly growing churches in those denominations have men as pastors.

[15] To take one example, I saw this happen at an influential evangelical church in Libertyville, Illinois, in 1996 and 1997. The pastor attempted over a period of months to add women to the governing board of the church, and as a result perhaps ten or more of the most conserva-

(2) Other members will stay even though they disagree with the egalitarian stance of their leaders. They will think that the leaders they respect are encouraging disobedience to Scripture, and this will tend to erode their confidence in Scripture in other areas as well.

(3) Those who are persuaded that the Bible allows women as pastors will usually accept one or more of the methods of interpretation I discuss in this book, methods that tend to erode and undermine the effective authority of Scripture in our lives. Therefore, they will be likely to adopt such methods in evading the force of other passages of Scripture or other topics in the future.

(4) A church with female elders or pastors will tend to become more and more "feminized" over time, with women holding most of the major leadership positions and men constituting a smaller and smaller percentage of the congregation.[16]

(5) Male leadership in the home will also be eroded, for people will reason instinctively if not explicitly that if women can function as leaders in the family of God, the church, then why should women not be able to function as well as men in leadership roles in the home? This influence will not be sudden or immediate, but will increase over time.

(6) The boys and girls growing up in the congregation will experience increasing gender identity confusion, since nobody in the church will be teaching them what it means to be a man instead of a woman, or to be a woman instead of a man (see chapter 30, below, for this trend among evangelical feminists). They will just be taught to grow up as Christian "persons" (with all instruction being gender-neutral, or even geared to teach boys how not to be

---

tive, most active families in the church left and joined the other main evangelical church in town, a Southern Baptist Church where I was an elder and where the pastor and church constitution clearly supported a complementarian position.

[16] See Leon Podles, *The Church Impotent: The Feminization of Christianity* (Dallas: Spence, 1999), who notes that in 1952 the adult attenders on Sunday morning in typical Protestant churches were 53 percent female and 47 percent male, which was almost exactly the same as the proportion of women and men in the adult population in the U.S. But by 1986 (after several decades of feminist influence in liberal denominations) the ratios were closer to 60 percent female and 40 percent male, with many congregations reporting a ratio of 65 percent to 35 percent (11-12). Podles focuses primarily on Roman Catholic and liberal Protestant churches in his study, and he concludes that, if present trends continue, the "Protestant clergy will be characteristically a female occupation, like nursing, within a generation" (xiii).

See also, *Why Men Hate Going to Church,* by David Murrow (Nashville: Thomas Nelson, 2005). Murrow describes in detail the increasing "feminization" of many churches, a trend that is driving men away.

different from girls, and to teach girls how not to be different from boys). As they enter their twenties, there will also be increased reluctance to marry because of confusion about what it means to be a husband or a wife.

All this is to say that the "evident blessing" that God gives when women preach the Bible is not the only result of such preaching. There will be many, far-reaching negative consequences as well.

It is not always easy to see the long-term consequences of any action. A better course is to have a settled conviction in our hearts that in the long run God will bring blessing to our churches and our lives when we obey all of his Word.

E. PUTTING EXPERIENCE ABOVE THE BIBLE IS A FORM OF "SITUATION ETHICS" AND IS ALSO THE FOUNDATIONAL PRINCIPLE OF MODERN LIBERALISM

What is right and wrong must be determined by the Bible, not by our experiences or our evaluation of the results of certain actions. Determining right and wrong by means of results is often known as "the end justifies the means." It is a dangerous approach to ethical decisions, because it so easily encourages disobedience to Scripture.

In 1966, Joseph Fletcher published *Situation Ethics: The New Morality.*[17] He argued that people at times needed to break God's moral laws in the Bible in order to do the greatest good for the greatest number of people. But as these ideas worked their way through American society, the "new morality" of Fletcher's situation ethics brought about a tremendous erosion of moral standards and widespread disobedience to all of God's moral laws.

If I say that women should be pastors because it brings good results, *even if I honestly believe the Bible says that women should not be pastors,* then I have simply capitulated to situation ethics. What is right and wrong must be determined by the teachings of Scripture, not by the seemingly good results of actions that violate Scripture.

J. I. Packer explains that one of the characteristics of theological liberalism is "an optimistic view of cultured humanity's power to perceive

---

[17] Joseph Fletcher, *Situation Ethics: The New Morality* (Philadelphia: Westminster, 1966).

God by reflecting on its experience."[18] Thus, *experience* rather than the Bible becomes the ultimate standard in theology. If we decide that women and men can have all the same roles in the church *primarily because we have seen blessing on the work of women preachers and Bible teachers,* such an egalitarian argument leads us toward theological liberalism.

I am not saying that experience or personal testimonies should be disregarded as we think about the teachings of the Bible. But experience and personal testimony can never prove something contrary to what the Bible teaches. If we begin to go in that direction, then we leave ourselves wide open to accepting such things as praying to the saints simply because some such prayers have been answered, or believing that Christians should always be "healthy and wealthy" simply because some who believe this have indeed become more healthy and wealthy. Basing doctrine on experience alone can lead us in any direction.

During the present controversy over women in leadership roles in the church, God has continued to allow some measure of blessing (for a time at least) on some churches that have women pastors and women elders, and on some women who teach the Bible to congregations of both men and women. This gives us an opportunity to decide whether we will follow God's Word or allow ourselves to be led away from his Word by experiences that seem to bring blessing to people. Though not everyone will agree with me at this point, I believe this is a test of our faithfulness to God and to his Word in our generation. Eventually the consequences of each decision will become plain.

Approving of women as pastors and elders *primarily because we see evidence of blessing on their ministries* and not primarily because we see it taught in the Bible is another step on the path toward liberalism.

---

[18] J. I. Packer, "Liberalism and Conservatism in Theology" in *New Dictionary of Theology,* ed. Sinclair B. Ferguson and David F. Wright (Leicester, UK: InterVarsity, 1988), 385.

"CALLING" TRUMPS SCRIPTURE

Some evangelical feminists put a subjective sense of "calling" above the Bible

Another liberal tendency to reject the authority of Scripture is seen when egalitarians claim that, if a woman has a genuine call from God for pastoral ministry, we have no right to oppose that call, and that call takes priority over any opposing argument that people might raise from Scripture. This argument is often made by women who believe that God has called them to become pastors.

Millicent Hunter, whom *Charisma* magazine identifies as "pastor of 3,000-member Baptist Worship Center in Philadelphia," says that the current generation of women ministers is emerging with more boldness. "They are coming out of the woodwork with an 'I don't care what you think; this is what God called me to do' type of attitude."[1]

Sarah Sumner insists that God called her to be a theology professor:

I didn't ask God to grant me the grace to enter seminary and complete my doctoral work. That was his idea. He designed the plan; he's the one who saw me through.[2]

---

[1] Millicent Hunter, as quoted in *Charisma*, May 2003, 40.
[2] Sarah Sumner, *Men and Women in the Church* (Downers Grove, Ill.: InterVarsity Press, 2003), 27.

She encourages other women to follow God's calling no matter what critics may say:

> It is not Anne Graham Lotz's spiritual obligation to sit down with the leaders of the Southern Baptist Convention and convince them that God gave her as a preacher. . . . If God gave her as a preacher, then she is a preacher, even if someone claims that that's impossible. . . . You are who you are no matter what. . . . God decides your calling. God decides your spiritual giftedness. . . . If the Spirit of God has given you as a pastor, you are a pastor, even if you're not employed as one.[3]

The following statement from a personal letter is typical of many that come to the office of the Council on Biblical Manhood and Womanhood:

> What will they answer, when before the throne of God, as to exactly why they didn't permit one that the Lord Himself *called* to teach, even a woman? . . . Am I any less called by God to do according to His purpose in my life because I am a woman?

Is this argument persuasive? Does God actually call some women to preach and teach his Word to men and women alike? Does he call some women to be pastors and elders?

God never calls people to disobey his Word. Our decision on this matter must be based on the objective teaching of the Bible, not on some person's subjective experience, no matter how godly or sincere that person is. This egalitarian claim is another form of the question, Will we take Scripture or experience as our ultimate guide?

I agree that people may have subjective experiences of God's presence and blessing that are genuine and real. But it is easy to make a mistake in understanding the meaning of those experiences. If a woman finds God's blessing and anointing when she preaches, then does that mean God is calling her to be a pastor, or does it mean that he is calling her to teach the Bible to women, in accordance with his Word, and that he will give much blessing in that task? If we had only the subjective

---

[3] Ibid., 318.

experience alone to go on, it would be impossible to be certain that we had reached the right answer, because we would have only our own human interpretations of the event, not an interpretation given in God's own words.

What a woman perceives as a call from God to a pastoral ministry *may be a genuine call to some other full-time ministry that is approved by Scripture.* Many ministries that include Bible teaching are open to women.[4] It may be that a strong sense of calling from God is in fact a calling from God to these kinds of ministries.

But I do not believe that God calls a woman to be a pastor or elder where she would teach God's Word and have governing authority over men. Women who dismiss any Scripture-based objections with a claim that a sense of God's calling has led them into such ministry are putting subjective experience above Scripture, and that is another step on the path toward liberalism.

---

[4] See Wayne Grudem, *Evangelical Feminism and Biblical Truth* (Sisters, Ore.: Multnomah, 2004), 84-101, for a list of many ministries that I think we should encourage for women.

"PROPHECIES" TRUMP SCRIPTURE

Some evangelical feminists put contemporary prophecies above the Bible

Another tendency leading toward rejection of the supreme authority of Scripture is the claim of Cindy Jacobs and other charismatics and Pentecostals that many contemporary prophecies are saying that God wants women to teach and preach to both sexes, or to be in pastoral leadership roles. When this claim is made, the contemporary prophecies take precedence over the teaching of Scripture. Jacobs, who speaks widely in charismatic and Pentecostal circles, writes,

> Of one thing I am certain: *God is calling women today in a greater way than He ever has before.* Major prophetic voices are prophesying all around the world that this is the time to find a way to release women into the ministry.[1]

This statement occurs at the beginning of Jacobs's section on the role of women in the church (171-244). It comes before she discusses the "difficult passages" on women in the church (225-244). As such, the prophecies play a foundational role in the discussion. They are not brought in as supplemental material after the teaching of Scripture has been established, but they are used to say, in effect, "This is what God

---

[1] Cindy Jacobs, *Women of Destiny* (Ventura, Calif.: Regal, 1998), 173.

is saying today. So this is right. Later we can discuss the 'difficult passages.'" When prophecies are appealed to in this way in an argument, it can seem to the reader that they are being given more weight than Scripture in how the matter is decided.

Although I quote only the published writings of Cindy Jacobs, there is substantial anecdotal evidence of such prophecies in many places. In addition, some things I have heard personally in circles where prophecies are allowed confirm that such prophecies are fairly common and that they have a real impact on decisions that leaders and churches make about women's ministries.

But are these prophecies genuine? Are they really from God? Elsewhere I have written extensively on the gift of prophecy and I affirm that this gift is in the New Testament, that it is one of the gifts of the Holy Spirit given for the new covenant age, and that there is a proper place for it in the church.[2] But it also carries the danger of abuse, and it must be tested by Scripture and used according to Scriptural guidelines.

What should we say, then, about people who claim that God is saying through "prophecies" today that women should be pastors and elders, and should teach the Bible to men? First, we have to ask carefully exactly what was said in these prophecies.

There may have been prophecies saying that a certain woman is gifted in Bible teaching, or that she should commit her life to full-time Christian ministry, or that God's anointing is on her Bible teaching. There is nothing contrary to Scripture in this, and the prophecies may well be from God. These gifts can all still be used in teaching women in the church, or teaching children in various ministries, with great effectiveness.[3]

But if the prophecies specifically say that a woman should become a pastor or an elder, I do not believe we should accept these prophecies as genuine. I do not think they are from God.

Paul commands that when Christians allow prophecies in the church, they are to "test everything" and to "hold fast what is good"

---

[2] See Wayne Grudem, *The Gift of Prophecy in the New Testament and Today*, rev. ed. (Wheaton, Ill.: Crossway, 2000). For a brief summary of my conclusions, see Grudem, *Systematic Theology* (Grand Rapids, Mich.: Zondervan, 1994), 1049-1061.

[3] For an analysis of which activities in the church should be encouraged for women and which should be restricted to men, see Wayne Grudem, *Evangelical Feminism and Biblical Truth* (Sisters, Ore.: Multnomah, 2004), 84-101.

(1 Thess. 5:20-21). This implies that some prophecies are not "good." Mature charismatic and Pentecostal leaders recognize that it is difficult, even for someone who has a prophetic gifting and has used it effectively for many years, to be sure whether any specific prophecy is from God, and whether all of it or just parts of it are from God. This is why Paul adds a provision for testing by others who hear the prophecy, both in 1 Thessalonians 5:20-21 and in 1 Corinthians 14:29. Prophecies must be tested especially for their conformity to Scripture.

The people who give prophecies saying it is time to release women into ministries of teaching and having authority over men may be sincere, committed Christians. But it is possible for sincere, committed Christians to make mistakes, and even to be led astray by their own desires or by evil spirits who masquerade as "angels of light," giving a subjective impression that feels so much like a genuine prophetic impulse: "even Satan disguises himself as an angel of light. So it is no surprise if his servants, also, disguise themselves as servants of righteousness" (2 Cor. 11:14-15).

The only safe way to guard against such deception is to test prophecies by Scripture. Prophecies that contradict Scripture are in error. We return to the fundamental question: what does the Bible teach? No genuine prophecy from the Holy Spirit is going to lead people to contradict or disobey God's Word.

Is accepting such prophecies a step toward liberalism? When people place them above Scripture it is. And when people allow such prophecies to influence their view of what the Bible teaches about women in ministry, it is. The Bible should test the prophecies; the prophecies should never be used to test Scripture. And when people have an attitude that says, "I don't know what the Bible teaches about women as pastors and elders and Bible teachers for men, but these prophecies lead me to approve of it," then this is clearly a step toward liberalism.

If people put contemporary prophecies above Scripture, they are denying the supreme authority of Scripture in our lives. If people allow contemporary prophecies rather than Scripture to determine what they think about women in ministry, this opens the door to receiving many more prophecies that contradict Scripture on many other areas of life. Even if people say, "We are looking *both* to Scripture and to these prophecies," they are then putting stock in these prophecies to help them decide the question of women's roles in the church today, a question that should be decided solely on the basis of what Scripture says. (And people who say they are looking both to Scripture and to prophecies in actual practice will likely put more weight on the prophecies than on Scripture.)

Many of the evangelical feminists who adopt such approaches to contemporary prophecies about women in ministry have good intentions and are seeking to honor God. But giving such weight to prophecies in deciding a major doctrinal question is in actual fact undermining the authority of Scripture. Leaders who follow this approach are thus taking their churches another step toward liberalism.

16

CIRCUMSTANCES TRUMP SCRIPTURE

*Some evangelical feminists put unique circumstances
above the Bible*

Yet another rejection of the ultimate authority of Scripture is found in claims like that of John Arnott, pastor of the Toronto Airport Christian Fellowship, that this is a unique time in history and therefore the old prohibitions against women being pastors or teaching the Bible to men no longer apply:

> Women readers, be encouraged: your anointing will make room for you! The desperate need of the hour is not merely for people who are trained and educated, but for people of God who are anointed and can bring God's kingdom to a broken, hurting, desperate world through signs, wonders and the power of the Holy Spirit.
>
> All Christians must come to terms with the fact that about 85 percent of the world's population is lost. And the lost are really lost! Under these desperate conditions, why would anyone stand in the way of another who felt called of God to help bring in the harvest?[1]

In a similar vein Cindy Jacobs writes,

---

[1] John Arnott, "All Hands to the Harvest," *Spread the Fire,* October 1997, 1; this journal was published by the Toronto Airport Christian Fellowship (see www.tacf.org).

> As I have traveled around the world and seen great revivals in places such as Colombia and Argentina, I have seen churches in major revival so busy trying to get the converts discipled that they are happy for laborers—either men or women![2]

They use these statements as support for their claims that all areas of ministry are open to women and men alike.

But if we are to be obedient to God's Word, we are not free to say that "this is an unusual time, so we don't have to obey the Bible." God knew that these days would come, and his Word is not obsolete! He has made provision in his Word for every period of history up until the day Christ returns. We are not free to disregard it.

We should also realize that the period recorded in the Book of Acts was a time of great revival and a great work of the Holy Spirit, yet there were no women pastors or elders. The Reformation in Europe and the Great Awakenings in the United States were times of great revival and blessing from God, yet they did not require Christians to disobey God's Word.

In other circumstances and at other times, people who have thought they could disobey God's Word because of unique circumstances have not been blessed by God. Think, for example, of Saul, who disobeyed the words of the prophet Samuel and offered a burnt offering himself (1 Sam. 13:9) because he thought the circumstances were so pressing and he was going to lose the people who had gathered to him (see vv. 8, 11-12). As a result, Samuel told Saul, "now your kingdom shall not continue" (1 Sam. 13:14). Abram decided that he had waited long enough without a child and chose (at the prompting of his wife Sarai) to have a child with Hagar, Sarai's Egyptian servant (Gen. 16). But Abram's decision not to wait and trust God, but to take matters into his own hands because of the apparent urgency of the situation, was not blessed by God. His lack of faith resulted in the birth of Ishmael, whose descendants continue to be at enmity with the people of Israel to this day.

Any argument that says the great needs of the hour should decide the question of women's roles in the church is just another way of say-

---

[2] Cindy Jacobs, *Women of Destiny* (Ventura, Calif.: Regal, 1998), 234.

ing that experience, not Scripture, should decide this question. And that is just a way of saying that we are free to disregard or even disobey Scripture. But disregarding or disobeying Scripture can never be right.

Another argument from "unique circumstances" might be the objection of some people who fear, "We will be subject to a lawsuit if we refuse to consider a woman for the job of pastor." But this fear is groundless at the present time at least in the United States, because case law has consistently given wide deference to churches and religious organizations in the way they select people entrusted with ministry responsibilities.[3] In other countries where laws may threaten the church, or in the United States if the legal situation ever changes, we would still be obligated to obey the Word of God even if it conflicted with the laws of human society (see Acts 5:29, "We must obey God rather than men").

Again and again, we keep returning to this question: what does the Bible say? If it forbids women from taking the office of pastor or elder (as I have argued extensively elsewhere),[4] then we have no right to say this is a "unique time" when we can disobey what God's Word says.

Therefore those who argue that women should have all ministry roles open to them because this is a "unique time" in history are taking the church another step down the path toward liberalism.

---

[3] See Donald A. Balasa, "Is It Legal for Religious Organizations to Make Distinctions on the Basis of Sex?" in *Recovering Biblical Manhood and Womanhood: A Response to Evangelical Feminism*, ed. John Piper and Wayne Grudem (Wheaton, Ill.: Crossway, 1991), 332-341.

[4] See Wayne Grudem, *Evangelical Feminism and Biblical Truth* (Sisters, Ore.: Multnomah, 2004), especially pages 62-102.

17

CALLING A HISTORICAL PASSAGE A JOKE

One evangelical feminist nullifies a Bible passage on Sarah obeying Abraham by saying that it was intended as humor

Gilbert Bilezikian, retired theology professor from Wheaton College and one of the founding elders of Willow Creek Community Church, uses another procedure to evade the force of New Testament teaching on roles for men and women. He claims that the author did not really mean what he said, but wanted us to take it as a humorous statement.

This occurs in Bilezikian's treatment of 1 Peter 3:1-6, which reads as follows:

> Likewise, *wives, be subject to your own husbands,* so that even if some do not obey the word, they may be won without a word by the conduct of their wives—when they see your respectful and pure conduct. Do not let your adorning be external—the braiding of hair and the putting on of gold jewelry, or the clothing you wear—but let your adorning be the hidden person of the heart with the imperishable beauty of a gentle and quiet spirit, which in God's sight is very precious. *For this is how the holy women who hoped in God used to adorn themselves, by submitting to their own husbands, as Sarah obeyed Abraham,* calling him lord. And you are her children, if you do good and do not fear anything that is frightening.

How does Bilezikian avoid the force of Peter's command to wives to be subject to their husbands and to imitate the example of Sarah, who "obeyed Abraham"? He says it was a humorous statement—in other words, the statement does not tell us what Peter actually meant. It was a joke. Here is what Bilezikian says:

> The use of Sarah as an example of obedience shows that *Peter was not devoid of a sense of humor.* In Genesis, Abraham is shown as obeying Sarah as often as Sarah obeyed Abraham—once at God's behest as he was told, "Whatever Sarah says to you, do as she tells you" (Gen. 16:2, 6; 21:11-12). . . . Sarah obeyed Abraham, but Christian wives, her spiritual daughters, are never told to "obey" their husbands neither here nor anywhere else in the Bible.[1]

But to say that a straightforward biblical statement is an example of humor is simply an easy way to avoid the force of a verse whose plain meaning contradicts one's position. This is not the kind of argument that reflects submission to Scripture.

Did Abraham actually "obey Sarah," as Bilezikian claims?

The Old Testament texts Bilezikian cites do not show Sarah taking over leadership of her household or Abraham obeying Sarah. Here are the verses he refers to:

> And Sarai said to Abram, "Behold now, the LORD has prevented me from bearing children. Go in to my servant; it may be that I shall obtain children by her." And Abram listened to the voice of Sarai (Gen. 16:2).

> But Abram said to Sarai, "Behold, your servant is in your power; do to her as you please." Then Sarai dealt harshly with her, and she fled from her (Gen. 16:6).

> So she said to Abraham, "Cast out this slave woman with her son, for the son of this slave woman shall not be heir with my son Isaac." And the thing was very displeasing to Abraham on account of his

---

[1] Gilbert Bilezikian, *Beyond Sex Roles: What the Bible Says About a Woman's Place in Church and Family*, 2nd ed. (Grand Rapids, Mich.: Baker, 1985), 191, italics added.

son. But God said to Abraham, "Be not displeased because of the boy and because of your slave woman. Whatever Sarah says to you, do as she tells you, for through Isaac shall your offspring be named" (Gen. 21:10-12).

These are not examples of Abraham "obeying" Sarah, as Bilezikian claims. Genesis 16:2 is an example of a husband giving in to a wrongful request from his wife, resulting in disobedience to God, for in this verse Abraham gives in to Sarah's urging and has a son by Hagar. For a husband to *grant his wife's request* surely does not prove that she has authority over him, any more than it shows a reversal of authority when God grants one of our requests, or when a parent grants a child's request. And when Abraham grants Sarah's wrongful request, with disastrous consequences, it proves even less. Bilezikian shows no awareness that the Bible does not hold up this incident of sin as a pattern for us to imitate.

In Genesis 16:6, Abraham does not obey Sarah but is clearly the family authority who (again wrongfully) gives in to Sarah's recriminations and allows her to mistreat Hagar and Ishmael. Why does Bilezikian refer to these examples of sin as positive examples of a husband's obeying his wife? To use such a procedure is to contradict the force of these passages.

Then in Genesis 21:11-12, God tells Abraham, "Listen to whatever Sarah tells you," but this was specifically about casting out Hagar and Ishmael. Abraham did what Sarah asked here not because he was obeying his wife but because at this specific point God told him to do what Sarah said. God used Sarah to convey his will to Abraham, but no pattern of husbands obeying their wives is established here. In fact, the exceptional intervention of God suggests that Abraham would not ordinarily have acceded to such a request from his wife.

So is Bilezikian right to say that Peter's statement is an example of "humor" and to imply that Peter uses Sarah ("as Sarah obeyed Abraham") as a negative example? Certainly not. But in actual fact, in this same discussion Bilezikian goes beyond his statement about Peter's "sense of humor" and overturns everything that Peter says about wives submitting to their husbands. Bilezikian says, the point of Peter's reference to Sarah is that wives in the new covenant can learn from their spiritual ancestress . . . who lived in the "dark side" of the old-covenant compromise, when she had to "obey" her husband. . . . Sarah obeyed Abraham, but Christian wives, her spiritual daughters, are never told to "obey" their husbands neither here nor anywhere else in the Bible.[2]

But this is just turning Peter's words into the opposite of what he says. Peter uses Sarah as a positive example for Christian wives to imitate, but Bilezikian uses her as a *negative* example showing what Christian wives are not supposed to do. Peter tells wives to act like "the holy women who hoped in God . . . by submitting to their own husbands" (1 Pet. 3:5), but Bilezikian says this was on the "dark side" of the "old-covenant compromise," implying that it should *not* be a pattern for women today.

Peter tells wives to act like Sarah, who "obeyed Abraham" (v. 6), but Bilezikian says that this verse does *not* tell wives to obey their husbands.

We should note carefully the result of Bilezikian's analysis of 1 Peter 3:1-7, because at several points he ends up denying what the text says and affirming what the text does not say. Peter says that wives *should* be subject to their husbands, but Bilezikian says that the motivations for a Christian wife's behavior should "have nothing in common with submission defined as obedience to authority."[3] Peter *does not say* that husbands should be subject to their wives, but Bilezikian says that husbands should undergo a "traumatic role reversal" whereby "now it is husbands who must show consideration for their wives and bestow honor upon them, much like a servant to his master."[4] Peter says that *Sarah obeyed Abraham*, but Bilezikian claims that *Abraham obeyed Sarah*. Peter says that wives *should* follow the example of Sarah, who obeyed her husband, but Bilezikian says that wives are *nowhere* told to be obedient to their husbands.

Bilezikian teaches just the opposite of what the Bible teaches regarding Sarah and Abraham. Under the guise of saying that Peter had a

---

[2] Ibid.
[3] Ibid., 190.
[4] Ibid., 192.

"sense of humor," Bilezikian advocates a position that is repeatedly unwilling to submit to the authority of the actual words of Scripture and simply changes the teaching of Scripture again and again.

Changing the plain words of Scripture into their opposite by claiming that they are an example of "humor" is another way to undermine the authority of Scripture. It is another step on the path toward liberalism.

18

THE RESULT OF REJECTING THE AUTHORITY OF THE BIBLE IN THESE WAYS

The previous chapters detail fifteen ways in which evangelical feminists, either directly or by implication, undermine and deny the authority of Scripture. Various evangelical feminists

(1) deny the authority or truthfulness of Genesis 1–3
(2) say that Paul was wrong
(3) say that some verses that appear in every ancient manuscript are not part of the Bible
(4) say that our ultimate authority is found not in what is written in Scripture but in developments that came after the Bible
(5) follow a "redemptive-movement hermeneutic" that casts all the ethical commands of the New Testament into doubt
(6) claim that everyone's position just depends on what Bible passages people choose to prioritize
(7) silence the most relevant Bible passages on men and women by saying they are "disputed"
(8) say that women can teach under the authority of pastors and elders
(9) evade New Testament commands by saying, "We are not a church"
(10) put church tradition above the Bible
(11) put experience above the Bible
(12) put a subjective sense of "calling" above the Bible
(13) put contemporary prophecies above the Bible
(14) put unique circumstances above the Bible
(15) nullify the Bible's statements by saying they are a joke

These methods of undermining the authority of Scripture indicate a deeply troubling trend toward theological liberalism.

But are these representative of the mainstream evangelical feminist movement? Yes, clearly they are. The claims that I have mentioned are promoted by prominent egalitarian writers and published by leading evangelical publishers such as (most often) Baker Book House and InterVarsity Press. And Christians for Biblical Equality, the flagship egalitarian organization, promotes on their website many of the evangelical books I have criticized in the previous section.[1]

Where are the voices challenging these approaches? Although there have been a few notable exceptions,[2] in general there is widespread silence from *other* egalitarian authors, who do not deny the authority of Scripture in these ways but who refrain from making any public criticism of those who do.

And what will happen to churches and organizations who allow these approaches to stand as acceptable options? As evangelicals accept the validity of these claims one after the other, and as evangelical pastors preach sermons adopting the methods found in these claims, evangelicals are quietly and unsuspectingly being trained to reject this verse of Scripture and that command of Scripture, and this passage, and that teaching, here and there throughout the Bible. As this procedure goes on, we will begin to have whole churches who no longer "tremble" at the Word of God (Isa. 66:2), and who no longer live by "every word that comes from the mouth of God" (Matt. 4:4), but who pick and choose the things they like and the things they don't like in the Bible, using the very same methods they have been taught by these egalitarian writers. The church will thus be led step by step, often without knowing what is happening, to a new liberalism for the twenty-first century.

And in this way the authority of God's Word, and the ultimate authority of God himself over our lives, will be diminished and increasingly rejected.

---

[1] See www.cbeinternational.org.

[2] For example, Anthony Thiselton has criticized Gordon Fee's claim that Paul did not write 1 Corinthians 14:34-35, as I noted in chapter 5, above.

PART III
EVANGELICAL FEMINIST VIEWS BASED ON UNTRUTHFUL OR UNSUBSTANTIATED CLAIMS

INTRODUCTION TO
PART III

In addition to these fifteen ways that directly or implicitly deny the
authority of Scripture, there is another whole category of egalitarian
claims that should trouble evangelical Christians today. This category
does not concern a *direct* denial of the authority of the Bible, but it nullifies the authority of the Bible in another way, through promoting
untruthful or unsubstantiated claims about what certain words in the
Bible "really mean," or about some historical facts that change our
understanding of the situation to which a book of the Bible was written.

These egalitarian claims are significant because they contain several
important historical and linguistic "facts" that egalitarian writers *allege*
to be true, and these alleged facts *change* people's understanding of what
the Bible teaches. But *if those alleged facts are incorrect* and people
believe them anyway, then people will think the Bible says something different from what it does say, and then *they will no longer believe or obey
what the Bible really says.* And thus, in a different way, the effective
authority of the Bible is undermined in our churches.

Here is a hypothetical example of what I am talking about, showing that if you change the meaning of some key words in the Bible, you
change the Bible and take away its authority. Consider this verse:

Children, *obey* your parents in the Lord, for this is right (Eph. 6:1;
compare Col. 3:20).

Now what if I write a scholarly article and claim that the Greek
word *hypakouō*, translated "obey," really means, "criticize"? Then the
verse would mean,

Children, *criticize* your parents in the Lord, for this is right (Eph. 6:1) (!).

By changing the meaning of a word, I have changed the whole point of the verse. And then I could make the same change with any other verses that tell children to obey their parents. Then I could claim, "The Bible nowhere says that children are to *obey* their parents. The verses that say that are all mistranslations."

However, if my claim is false, if in fact the word *hypakouō* does mean "obey," then I have undermined the authority of Scripture in another way. *By wrongly changing the meaning of the words, I have taken away some of the words of the Bible and replaced them with other words that God did not say.* In this way I have violated the commands that warn against adding to or taking from the words of Scripture:

Deuteronomy 4:2: "You shall not add to the word that I command you, nor take from it, that you may keep the commandments of the LORD your God that I command you."

Deuteronomy 12:32: "Everything that I command you, you shall be careful to do. You shall not add to it or take from it."

Proverbs 30:5-6: Every word of God proves true; he is a shield to those who take refuge in him. Do not add to his words, lest he rebuke you and you be found a liar.

Revelation 22:18-19: I warn everyone who hears the words of the prophecy of this book: if anyone adds to them, God will add to him the plagues described in this book, and if anyone takes away from the words of the book of this prophecy, God will take away his share in the tree of life and in the holy city, which are described in this book.

A second way I can change the meaning of words is by claiming there was a *special situation* that the author was writing to, and that means *the verse applies only to people in that same situation.* For example, take this same verse:

Children, obey your parents in the Lord, for this is right (Eph. 6:1).

Now, what if I write a scholarly article and claim that in Ephesus (and Colossae) when Paul wrote, there was a special problem of violent children who traveled in gangs, and those were the children Paul was writing about? I could argue that the Ephesian Christians would have known about that and they would have understood that Paul was not talking about all children, but only these violent ones. Then I would say the verse really means this:

> *You violent children who travel in gangs,* obey your parents in the Lord, for this is right (Eph. 6:1).

Then I could say, "The Bible nowhere tells all children to obey their parents. In fact, that could damage the child's self-esteem! This verse was only a corrective measure Paul imposed for a special circumstance. For today, the verse just means that violent children who are traveling in gangs should go home and be obedient to their parents."

By saying there was a special background situation, I have limited the general application of the verse. I have changed the meaning of "children" so that it is restricted to only a narrow group of children. So the word "children" no longer means what it used to mean. And the Bible no longer tells children today to obey their parents.

But what if my scholarly article is wrong? What if there were no violent children in gangs in Ephesus, and what if that wasn't what Paul meant? *Then again, by wrongly narrowing the meaning of the words to a special group at that time, I have taken away some of the words of Scripture and replaced them with words that God did not say.*

In fact, this is exactly what is done by people who argue that the Bible does not condemn homosexual conduct. For example, Paul speaks about homosexuality in Romans 1:26-27:

> For this reason God gave them up to dishonorable passions. For their women exchanged natural relations for those that are contrary to nature; and the men likewise gave up natural relations with women and were consumed with passion for one another, men committing shameless acts with men and receiving in themselves the due penalty for their error.

Some homosexual rights advocates say that Paul was speaking to a *special situation.* They say that, in the ancient world, only abusive homosexual relationships and homosexual prostitution were condemned, not faithful relationships between consenting adults. In addition, they say that when Paul spoke of people giving up "natural relations" he was speaking only about people whose "natural" desires were for heterosexual relationships. But there are other people whose "natural" desires are for homosexual relationships, and Paul was not speaking about them. In essence, then they narrow the meaning of Romans 1:26-27 as follows:

> For this reason God gave them up to dishonorable passions. For their women *who were not born with homosexual desires* exchanged natural relations for those that are contrary to nature; and the men *who were not born with homosexual desires* likewise gave up natural relations with women and were consumed with passion for one another, men committing shameless acts with men and receiving in themselves the due penalty for their error.

Thus, they claim, the Bible does not condemn all homosexual conduct, only that by people who are naturally inclined to be heterosexuals. For these people, homosexuality is "unnatural."[1] But they say these verses are not even speaking about people who were born with homosexual desires, and so the verses do not apply to many homosexuals today.

Once again, by incorrectly limiting the verses to a special situation, these people change the meaning of the words of Scripture. And in that way they undermine the authority of the Word of God.

In the material that follows, I see similar patterns of wrongly changing the meaning of key words, or wrongly limiting the application of verses because of incorrect claims about "special background situations" that limit the application of the verses today. Such changes to the key verses are supported by claims about words or claims about historical situations that I believe to be wrong because they are either (a) contrary to the evidence we have or (b) mere speculation based on no hard evidence at all. Because these claims change the meanings of several

---

[1] These claims about the ancient world, and about the meaning of Romans 1:26-27, are extensively refuted in several writings. See, for example, Thomas E. Schmidt, *Straight and Narrow?* (Downers Grove, Ill.: InterVarsity Press, 1995); and Thomas R. Schreiner, *Romans* (Grand Rapids, Mich.: Baker, 1998), 92-97.

verses of Scripture, they effectively nullify the force of what God actually said in his Word. They take away what God said and replace it with some other idea, something that God did not say.

I am troubled to see that several of the egalitarian claims in the following chapters are repeatedly promoted to unsuspecting readers *as if they were established fact,* when actually *no proof for them has ever been found* in established historical facts, and several of the claims are even *contradicted by the facts we have.* If egalitarians regularly presented such claims as "an interesting idea that may turn out to be true if facts can be found to support it," this would be a different matter. But very often these claims are presented as facts that have already been proven, when that is far from the actual situation.

Our God is a God of truth (Prov. 30:5; Titus 1:2; Heb. 6:18), and he cares about truth (Ex. 20:16; 2 Cor. 4:2; Eph. 4:25; Col. 3:9). Therefore it is of utmost importance that readers and authors on both sides of this controversy never become careless with regard to truth or fail to exercise the greatest care for accuracy regarding the historical or linguistic data that we depend on in interpreting the Bible.

The following egalitarian claims are some examples of promoting as true something that either is *unsubstantiated* by actual historical data or must be judged *untruthful* in the light of the actual data we have. In each case, I have given an abbreviated response, but fuller discussion can be found in my book *Evangelical Feminism and Biblical Truth.*[2]

---

[2] Wayne Grudem, *Evangelical Feminism and Biblical Truth* (Sisters, Ore.: Multnomah, 2004).

19

DISRUPTIVE WOMEN IN CORINTH?

Some evangelical feminists claim that Paul told the women in Corinth to "keep silent" because they were disrupting the church services

Several egalitarians claim that the reason Paul wrote that "the women should keep silent in the churches" (1 Cor. 14:34) was that women were being disorderly and disrupting the church services at Corinth. Perhaps they were rudely shouting questions to their husbands (or to other men) seated across the room, or perhaps (according to a variant of this position) even giving loud shouts characteristic of near-ecstatic worship. Advocates of this interpretation say that Paul wanted to stop these disruptions and restore order to the service.

Craig Keener, professor of New Testament at Palmer Theological Seminary (formerly Eastern Baptist Theological Seminary) in Philadelphia, says,

> We will turn to what seems to be the most likely interpretation of 1 Corinthians 14:34-35: Paul was addressing relatively uneducated women who were disrupting the service with irrelevant questions. The immediate remedy for this situation was for them to stop asking such questions; the long-term solution was to educate them.[1]

---

[1] Craig Keener, *Paul, Women, and Wives: Marriage and Women's Ministry in the Letters of Paul* (Peabody, Mass.: Hendrickson, 1992), 70.

Stanley Grenz writes,

> The most widely held view among egalitarians claims that the problem in Corinth focused on certain women who were asking many questions that disrupted the worship services. . . . The women may have been recent converts . . . or perhaps they were uneducated women voicing irrelevant questions. . . . Or perhaps the women were interrupting either the Scripture exposition in the services or the evaluation of the prophetic messages. . . . Regardless of the actual details, the results were the same. The adamant questioning resulted in chaos. In response, Paul rules the women out of order.[2]

One detailed explanation of this view is from Linda Belleville, who says that married Corinthian women were less educated than their husbands and were asking questions because they wanted to learn. She says, "It is likewise plain that the questions of these women were directed at men other than their husbands, for Paul instructs them to ask their *own* men."[3] (Linda Belleville was until 2005 a professor of New Testament at North Park Theological Seminary in Chicago, and is a widely published egalitarian author.)

The first thing to be said about this claim is that there are no facts to support it. There are no data in the book of 1 Corinthians itself to support this claim, nor are there any extrabiblical data to corroborate it. It is true that Craig Keener cites some twenty-six extrabiblical references, and with such a long string of references readers may imagine that there is abundant historical information to support his claim.[4] But when we actually look up these references, they are all references to Graeco-Roman and Jewish writings that talk about concerns for decency and order in public assemblies. Not one of them mentions women in the Corinthian church. Not one of them mentions women in any Christian church, for that matter! Proving that Greeks and Romans and Jews had

---

[2] Stanley Grenz, *Women in the Church: A Biblical Theology of Women in Ministry* (Downers Grove, Ill.: InterVarsity Press, 1995), 123-124. See also J. Lee Grady, *Ten Lies the Church Tells Women* (Lake Mary, Fla.: Creation House, 2000), 61-64.

[3] Linda Belleville, "Women in Ministry," in *Two Views on Women in Ministry*, ed. James Beck and Craig Blomberg (Grand Rapids, Mich.: Zondervan, 2001), 116. See also Cindy Jacobs, *Women of Destiny* (Ventura, Calif.: Regal, 1998), 233; Judy L. Brown, *Women Ministers According to Scripture* (Springfield, Ill.: Judy L. Brown, 1996), 271-273.

[4] Keener, *Paul, Women, and Wives*, 89n4.

concerns for order in public assemblies does not prove that women in the church at Corinth were being disruptive or disorderly![5]

This theory attempts to make the Corinthian situation a special one, when in fact Paul applies his rule to "all the churches" (1 Cor. 14:33b).[6] Thus his rule cannot be restricted to one local church where there supposedly were problems. Instead, Paul directs the Corinthians to conform to a practice that was universal in the early church.

Moreover, this "noisy women" theory either does not make sense of Paul's solution or else it makes his remedy unfair.

First, it does not make sense. If women were being disruptive, Paul would just tell them to act in an orderly way, not to be completely silent. In other cases where there are problems of disorder, Paul simply prescribes order (as with tongues or prophecy in 14:27, 29, 31, and as with the Lord's Supper in 11:33-34). If noise had been the problem in Corinth, he would have explicitly forbidden *disorderly* speech, not all speech.

Second, it would be unfair. With this view, Paul would be punishing all women for the misdeeds of some. If there were noisy women, in order to be fair, Paul should have said, "The *disorderly* women should keep silent." But this egalitarian position makes Paul unfair, for it makes him silence all women, not just the disorderly ones. It is unlike Paul, or any other New Testament writer, to make unfair rules of this sort. Also, Paul would be unfair to punish only the disorderly women and not any disorderly men. And to say that only women and no men were disorderly is merely an assumption with no facts to support it.

Finally, and perhaps most important, we should note the reason that

---

[5] For a more detailed response to this claim and other variations of it see Wayne Grudem, *Evangelical Feminism and Biblical Truth* (Sisters, Ore.: Multnomah, 2004), 243-247. In Keener's subsequent essay, "Learning in the Assemblies: 1 Cor. 14:34-35," in *Discovering Biblical Equality*, ed. Ronald W. Pierce and Rebecca Merrill Groothuis (Downers Grove, Ill.: InterVarsity, 2004), 161-171, he still holds that "women were interrupting the service with questions" (165), but he gives additional emphasis to the lower educational status of women as the probable reason for this: "women on average were less educated than men" (169). What is noteworthy, however, is that this recent essay provides no more evidence for the fundamental premise that women were being disruptive: this "event" is *assumed* to be true, and after that Keener goes on to provide historical factors that might have caused this event. But the existence of the "event" itself remains without proof or evidence.

[6] See Grudem, *Evangelical Feminism and Biblical Truth*, 254, for my discussion of how the phrase "as in all the churches of the saints" (v. 33b) relates best to verse 34. But even if someone thinks that phrase goes with the preceding sentence, Paul still says, in verse 34, "the women should keep silent *in the churches.*"

Paul does give for instruction on this matter. Paul does not give "noisy women" as a reason for his instruction, but rather he cites the Old Testament law. He says, "For they are not permitted to speak, *but should be in submission, as the Law also says*" (1 Cor. 14:34). "Law" here most likely refers to the teaching of the Old Testament in general on men and women, because Paul does not quote any specific Old Testament passage. He frequently uses "law" (Greek *nomos*) to refer to the Old Testament, and especially with this formula, "as the Law . . . says" (see the other two instances in Rom. 3:19 and 1 Cor. 9:8).[7] It is unlikely that "law" refers to Roman law or to Jewish oral traditions, for Paul does not elsewhere use *nomos* in those ways.[8]

Paul therefore gives "the Law" as the reason for his statement, not "noisy women." It is precarious to remove from our explanation of Paul's instruction the reason that Paul does give and replace it with a reason he does not give. Paul here is not saying,

> Let the women be silent *because they should not be asking disruptive questions.*

or

> Let the women be silent *because God wants orderly worship services.*

but rather,

---

[7] This was pointed out by D. A. Carson, "'Silent in the Churches': On the Role of Women in 1 Corinthians 14:33b-36," in *Recovering Biblical Manhood and Womanhood*, ed. John Piper and Wayne Grudem (Wheaton, Ill.: Crossway, 1991), 148.

[8] Linda Belleville says "law" here refers to Roman law ("Women in Ministry," 119). As evidence, she says, "Official religion of the Roman variety was closely supervised," but the only proof she gives is a reference to her book, *Women Leaders and the Church: Three Crucial Questions* (Grand Rapids, Mich.: Baker, 2000), 36-38. On those pages, we look in vain for any reference to Roman law regulating anyone's conduct within any religious service. She mentions the Emperor Tiberias's attempt to abolish the cult of Isis, but that proves nothing about attempts to regulate Christian conduct or any other religious activity within a worship service. Belleville asks us to believe, without proof, the rather remarkable position that Roman laws prohibited women from asking disruptive questions *within a worship service such as found in a Christian church*. And she gives not one shred of proof.

Paul never uses "law" (Greek *nomos*) to refer to Roman law, but often uses it, as here, to refer to the teachings of the Old Testament taken as a whole.

Walter Kaiser, *Hard Sayings of the Old Testament* (Downers Grove, Ill.: InterVarsity Press, 1988), 36, claims that "the law" here means Rabbinic teaching, but he provides no supporting evidence, and, again, Paul does not use the word "law" in that way.

> As in all the churches of the saints, the women should keep silent in
> the churches. *For they are not permitted to speak, but should be in*
> *submission, as the Law also says* (1 Cor. 14:33b-34).

Paul does not speak here about disorder but about the principle of
submission—in this case, submission to male leadership among God's
people.

A far better interpretation of this passage comes from the very context of these verses themselves. Paul is speaking in this context about
people giving prophecies in the church meeting and about others judging those prophecies: "Let two or three prophets speak, and let the others weigh what is said" (1 Cor. 14:29). In the context of judging
prophecies, Paul says, "the women should keep silent in the churches."
He does not allow women to speak out and judge prophecies in front of
the whole congregation, but he leaves that governing task to men, which
is consistent with what he says in 1 Timothy 2:12 about women not having authority over a man. The verse says nothing about noisy women,
but the context clearly talks about judging prophecies.[9]

So where is the actual *historical evidence* that women were disrupting the worship service at Corinth? None has been found. The idea
is mere speculation supported by frequent repetition but not by one
shred of hard historical data.

When egalitarians claim that 1 Corinthians 14:33-35 applies only
to a special situation of disruptive women in the church at Corinth, they
are changing the meaning of a verse by restricting it to a very narrow
situation. And they are basing this on mere speculation, not on any hard
facts. In doing this they are setting up a pattern of interpretation that
will be imitated by others who will speculate (without any hard facts)
about "special situations" that can be used to invalidate other New
Testament commands as well. And in that way they take another step
on the path to liberalism.

---

[9] For further explanation of this view, see Grudem, *Evangelical Feminism and Biblical Truth*,
78-80.

WOMEN HOMEOWNERS
AS ELDERS?

Some evangelical feminists claim that women homeowners were overseers (or elders) in early churches

Linda Belleville claims that "Mary (Acts 12:12), Lydia (16:15), Chloe (1 Cor 1:11), and Nympha (Col 4:15)" were "overseers of house churches," and other egalitarians make similar claims.[1] The reason Belleville gives for this is that "the homeowner in Greco-Roman times was in charge of any and all groups that met under their roof."[2] The example she gives is Jason, who was responsible to "post bond" in Acts 17:7-9.

The problem with this claim is that Belleville and others go beyond the text of Scripture and claim far more than it actually says. Jason was required by the city authorities to post some "money as security" (Acts 17:9), probably as a guarantee against any property damage or violence

---

[1] Linda Belleville, "Women in Ministry," in *Two Views on Women in Ministry*, ed. James Beck and Craig Blomberg (Grand Rapids, Mich.: Zondervan, 2001), 95. See also Judy L. Brown, *Women Ministers According to Scripture* (Springfield, Ill.: Judy L. Brown, 1996), 170, 175; and Cindy Jacobs, *Women of Destiny* (Ventura, Calif.: Regal, 1998), 200. Jacobs says that the "presiding elder" of a house church "was also the head of the household where the church met." Therefore she concludes that "Lydia and Mary . . . and others very possibly functioned as 'presiding elders' (or at least the deacons) of the churches in their houses. In fact, if this is so, most of the house churches listed in Scripture were 'pastored' by women!" (200). A few pages earlier she quotes with approval a comment of C. Peter Wagner that there were no church buildings as we know them in the early church, and therefore meeting in private homes was the "norm" (197). Thus, reasoning from one unsubstantiated assumption about the role of a woman who owned a house, Jacobs suddenly has women pastors in most of the house churches in the New Testament! And all of this without one shred of clear supportive evidence.
[2] Ibid., 83; also 96.

that the authorities suspected might happen. But that does not prove that Jason was ruling over the meetings of Christians in his house, and even over Paul and Silas when they conducted those meetings!

Belleville would have us believe that homeowners could bypass all the qualifications for elders in 1 Timothy 3 and Titus 1, and, simply by virtue of having a church meet in their home, become overseers or elders. She would also have us believe that Lydia, who was a brand-new convert and who had just been baptized, became the overseer of the church at Philippi simply because she said to Paul, "come to my house and stay" (Acts 16:15).

This claim is going far beyond the evidence in Scripture. The extrabiblical references that Belleville cites do not prove anything about homeowners having such a leadership role in the churches either.[3] This claim is speculation with no facts to support it, and several factors in Scripture contradict it.

But by making this unsubstantiated claim, Belleville leads readers to think that "Mary (Acts 12:12), Lydia (16:15), Chloe (1 Cor 1:11), and Nympha (Col 4:15)" were "overseers of house churches."[4] She leads readers to believe that several such women were overseers or elders. And so she makes these verses say something they do not say. This leads people to disbelieve or seek some way to explain away the passages that restrict the office of elder to men, and so it undermines the authority of Scripture. Therefore this claim takes another step on the path to liberalism.

---

[3] For additional comments concerning this claim see Wayne Grudem, *Evangelical Feminism and Biblical Truth* (Sisters, Ore.: Multnomah, 2004), 262-263. Belleville makes similar claims about women homeowners in "Women Leaders in the Bible," in *Discovering Biblical Equality*, ed. Ronald W. Pierce and Rebecca Merrill Groothuis (Downers Grove, Ill.: InterVarsity, 2004), 122-124.

[4] Belleville, "Women in Ministry," 95.

WOMEN DEACONS WITH AUTHORITY?

Some evangelical feminists claim that women deacons
had governing authority in early church history

Linda Belleville helpfully points out a number of writings from the early church fathers and other documents that give evidence of women serving as deacons in at least some parts of the early church.[1] However, then she goes on to say, *"Canon #15 of the Council of Chalcedon (fifth century) details the ordination process for women deacons and places them in the ranks of the clergy."*[2]

But is it correct that some early church documents place women deacons "in the ranks of the clergy"? When we look at the actual documents, they turn out to contradict what Belleville says.

It is true that there was a "laying on of hands" to establish a woman in the role or office of deaconess, but there is no indication that this is parallel to what we today refer to as ordination for pastors or elders, and it is not true that this canon places a woman "in the ranks of the clergy." Here is what it says:

> A woman shall not receive the laying on of hands as a deaconess under forty years of age, and then only after searching examination. And if, after she has had hands laid on her and has continued for a

---

[1] Linda Belleville, "Women in Ministry," in *Two Views on Women in Ministry*, ed. James Beck and Craig Blomberg (Grand Rapids, Mich.: Zondervan, 2001), 89-90.
[2] Ibid., 90, italics added.

time to minister, she shall despise the grace of God and give herself in marriage, she shall be anathematized and the man united to her.[3]

An explanatory note to this canon refers the reader to an excursus on deaconesses that says,

The principal work of the deaconess was to assist the female candidates for holy baptism. At that time the sacrament of baptism was always administered by immersion . . . and hence there was much that such an order of women could be useful in. Moreover they sometimes gave to the female catechumens preliminary instruction, but *their work was wholly limited to women*, and *for a deaconess of the Early Church to teach a man or to nurse him in sickness would have been an impossibility.* The duties of the deaconess are set forth in many ancient writings. . . .

[The author then quotes Canon 12 of the Fourth Council of Carthage (398)] "Widows and dedicated women . . . who are chosen to assist at the baptism of women, should be so well instructed in their office as to be able to teach aptly and properly unskilled and rustic women how to answer at the time of their baptism to the questions put to them, and also how to live godly after they have been baptized."[4]

In light of this evidence, it is misleading for Belleville to say that these deaconesses were placed "in the ranks of the clergy." Women who were deacons in the early church were honored, and they performed valuable functions, but they did not teach or govern men, and they were not counted among the clergy.

Were women actually deacons at the time of the New Testament? There are differences of opinion among New Testament scholars with regard to that question. In fact, the question is not easy to decide. But it does not make much difference regarding the question of whether women can be pastors or elders today, because in the New Testament the office of deacon does not include the governing and teaching authority that is reserved for elders.[5]

---

[3] Cited in *Nicene and Post-Nicene Fathers*, 2nd ser., 14:279.
[4] "Excursus on the Deaconess of the Early Church," unsigned article in ibid., 14:41, italics added.
[5] For further discussion of the question of women as deacons, see Wayne Grudem, *Evangelical Feminism and Biblical Truth* (Sisters, Ore.: Multnomah, 2004), 263-268.

Belleville's claim that women deacons were among the "clergy" is another example of changing the meaning of Scripture by claiming something that is unsupported by any facts and that in fact is contradicted by the facts we have. Her claim will lead readers to think that when they see the word "deacon" (or the Greek word *diakonos*, which can mean either "servant" or "deacon") applied to women in the New Testament, that is equivalent to being a pastor or elder, a member of the "clergy." But that is not what *diakonos* means.[6] And thus Belleville takes away from readers the actual meaning of those verses and replaces it with something they do not mean.

In this way the claim that women deacons had governing authority in the early church is another way of undermining the authority of Scripture, and another step on the path to liberalism.

---

[6] For a discussion of the meaning of "elder" and "deacon" in the New Testament, see Wayne Grudem, *Systematic Theology* (Grand Rapids, Mich.: Zondervan, 1994), chapter 47.

UNEDUCATED WOMEN IN EPHESUS?

Some evangelical feminists claim that Paul told the women in Ephesus not to teach or exercise authority over men because they were uneducated and therefore unqualified to do so

According to many evangelical feminists, the reason that Paul prohibits women from teaching or exercising authority over men in 1 Timothy 2:12 ("I do not permit a woman to teach or to exercise authority over a man . . .") is that the women of ancient Ephesus were uneducated and therefore unqualified to be pastors or teachers. They cite verses 13-14, "For Adam was formed first, then Eve; and Adam was not deceived, but the woman was deceived and became a transgressor," and say this refers to the fact that Adam received instructions directly from God, while Eve was less well trained.

Gilbert Bilezikian, whom we discussed in chapter 17, says this:

> In the fateful story of the fall, it was Eve, *the lesser informed* person, who initiated a mistaken course of action and who led herself into error. Eve was not created first or at the same time as Adam. She was the late-comer on the scene. . . .
>
> Paul's teaching in this passage [1 Timothy 2:11-15] has an absolute and universal relevance. The principle he lays down to protect the teaching ministry and the exercise-of-authority functions from incompetent persons is valid for all times and for all churches.

Christian communities should always remain watchful to authorize in positions of leadership only those persons who have received adequate training . . . [1]

Craig Keener also thinks that the most likely reason for Paul's prohibition in 1 Timothy 2 against women teaching is their inadequate education:

The third possibility [which Keener thinks most likely] is that Paul intends to connect Eve's later creation to why she was deceived: She was not present when God gave the commandment, and thus was dependent on Adam for the teaching. In other words, she was inadequately educated—like the women in the Ephesian church. [2]

Cindy Jacobs says (in her discussion of 1 Cor. 14:34-35), "Also, at that time, most women were illiterate and hadn't had the privilege of an education." [3]

J. Lee Grady, editor of *Charisma* magazine, agrees with this position, claiming, "The women in Ephesus needed more instruction. . . . women in this culture had been denied all educational opportunities. Except for some Roman women in the upper class, women in the Middle East and Asia Minor were sequestered at home and kept away from books and learning." [4]

These egalitarians then say that the prohibition against women teaching men does not apply today, when both women and men are well educated.

But is it true that women in ancient Ephesus were not sufficiently

---

[1] Gilbert Bilezikian, *Beyond Sex Roles: What the Bible Says About a Woman's Place in Church and Family,* 2nd ed. (Grand Rapids, Mich.: Baker, 1985), 180-181. He elaborates on this later: "Paul's understanding of the primacy of Adam as a safeguard against deception shows that he is concerned with competency. The reference to Eve . . . provides further evidence that Paul is establishing a principle based not on chronology but on competency" (297). See also Cindy Jacobs, *Women of Destiny* (Ventura, Calif.: Regal, 1998), 230; Judy L. Brown, *Women Ministers According to Scripture* (Springfield, Ill.: Judy L. Brown, 1996), 297-298; Andrew Perriman, *Speaking of Women* (Leicester, UK: Apollos, 1998), 165-168; Rich Nathan, *Who Is My Enemy?* (Grand Rapids, Mich.: Zondervan, 2002), 150, 153.

[2] Craig Keener, *Paul, Women, and Wives: Marriage and Women's Ministry in the Letters of Paul* (Peabody, Mass.: Hendrickson, 1992), 116.

[3] Jacobs, *Women of Destiny,* 230.

[4] J. Lee Grady, *Twenty-five Tough Questions About Women and the Church* (Lake Mary, Fla.: Charisma, 2003), 141. Grady cites Bilezikian for support.

educated to be teachers, and that this is why Paul forbade them to teach? The actual historical evidence shows a much different picture:

(1) Many men and women in the first century had basic literary skills, and very few men or women had education beyond this level. Steven Baugh, an expert in the history of ancient Ephesus, writes,

> Because women's education in antiquity usually took place privately, we get only a glimpse of it here and there. As for women's literacy, daughters of the upper classes needed some level of education for their duties in managing large households. And though they were not commonly found in fields like philosophy, women did read and write literature and poetry during this period.[5]

Baugh mentions that from Ephesus we have several examples of writing by women, including some poems and prayers.[6]

Other sources indicate that in Greek culture, the "Hellenistic school" form of education "endured with but slight changes to the end of the ancient world," and, "girls, too, were educated at all age levels. In some cases they came under the control of the same officials as the boys and shared the same teachers. . . . In other cases separate state officials were responsible for them."[7]

In Roman society, one of the characteristics of schools was "the inclusion of girls in the benefits of education."[8] *The Oxford Classical Dictionary* notes that both Plato and Aristotle "believed that men and women should have the same education and training."[9] And in earlier Greek society, "Papyri (private letters, etc.) show widespread literacy among the Greeks of Egypt," while in Rome, "upper-class Roman women were influential . . . many women were educated and witty."[10]

---

[5] S. M. Baugh, "A Foreign World: Ephesus in the First Century," in *Women in the Church: A Fresh Analysis of 1 Timothy 2:9-15*, ed. Andreas Köstenberger, Thomas Schreiner, and H. Scott Baldwin (Grand Rapids, Mich.: Baker, 1995), 46, with reference to H. I. Marrou, *Education in Antiquity*, trans. George Lamb (New York: Sheed & Ward, 1956), 46.

[6] Ibid., 47n140; additional evidence from several other sources is given on page 46nn136, 138, and 139.

[7] F. A. G. Beck, "Education," in *The Oxford Classical Dictionary*, 2nd ed., ed. N. G. L. Hammond and H. H. Scullard (Oxford: Clarendon, 1970), 371.

[8] Ibid., 372.

[9] Walter K. Lacey, "Women," in *Oxford Classical Dictionary*, 2nd ed., 1139.

[10] Ibid.

In *Women and Men in Ministry: A Complementary Perspective*,[11] Clinton Arnold and Robert Saucy report further evidence of the significant educational achievements of women in ancient Ephesus:

> In a very important recent study, Paul Trebilco has accumulated and presented the inscriptional evidence attesting to the role of women in civic positions in western Asia Minor. . . .[12]
>
> There is now inscriptional evidence that women served in some of the cities in a position that would be a close functional equivalent of our "superintendent of schools," that is, in the capacity of a gymnasiarch (*gymnasiarchos*). The "gymnasium" was the center for education in a Greek city. . . . The "gymnasiarch" had oversight of the intellectual training of the citizens and for the general management of the facility. Inscriptions dating from the first to the third centuries attest to forty-eight women who served as gymnasiarchs in twenty-three cities of Asia Minor and the coastal islands. This suggests that women not only had access to education, but also that in many places they were leading the educational system.
>
> This evidence stands in contrast to what we generally know of the plight of women at the beginning of the Roman Empire. . . . But beginning in the late republic (2nd Century B.C.) and early Imperial Period, a much greater array of opportunities opened up for women. The famous British classicist, Michael Grant, observed that "The Roman women of the late republic possessed a freedom and independence almost unparalleled until the present century."[13]

(2) The Bible never requires advanced degrees for people who teach God's Word or have governing authority in the church. The fact that many women as well as men had basic literacy skills in Greek, Roman, and Jewish cultures is enough by itself to disprove the egalitarian claims

---

[11] Robert L. Saucy and Judith K. TenElshof, eds., *Women and Men in Ministry: A Complementary Perspective* (Chicago: Moody, 2001).

[12] Clinton Arnold and Robert Saucy, endnotes to "The Ephesian Background of Paul's Teaching on Women's Ministry," in *Women and Men in Ministry*, 366n4. Arnold and Saucy at this point referred to Paul Trebilco, *Jewish Communities in Asia Minor*, Society for New Testament Studies Monograph Series 69 (Cambridge: Cambridge University Press, 1991), especially chapter 2, "The Prominence of Women in Asia Minor," 104-126.

[13] Clinton Arnold and Robert Saucy, "The Ephesian Background of Paul's Teaching on Women's Ministry," in *Women and Men in Ministry*, 281-283. The quotation from Michael Grant at the end of this statement was from Michael Grant, *A Social History of Greece and Rome* (New York: Scribner, 1992), 30-31.

about 1 Timothy 2. If absolutely *no* women and *only* men could read and write in ancient Ephesus, and if that practice had carried over into the church so that *no* Christian women learned the Bible, then the egalitarian claim would deserve some consideration. But that is simply not the case. *Both women and men could read and write.*

Formal academic training in Scripture (as in a modern seminary, or in an ancient school for rabbis) was not required for leaders in the New Testament church. We even see that several of the apostles did not have formal biblical training or schooling as the rabbis did (see Acts 4:13). The ability to read and study Scripture was available to men and women alike, and *both men and women learned and studied Scripture in the ancient church* (note Acts 18:26, where Priscilla and Aquila *together* instruct Apollos; also 1 Tim. 2:11, which encourages women to "learn," and Titus 2:3-4, where older women are to *"teach* what is good, and so *train* the young women"). This certainly would have been true in a major metropolitan center like Ephesus, where there would have been many literate, educated women in the church.

(3) It is untrue to state that *no* women in the first-century churches possessed adequate education to be teachers or rulers in the church. The New Testament shows several women who had a considerable level of understanding of Scripture. Many women accompanied Jesus and learned from him during his earthly ministry. (See Luke 8:1-3; 10:38-42; also John 4:1-27; 11:21-27.) In this very passage in 1 Timothy 2, Paul says that women should "learn" (v. 11).

Perhaps the best example of a woman well trained in knowledge of the Bible is Priscilla. When Paul went to Corinth, he stayed with Aquila and Priscilla: "because he was of the same trade he stayed with them and worked, for they were tentmakers by trade" (Acts 18:3). Paul stayed a year and six months at Corinth (Acts 18:11), and we may ponder just how much Bible and theology Priscilla would have learned while having the apostle Paul as a house guest and business partner during that time! Then Priscilla and Aquila went with Paul to Ephesus (Acts 18:18-19). It was at Ephesus in A.D. 51 that Priscilla and Aquila together "explained" to Apollos "the way of God more accurately" (Acts 18:26). So in A.D. 51 Priscilla knew Scripture well enough to help instruct Apollos.

After that, Priscilla probably learned from Paul for another three years while he stayed at Ephesus teaching "the whole counsel of God" (Acts 20:27; compare 1 Cor. 16:19, where Priscilla is called Prisca, and Paul sends greetings to Corinth from Aquila and Prisca and the church that meets "in their house"). By the end of Paul's three-year stay in Ephesus, *Priscilla had probably received four and a half years of teaching directly from the apostle Paul.* No doubt many other women in Ephesus also learned from Paul—and from Priscilla!

Aquila and Priscilla went to Rome sometime later (Rom. 16:3, perhaps around A.D. 58), but they returned to Ephesus, for they were in Ephesus again at the end of Paul's life (in 2 Tim. 4:19, Paul writes to Timothy at Ephesus, "Greet Prisca and Aquila"). Now, 2 Timothy was probably written in A.D. 66 or 67 (Eusebius says that Paul died in A.D. 67), and 1 Timothy a short time before that, perhaps in A.D. 65. In addition, before he wrote 1 Timothy, Paul seems to have been in Ephesus and it seems he had told Timothy to remain there when he left for Macedonia (see 1 Tim. 1:3: "As I urged you when I was going to Macedonia, remain at Ephesus . . ."). Therefore, both because 1 Timothy is near in time to 2 Timothy, and because Paul had recently been in Ephesus to know who was there before he wrote 1 Timothy or 2 Timothy, it seems likely that Aquila and Priscilla were back in Ephesus by the time Paul wrote 1 Timothy, about A.D. 65. This was fourteen years after Priscilla and Aquila had explained the way of God to Apollos in Ephesus.

What is the point of this detailed timeline? Not even well-educated Priscilla, nor any other well-educated women of Ephesus who followed her example and listened to Paul's teaching for several years, were allowed to teach men in the public assembly of the church. Writing to a church where many women had received significant training in the Bible, Paul said, "I do not permit a woman to teach or to exercise authority over a man" (1 Tim. 2:12). Paul's reason was certainly not lack of education.

(4) Paul does give a reason for the restriction of teaching and governing roles to men, but it is not lack of education. It is the order of creation. We should not deny the reason Paul gives and substitute a reason he does not give. Paul does not say, "I do not permit a woman to teach or to exercise authority over a man; rather, she is to remain quiet, *for women are not as well educated as men.*" That is not the reason Paul gives. The reason he gives is the order that God established when he cre-

ated Adam and Eve: *"For Adam was formed first, then Eve;* and Adam was not deceived, but the woman was deceived and became a transgressor" (1 Tim. 2:13-14).

(5) If lack of education were the reason for Paul's prohibition of public teaching roles for women in the church, it would be unfair and inconsistent for Paul not to prohibit teaching by uneducated men as well. Surely there were untrained men in the congregations at Ephesus, including new converts and perhaps some poorly educated and illiterate slaves or day laborers. But Paul does not mention them. Why does he focus on women? The egalitarian position is inconsistent at this point, for it cannot explain why Paul excludes all women (even the well-educated ones) and does not exclude any men (even the poorly educated ones).

(6) Finally, the phrase, "Adam was formed first, then Eve," cannot be made to mean that Eve had less education than Adam without doing violence to the text.[14] The statement does not refer to education but refers to Genesis 2, where God "formed the man of dust from the ground" (Gen. 2:7).

So where is the historical evidence that women were not sufficiently educated to serve as pastors or elders in the church in Ephesus? It has not been found, and the idea is contrary to the evidence that does exist both from the ancient world and from the text of Scripture itself. Yet egalitarians continue to repeat it as if it were established fact.

What is the result of this? Evangelical feminists have changed the meaning of a text of Scripture. 1 Timothy 2:12 used to say,

---

[14] See this argument, for example, in Bilezikian, *Beyond Sex Roles,* 180; also Walter Kaiser, "Paul, Women, and the Church," *Worldwide Challenge* 3 (1976): 9-12. The problem with this "lack of education" interpretation of "For Adam was *formed* first, then Eve," is that the Greek word that Paul uses, *plassō,* does not mean "educated" anywhere in the Bible (sometimes outside the Bible it can refer to things like training/forming the soul or training/forming the voice, but the part of the person being trained is always specified in the context, and that is not the case here).

More significantly, Paul is quoting the Greek translation of the Old Testament (the Septuagint), which uses the verb *plassō* four times in the very story of creation Paul is referring to (Gen. 2:7, 8, 15, 19). The word *plassō* is commonly used in the Septuagint to refer to God's act of creation (31 of 49 instances of *plassō* in the Septuagint refer to creation). In no case in the Septuagint does this word mean "educate." So how could Paul mean "educate" when he used *plassō* to refer to this very passage in Genesis 2? Paul's words clearly and simply refer to the creation of Adam first, and then Eve, as the usage of *plassō* in the Greek translation of Genesis 2 indicates. That is surely what the original readers would have understood by Paul's words. See Wayne Grudem, *Evangelical Feminism and Biblical Truth* (Sisters, Ore.: Multnomah, 2004), 293-295 for further discussion.

> I do not permit *a woman* to teach or to exercise authority over a man; rather, she is to remain quiet.

But if people believe this egalitarian claim about uneducated women they will think it means,

> I do not permit *an uneducated woman like those in ancient Ephesus* to teach or to exercise authority over a man; rather, she is to remain quiet.

This is an entirely different meaning! But if this "uneducated women" claim is false (as the evidence indicates) then this different meaning is not what the Bible really says. And that means that egalitarians who promote this view have wrongly removed the authority of this verse of Scripture from everyone who believes their claim.

Holding the "uneducated women" view of 1 Timothy 2:12 is therefore another way of undermining the authority of Scripture. Believing a view that is unsubstantiated by hard facts and that completely changes the meaning of a passage of Scripture is another step on the path to liberalism.

WOMEN TEACHING FALSE DOCTRINE IN EPHESUS?

Some evangelical feminists claim that Paul told the women in Ephesus not to teach or exercise authority over men because they were teaching false doctrine

Some evangelical feminists claim that there was a unique situation in Ephesus in which women were teaching false doctrine. Therefore Paul's command would be relevant only for that particular situation.

This view is very commonly argued by egalitarians. Richard and Catherine Kroeger argue that women were teaching false doctrine, perhaps connected either to Gnosticism or to proto-Gnosticism. (Catherine Kroeger is associate professor of classical and ministry studies at Gordon-Conwell Theological Seminary.) They write,

> Our hypothesis will deal with the possibility that the false teachers were indeed Gnostics, proto-Gnostics, or some group with a mythology remarkably like that of the Gnostics. . . . We maintain that those involved with the false doctrines included both men and women, and that the women were involved in telling stories which contradicted the Scriptures.[1]

---

[1] Richard Clark Kroeger and Catherine Clark Kroeger, *I Suffer Not a Woman: Rethinking 1 Timothy 2:11-15 in Light of Ancient Evidence* (Grand Rapids, Mich.: Baker, 1992), 65-66. Cindy Jacobs, *Women of Destiny* (Ventura, Calif.: Regal, 1998), 240-241, shows sympathy for this "Gnostic heresy" view, depending only on the Kroegers for support. J. Lee Grady, *Twenty-five Tough Questions About Women and the Church* (Lake Mary, Fla.: Charisma,

Craig Keener says, "Much of the false teaching in Ephesus was being spread through women in the congregation. . . . Presumably, Paul wants them to learn so that they could *teach*."[2]

Gordon Fee writes (regarding 1 Tim. 2:12),

> It is probably because some of them have been so terribly deceived by the false teachers, who are specifically abusing the OT. . . . The word translated *authority*, which occurs only here in the NT, has the connotation "to domineer." In context it probably reflects again on the role the women were playing in advancing the errors—or speculations—of the false teachers and therefore is to be understood very closely with the prohibition against teaching.[3]

And J. Lee Grady states,

> What is translated as "certain men" [in 1 Tim. 1:3] is the indefinite Greek pronoun *tisi*. An indefinite pronoun does not indicate gender. Paul is saying, "Instruct certain *people* not to teach strange doctrines." Later in 1 Timothy, it becomes evident that women were doing the teaching of these strange doctrines, at least in part. A major purpose of this entire epistle was to correct unbiblical teachings being presented by women.[4]

Don Williams says, "Could some of those teaching falsely be women? Quite probably so."[5]

2003), also agrees with the Kroegers' view, saying, "The Gnostics . . . concocted the notion that Eve was created before Adam. . . . It is possible that one or more female false teachers had invaded the church at Ephesus and were spreading this detestable doctrine" (144). Sarah Sumner, *Men and Women in the Church* (Downers Grove, Ill.: InterVarsity Press, 2003), also supports this view in her statement, "Perhaps the most insidious thing is that the false teachers, like Satan, were twisting the Scriptures, lying to the people by saying that Eve was created first and that Eve was not deceived" (259).

[2] Craig Keener, *Paul, Women, and Wives: Marriage and Women's Ministry in the Letters of Paul* (Peabody, Mass.: Hendrickson, 1992), 111-112.

[3] Gordon D. Fee, *1 and 2 Timothy, Titus*, New International Biblical Commentary (Peabody, Mass.: Hendrickson, 1984, 1988), 73.

[4] J. Lee Grady, *Ten Lies the Church Tells Women* (Lake Mary, Fla.: Creation House, 2000), 57. See also Andrew Perriman, *Speaking of Women* (Leicester, UK: Apollos, 1998), 141-142. I. Howard Marshall also thinks that behind 1 Timothy 2:12 "lies some particular false teaching by some women" (Marshall, in collaboration with Philip H. Towner, *A Critical and Exegetical Commentary on the Pastoral Epistles* [London, New York: T & T Clark, 2004], 458).

[5] Don Williams, *The Apostle Paul and Women in the Church* (Glendale, Calif.: Regal, 1977), 111.

But where is the hard evidence that women were teaching false doctrine at Ephesus? The evidence we do have points in another direction:[6]

(1) The only false teachers named at Ephesus are men, not women. In 1 Timothy 1:19-20 we read of two men, Hymenaeus and Alexander: ". . . holding faith and a good conscience. By rejecting this, some have made shipwreck of their faith, among whom are *Hymenaeus and Alexander,* whom I have handed over to Satan that they may learn not to blaspheme."

In 2 Timothy 2:17-18 we again encounter two men who are false teachers, Hymenaeus and Philetus: "and their talk will spread like gangrene. Among them are *Hymenaeus and Philetus,* who have swerved from the truth, saying that the resurrection has already happened. They are upsetting the faith of some."

Then in Acts 20, Paul speaks of the false teachers that would come to the church as "men" (Greek *andres*): "and from among your own selves will arise *men* speaking twisted things, to draw away the disciples after them" (v. 30).

So all three of the verses in the Bible that specifically identify false teachers at Ephesus show that the false teachers were men. All three of these references are clearly to men, as all three are marked with masculine gender in the Greek text. Yet the Kroegers nevertheless conjecture that there *must have been* false female teachers in addition to these men teaching false doctrine.

The Kroegers, after naming Hymenaeus, Alexander, and Philetus, do not dispute that these names refer to men. However, they then add, "We shall suggest that at least one of the individuals who was teaching a different doctrine was a woman."[7] It does not appear that they are attempting to claim that any of these three names (which all have masculine gender forms in the Greek text) refers to a woman, and no later argument is made in their book (as far as I can tell) that one of these names refers to a woman. The statement must mean, rather, that their general argument *suggests* that there were one or more women *in addition to these three men* teaching false doctrine in Ephesus. But the fact

---

[6] For more detailed treatments of this objection see Wayne Grudem, *Evangelical Feminism and Biblical Truth* (Sisters, Ore.: Multnomah, 2004), 280-288.

[7] Kroeger and Kroeger, *I Suffer Not a Woman,* 59-60.

remains that three men and no women are named. The Kroegers give no evidence to support their statement. They have simply made a "suggestion" with no facts to support it.

I am saddened, therefore, to see a more popular writer like Cindy Jacobs accept their unsupported "suggestion" as something true. Jacobs actually misunderstands the Kroegers' statement, for in reference to this passage in their book she writes,

> We see that three people are mentioned who opposed sound doctrine: Hymenaeus, Alexander and Philetus (see 1 Tim. 1:20; 2 Tim. 2:17; 4:14). The Kroegers suggest that at least *one of these individuals* was a woman and that 1 Timothy 2:12 forbids her to teach a heresy which was creating serious problems in the Church.[8]

But the names are all masculine in Greek and all refer to men.

(2) No clear proof of women teaching false doctrine at Ephesus has been found either inside or outside the Bible.[9] First Timothy 5:13 warns that younger women who do not marry again will become "gossips and busybodies, *saying what they should not.*" But this does not indicate that any women were teaching false doctrine. To "gossip" means to spread "intimate or private rumors or facts,"[10] but spreading such personal details about other people, whether rumors or facts, is not the same as teaching false doctrine. Most of us probably can think of people in our local churches or communities who gossip, but they are not teachers of false doctrine! The two speech activities are quite distinct.[11]

When Paul says in 1 Timothy 5:13 that such young women will become "*gossips* and busybodies, *saying what they should not,*" the natural interpretation of "saying what they should not" is to take it as an expansion of what Paul means by "gossips." These younger widows who go from house to house will be saying things they should not say, spreading rumors and misinformation about other people. But this does

---

[8] Jacobs, *Women of Destiny*, 235, italics added.

[9] For elaboration of this point see Grudem, *Evangelical Feminism and Biblical Truth*, 282-284.

[10] *American Heritage Dictionary*, 3rd ed. (Boston: Houghton Mifflin, 1996), 783. The Greek term *phluaros* is an adjective meaning "gossipy" (Bauer-Danker-Arndt-Gingrich, *A Greek-English Lexicon of the New Testament and Other Early Christian Literature*, 3rd ed. [Chicago: University of Chicago Press, 1999], 1060).

[11] For further evidence showing that "gossips" in 1 Timothy 5:13 does not mean "teachers of false doctrine," see Grudem, *Evangelical Feminism and Biblical Truth*, 282-284.

not mean they are spreading false doctrine such as denying the resurrection of Christ, or saying that the resurrection is past already, or uttering blasphemies as Hymenaeus and Alexander did (1 Tim. 1:20), or speaking twisted things to gain a following as Paul predicted false teachers would do (Acts 20:30). There is good evidence that Paul was concerned about gossip becoming a problem among some women at Ephesus, but the needed evidence for women *teaching false doctrine* at Ephesus simply cannot be found in 1 Timothy 5:13.

Second Timothy 3:6-7 is another passage egalitarians sometimes use to claim there were women teaching false doctrine at Ephesus:

> For among them are those who creep into households and capture weak women, burdened with sins and led astray by various passions, always learning and never able to arrive at a knowledge of the truth.

This passage indicates that some women were *led astray* by false teachers. That is not surprising, for when false teaching comes into a church, some men and some women will be led astray—God does not give immunity from wrong belief to either men or women in general. But the passage does not say that the women were *doing the false teaching;* it simply says they were being led astray.

There is no proof that any woman or any group of women were engaged in teaching false doctrine at Ephesus. But even if that could be established, the egalitarian claim is not persuasive because it does not show that women were *primarily* responsible for spreading the false teaching—of which the only named proponents are men. And unless women were *primarily* responsible for spreading the false teaching, Paul's silencing of the women (in the egalitarian view) would not make sense.

Is there any other proof of women in the Ephesian church being engaged in false teaching? Some have mentioned the passage about Jezebel in Revelation 2, where Jesus says to the church in Thyatira,

> But I have this against you, that you tolerate that woman Jezebel, who calls herself a prophetess and is teaching and seducing my servants to practice sexual immorality and to eat food sacrificed to idols (Rev. 2:20).

Does this prove there were women teaching false doctrine at Ephesus? It does prove there was one woman in the church at Thyatira, a different church at a later time, teaching false doctrine and claiming to be a prophetess. And I do not deny that there have been women who have taught false doctrine at various points in the history of the church. But *one woman teaching false doctrine at Thyatira* does not prove that there were *any women teaching false doctrine at Ephesus!* There may or may not have been women teaching false doctrine at Ephesus. My point is simply that there is *no evidence* that women were teaching false doctrine at Ephesus. And so the claim turns out to be speculation without any hard evidence to support it. Should we base our interpretation of a passage on a claim with no supporting evidence?

At this point someone may object, "Well, there *might have been* women teaching false doctrine at Ephesus!" But should we nullify a direct Scriptural command based on a "might have been"? People can say "might have been" about most anything they wish, but "might have been" does not constitute legitimate evidence and should not be allowed to influence an argument. And in this case it has even less legitimacy, because this claim for what "might have been" goes contrary to the actual evidence we have in the text.

(3) If the fact that some people were teaching false doctrine disqualified everyone of the same gender, then all men would have been disqualified from teaching. So the egalitarian argument simply is not consistent. Even if *some* women were teaching false doctrine at Ephesus, why would that lead Paul to prohibit *all* women from teaching? It would not be fair or consistent to do so.

As we saw above, the only false teachers we know about with certainty at Ephesus are men, not women. Therefore if the egalitarian argument were consistent, it would have Paul *prohibiting all men from teaching,* just because some men were teaching false doctrine! But Paul does not do that, and this shows the inconsistency of the egalitarian argument.

(4) Once again, Paul gives the reason for his command, and it is the creation order (1 Tim. 2:13-14), not any false teaching by women. It is precarious to substitute a reason Paul does *not* give for one that he *does* give. Paul does not mention false teaching by women as a reason for his command. He does not say, "I do not permit a woman to teach or to

exercise authority over a man; rather, she is to remain quiet, *for some women are teaching false doctrine there at Ephesus.*" Rather, Paul's reason is the creation order: *"For Adam was formed first, then Eve."* We should be reluctant, then, to accept a position based on a reason Paul does not give, especially when it minimizes, ignores, or presents an eccentric interpretation of the reason Paul actually does give (as several egalitarian positions do).

Should we base our understanding of such a key verse on a speculative claim with no hard evidence to support it? Should we change our entire understanding of the verse based on no evidence? Is this a responsible way to interpret the Bible? I do not believe it is.

So what is the result of this "women were doing false teaching" interpretation of 1 Timothy 2:12? It effectively substitutes a different meaning for the verse:

Previous meaning: I do not permit a woman to teach or to exercise authority over a man; rather, she is to remain quiet.

New meaning: *In a church where most or all the women are teaching false doctrine,* I do not permit a woman to teach or to exercise authority over a man; rather, she is to remain quiet.

Since no churches today have most or all the women teaching false doctrine, the verse (with this new meaning) has no direct application for today. And it no longer prohibits women from being pastors and elders.

But if we substitute a different meaning for the verse, and if the new meaning is wrong, then we have nullified the authority of the Bible at that verse. People will no longer obey what God actually said in his Word, because they will no longer know what he said. They will think he said something else.

So if this new meaning is wrong, then this "women were doing false teaching" interpretation actually does undermine the effective authority of Scripture at this key verse. And when it undermines the effective authority of Scripture in this way, it is another step on the path to liberalism.

WOMEN TEACHING A GNOSTIC HERESY IN EPHESUS?

Some evangelical feminists claim that Paul told the women in Ephesus not to teach or exercise authority over men specifically because they were teaching a Gnostic heresy about Eve being created before Adam

One specific form of the "women teaching false doctrine" position that we considered in the previous chapter is found in the extensive argument of Richard and Catherine Kroeger regarding a Gnostic heresy in the church at Ephesus. Because this viewpoint is so detailed and so widely quoted, I have devoted a separate chapter to it in this book.

The Kroegers argue extensively for the presence of a Gnostic or proto-Gnostic heresy in Ephesus, probably propagated by women in the church, that taught that Eve was created before Adam and that she taught Adam spiritual knowledge.[1] They suggest that it was the presence of this specific Gnostic heresy at Ephesus that led Paul to write what he

---

[1] Richard Clark Kroeger and Catherine Clark Kroeger, *I Suffer Not a Woman: Rethinking 1 Timothy 2:11-15 in Light of Ancient Evidence* (Grand Rapids, Mich.: Baker, 1992), 59-66, 119-125.

Gnosticism was an ancient heretical religion that opposed true Christianity. The name Gnosticism comes from the Greek word *gnōsis*, which means "knowledge." Gnosticism stressed salvation through acquiring hidden knowledge and taught that the material world was evil and only the nonmaterial, spiritual world was good. For an excellent brief summary of Gnosticism and current scholarly viewpoints about it, with an extensive bibliography, see E. M. Yamauchi, "Gnosticism," in *Dictionary of New Testament Background*, ed. Craig A. Evans and Stanley E. Porter (Downers Grove, Ill.: InterVarsity Press, 1993), 414-418.

did about women in 1 Timothy 2, but that was a unique situation unlike any situation in today's churches.

But once again, where is the actual evidence? The Kroegers offer no proof from any first-century material outside the New Testament, and their lack of care in the use of later sources has opened up their work to significant criticism. For example, Thomas Schreiner says,

> Unfortunately, the Kroegers' reconstruction is riddled with method-ological errors. They nod in the direction of saying that the heresy is *"proto-gnostic,"* but consistently appeal to later sources to establish the contours of the heresy. The lack of historical rigor, if I can say this kindly, is nothing less than astonishing. They have clearly not grasped how one should apply the historical method in discerning the nature of false teaching in the Pauline letters.[2]

Other reviews of the Kroegers' work by New Testament experts offer deeply troubling evaluations. Steven Baugh, New Testament pro-fessor at Westminster Seminary (California), whose Ph.D. thesis is on the history of ancient Ephesus, wrote an extended review called "The Apostle Among the Amazons."[3] As Baugh's title indicates, the Kroegers rely heavily on nonfactual myths (such as myths of Amazon women "warriors") to paint a picture of ancient Ephesus where women had usurped religious authority over men: a "feminist Ephesus" in the reli-gious realm. But their historical reconstruction is just not true. Baugh says, "the Kroegers . . . have painted a picture of Ephesus which wan-ders widely from the facts" (155). With his expertise in the history of Ephesus, Baugh affirms, "No one has established historically that there was, in fact, a feminist culture in first-century Ephesus. It has merely been assumed" (154). He says the Kroegers' foundational claim that the religious sphere of life could be led by women, but not the social-civic spheres, "betrays an astonishing innocence of how ancient societies worked" (160). After analyzing their data, he concludes, "It is difficult

---

[2] Thomas Schreiner, "An Interpretation of 1 Timothy 2:9-15: A Dialogue with Scholarship," in *Women in the Church: A Fresh Analysis of 1 Timothy 2:9-15*, ed. Andreas Köstenberger, Thomas Schreiner, and H. Scott Baldwin (Grand Rapids, Mich.: Baker, 1995), 109-110.
[3] Steven Baugh, "The Apostle Among the Amazons," *Westminster Theological Journal* 56 (1994): 153-171; also reprinted in Wayne Grudem, *Evangelical Feminism and Biblical Truth* (Sisters, Ore.: Multnomah, 2004), 658-674.

to imagine how such a momentous conclusion could have been erected upon such fragile, tottering evidence" (161). Other evidence used by the Kroegers is "wildly anachronistic" (163), and contains "outright errors of fact" (165). On the other hand, "they virtually ignore a vast body of evidence of a historically much more reliable and relevant quality: the approximately 4,000 Ephesian inscriptions and the burgeoning secondary literature surrounding them" (162).[4]

Another review of the book is by Albert Wolters, professor of religion and theology/classical studies at Redeemer College in Hamilton, Ontario.[5] Wolters first summarizes the Kroegers' argument that 1 Timothy 2:12 should be translated, "I do not permit a woman to teach nor to represent herself as originator of man, but she is to be in conformity [with the Scriptures]," and that Paul was opposing a specific feminist heresy at Ephesus. He then says,

> their proposal, both philologically and historically, is a signal failure. In fact, it is not too much to say that their book is precisely the sort of thing that has too often given evangelical scholarship a bad name. There is little in the book's main thesis that can withstand serious scrutiny, and there is a host of subordinate detail that is misleading or downright false.[6]

Citing several specific examples, Wolters observes that the Kroegers

> repeatedly misunderstand the sources they cite, and they fail to mention important recent literature which counts against their own interpretation. . . . Their scholarly documentation is riddled with

---

[4] In a response to Baugh in the egalitarian journal *Priscilla Papers*, Alan Padgett says that Baugh "nowhere even considers, much less refutes, the idea that a small group of philosophers (like the Gnostics) might have been teaching the equality of women, contrary to the rest of society" (Alan Padgett, "The Scholarship of Patriarchy [On 1 Timothy 2:8-15]," *Priscilla Papers* [Winter 1997]: 25-26). The word "might" in this statement reveals a desperate grasping at straws when there is no supporting evidence. I suppose someone could say there "might" have been people at Ephesus supporting all sorts of different doctrines, but a bare "might have been" in the absence of facts is hardly a sufficient basis on which to justify rejecting present-day obligations to obey the instructions of 1 Timothy 2:12. If they wish, people are free to believe something that has no contemporaneous facts supporting it and hundreds of facts against it, but such a decision can hardly be called rational.

[5] Al Wolters, "Review: *I Suffer Not a Woman*," *Calvin Theological Journal* 28 (1993): 208-213; reprinted in Grudem, *Evangelical Feminism and Biblical Truth*, 646-651.

[6] Ibid., 209-210.

elementary linguistic blunders. . . . Unfortunately, things are not much better with the Kroegers' historical argumentation. There is in fact no direct evidence that their postulated Gnostic sect ever existed in first-century Ephesus, or indeed that a Gnostic group fitting their description ever existed at all.[7]

So where is the historical evidence that proves the claim that Paul, in 1 Timothy 2, was opposing a specific Gnostic heresy at Ephesus? It has not been found. Yet a number of egalitarian writers continue to affirm the Kroegers' claim as established fact.

To take one example of mistakenly believing an egalitarian scholar's arguments "by faith" rather than because of hard evidence, consider Cindy Jacobs's acceptance of the arguments of Richard and Catherine Kroeger about the background for 1 Timothy 2:11-15. Jacobs writes, "In my study of this passage, I have found Richard and Catherine Clark Kroegers' book *I Suffer Not a Woman: Rethinking 1 Timothy 2:11-15 in Light of Ancient Evidence* (Baker, 1992) was particularly enlightening for understanding the historical and religious setting of Ephesus at the time 1 Timothy was written. Their study reveals a world of idolatrous paganism based upon a matriarchal society and goddess worship."[8]

But Jacobs does not seem to have any awareness of how severely the Kroegers' arguments have been criticized by competent New Testament scholars. Compare Jacobs's trust in the Kroegers' writings to the scholarly analyses of Thomas Schreiner, Robert W. Yarbrough, Albert Wolters, and S. M. Baugh mentioned above. (Schreiner is professor of New Testament at The Southern Baptist Theological Seminary in Louisville, Kentucky; Yarbrough is chairman of the New Testament department at Trinity Evangelical Divinity School in Deerfield, Illinois; Wolters is professor of religion and theology/classical languages at Redeemer University College, Ancaster, Ontario, Canada; and Baugh is professor of New Testament at Westminster Theological Seminary in Escondido, California.) These New Testament scholars do not simply say they disagree with the Kroegers (for scholars will always differ in

---

[7] Ibid., 211. For further discussion, see Robert W. Yarbrough, "I Suffer Not a Woman: A Review Essay," *Presbyterion* 18 (1992): 25-33.

[8] Cindy Jacobs, *Women of Destiny* (Ventura, Calif.: Regal, 1998), 235.

their *interpretation* of data), but they say that again and again the Kroegers are not even telling the truth about much of the historical data that they claim.

But in spite of this widespread rejection of the Kroegers' argument, evangelical leaders like Cindy Jacobs accept it as true.

What is the result of the Kroegers' claim? Once again it substitutes a different meaning for what Paul wrote.

> **Previous meaning:** I do not permit a woman to teach or to exercise authority over a man; rather, she is to remain quiet.

> **New meaning:** *In a church where all the women are promoting a Gnostic heresy about Eve being created before Adam,* I do not permit a woman to teach or to exercise authority over a man; rather, she is to remain quiet.

Since no churches like that exist today, the verse (with this new meaning) has no direct application for today. And then it no longer prohibits women from being pastors and elders.

But as I argued in the previous chapter, if we substitute a different meaning for the verse, and if the new meaning is wrong, then we have nullified the authority of the Bible at that verse. People will no longer obey what God actually said in his Word, because they will no longer know what he said. They will think he said something else.

So if the Kroegers' new meaning is wrong, then this "women were promoting a heresy about Eve being created before Adam" interpretation actually does undermine the effective authority of Scripture at this key verse. And when it undermines the effective authority of Scripture in this way, it is another step on the path to liberalism.

DOES "HEAD" MEAN "SOURCE"?

*Some evangelical feminists claim that the Greek word
kephalē ("head") often meant "source"
but did not mean "authority"*

Paul writes in Ephesians 5:23, "For the husband is the *head* of the wife even as Christ is the *head* of the church," and in 1 Corinthians 11:3 he writes, "But I want you to understand that the *head* of every man is Christ, the *head* of a wife is her husband, and the *head* of Christ is God." What does the word "head" mean in these verses?

According to many egalitarians, the word translated "head" (Greek *kephalē*) in Ephesians 5:23 and 1 Corinthians 11:3 does not mean "person in authority over" but has some other meaning, especially the meaning "source." Thus, the husband is the *source* of the wife (an allusion to the creation of Eve from Adam's side in Genesis 2), as Christ is the *source* of the church.[1] This is based on the egalitarian claim that the word

---

[1] Egalitarian writings holding that *kephalē* means "source" are numerous. Some of the most influential are: Berkeley Mickelsen and Alvera Mickelsen, "What Does *Kephale* Mean in the New Testament?" in *Women, Authority, and the Bible*, ed. Alvera Mickelsen (Downers Grove, Ill.: InterVarsity Press, 1986), 97-110; Philip B. Payne, "Response," in *Women, Authority, and the Bible*, 118-132; Bilezikian, "A Critical Examination of Wayne Grudem's Treatment of *kepahle* in Ancient Greek Texts," appendix to *Beyond Sex Roles: What the Bible Says About a Woman's Place in Church and Family*, 2nd ed. (Grand Rapids, Mich.: Baker, 1985), 215-252; Catherine Clark Kroeger, "The Classical Concept of *Head* as 'Source,'" appendix 3 in Gretchen Gaebelein Hull, *Equal to Serve* (Old Tappan, N.J.: Revell, 1987), 267-283; Gordon D. Fee, *The First Epistle to the Corinthians*, New International Commentary on the New Testament (Grand Rapids, Mich.: Eerdmans, 1987), 501-505; Catherine Kroeger, "Head," in

kephalē seldom meant "authority over" in ancient Greek and often meant "source" (with no necessary sense of authority).

It is important to realize the decisive significance of these verses, and particularly of Ephesians 5:23, for the current controversy about male-female roles in marriage. If "head" means "person in authority over," then there is a unique authority that belongs to the husband in marriage, and it is parallel to Christ's authority over the church. If this is the true meaning of "head" in these verses, then the egalitarian view of marriage is wrong.[2] But if "head" means "source" here, then two Scripture texts significant to complementarians have been shown to have no impact on the controversy.

What is the actual evidence? Is there evidence that *kephalē* frequently meant "source" in the ancient world, or that it ever meant "source"? Is "authority over" an unproven meaning?

In fact, *kephalē* is found in over fifty contexts where it refers to people who have authority over others of whom they are the "head."[3] But it never once takes a meaning "source without authority," as egalitarians would like to make it mean.[4]

Here are several examples where *kephalē* is used to say that one person is the "head" of another, and the person who is called head is the one in authority:[5]

Dictionary of Paul and His Letters, ed. Gerald F. Hawthorne, Ralph P. Martin, and Daniel G. Reid (Downers Grove, Ill.: InterVarsity Press, 1993), 375-377; Judy L. Brown, *Women Ministers According to Scripture* (Springfield, Ill.: Judy L. Brown, 1996), 213-215, 246.

[2] I realize that some egalitarians claim that Paul's teaching about marriage applied only to his time in history, and is not applicable to us today. This position is not affected by disputes over the meaning of *head*, but it is very difficult to sustain in light of the parallel with Christ and the church and in light of Paul's tying it to the statements about marriage before there was sin in the world (Eph. 5:31-32, quoting Gen. 2:24).

[3] I have quoted English translations for the more than fifty examples in *Evangelical Feminism and Biblical Truth* (Sisters, Ore.: Multnomah, 2004), 544-551, so readers can inspect them for themselves.

[4] I have published three extensive studies of the meaning of *kephalē*, in which the relevant texts are analyzed in detail: (1) Wayne Grudem, "Does *kephale* ('Head') Mean 'Source' or 'Authority Over' in Greek Literature? A Survey of 2,336 Examples," *Trinity Journal* 6 NS (Spring 1985): 38-59; (2) Wayne Grudem, "The Meaning of *kephalē* ('Head'): A Response to Recent Studies," *Trinity Journal* 11 NS (Spring 1990): 3-72; (3) Wayne Grudem, "The Meaning of *Kephalē* ('Head'): An Analysis of New Evidence, Real and Alleged," *Journal of the Evangelical Theological Society* 44/1 (March 2001): 25-65. The third article is reprinted, with some added material interacting with Anthony Thiselton, in *Evangelical Feminism and Biblical Truth*, 552-599. (The added material on Thiselton's view is on pages 590-597.)

[5] These texts are discussed in the first two of my previous articles on *kephalē* (mentioned above).

1. David as King of Israel is called the "head" of the people he conquered (2 Sam. [LXX 2 Kings] 22:44): "you kept me as the *head* of the nations; people whom I had not known served me"; similarly, Psalm 18 (LXX 17):43

2. The leaders of the tribes of Israel are called "heads" of the tribes (1 Kings [LXX 3 Kings] 8:1, Alexandrinus text): "Then Solomon assembled the elders of Israel and all the *heads* of the tribes" (similar statements in the second century A.D. Greek translation of Aquila, Deut. 5:23; 29:9 [English verse 10]; 1 Kings [LXX 3 Kings] 8:1)

3. Jephthah becomes the "head" of the people of Gilead (Judg. 11:11, "the people made him *head* and leader over them"; also stated in 10:18; 11:8, 9)

4. Pekah the son of Remaliah is the head of Samaria (Isa. 7:9, "the *head* of Samaria is the son of Remaliah")

5. The father is the head of the family (Hermas, *Similitudes* 7.3; the man is called "the *head* of the house")

6. The husband is the "head" of the wife (Eph. 5:23, "the husband is the *head* of the wife even as Christ is the *head* of the church")

7. Christ is the "head" of the church (Col. 1:18, "he is the *head* of the body, the church"; also in Eph. 5:23)

8. Christ is the "head" of all things (Eph. 1:22, "he put all things under his feet and gave him as *head* over all things to the church")

9. God the Father is the "head" of Christ (1 Cor. 11:3, "the *head* of Christ is God")

In related statements using not metaphors but closely related similes, (1) the general of an army is said to be "like the head" in Plutarch, *Pelopidas* 2.1.3: In an army, "the light-armed troops are like the hands, the cavalry like the feet, the line of men-at-arms itself like chest and breastplate, and the general is like the *head*." Similarly, (2) the Roman Emperor is called the "head" of the people in Plutarch, *Galba* 4.3: "Vindix . . . wrote to Galba inviting him to assume the imperial power, and thus to serve what was a vigorous body in need of a *head*" (compare a related statement in Plutarch, *Cicero* 14.4). And (3) the King of Egypt is called "head" of the nation in Philo, *Moses* 2.30: "As the *head* is the ruling place in the living body, so Ptolemy became among kings."

Then there are the additional (somewhat later) citations from

Chrysostom (c. A.D. 344/354–407) quoted in my 2001 article,[6] where (1) God is the "head" of Christ; (2) Christ is the "head" of the church; (3) the husband is the "head" of the wife; (4) Christ is the "head" of all things; (5) church leaders are the "head" of the church; and (6) a woman is the "head" of her maidservant. In all six of these cases, Chrysostom uses language of rulership and authority to explain the role of the "head" and uses language of submission and obedience to describe the role of the "body."

In addition, there are several statements from various authors indicating a common understanding that the physical head functioned as the "ruling" part of the body: (1) Plato says that the head "reigns over all the parts within us" (*Timaeus* 44.D). (2) Philo says, "the *head* is the ruling place in the living body" (*Moses* 2:30); "the mind is *head* and ruler of the sense-faculty in us" (*Moses* 2.82); "*head* we interpret allegorically to mean the ruling part of the soul" (*On Dreams* 2.207); and "Nature conferred the sovereignty of the body on the *head*" (*The Special Laws* 184). (3) Plutarch says, "We affectionately call a person 'soul' or '*head*' from his ruling parts" (*Table Talk* 7.7 [692.e.1]).

Moreover, the meaning "source" makes no sense in key passages like Ephesians 5:23, "the husband is the head of the wife." I am not the source of my wife in any meaningful sense of the word "source." And so it is with all husbands and wives. It is just not true to say, "the husband is the *source* of the wife as Christ is the source of the church." It makes the verse into nonsense.

To my knowledge, no one has yet produced one text in ancient Greek literature where a person is called the *kephalē* of another person or group *and that person is not the one in authority over that other person or group*. Nearly two decades after the publication of my 1985 study, the alleged meaning "source without authority" has still not been supported with *any* citation of *any* text in ancient Greek literature. Over fifty examples of *kephalē* meaning "ruler, authority over" have been found, but no examples of the meaning of "source without authority."

Finally, while all the recognized lexicons for ancient Greek, or their editors, now give *kephalē* the meaning "person in authority over" or something similar, none give the meaning "source" when the word is applied to persons.[7] Nor do any of these lexicons or any other ancient citations support other meanings claimed by egalitarians, such as the meaning "one who does not take advantage of his body" or "preeminent one."[8]

Once again the question is, *where is the evidence? Where is even one example of a statement that takes the form "person A is the head of person B," in which person A is not in a position of authority over person B?* Not one example has ever been produced by egalitarians. But if all the lexicons and all the citations of this kind of expression contradict the egalitarian position, why do egalitarian writers go on affirming it as if it were proven fact?

Here again we must ask, what is the result of this egalitarian interpretation? It changes the meaning of Ephesians 5:23:

Previous meaning: For the husband is the head of (= leader, authority over) the wife even as Christ is the head of the church, his body, and is himself its Savior.

New meaning: For the husband is the head (= source, care-giver) of the wife even as Christ is the head of the church.

Once again, if we substitute a different meaning for a verse, and if the new meaning is wrong, we have taken away the Word of God from

---

[7] For elaboration see Grudem, *Evangelical Feminism and Biblical Truth*, 206-208.

[8] Ibid., 208-211. In *Discovering Biblical Equality*, the section on the meaning of *kephalē* by Gordon Fee adopts the meaning "source" for 1 Corinthians 11:3 and Ephesians 5:33: see Gordon Fee, "Praying and Prophesying in the Assemblies: 1 Cor. 11:2-16," in *Discovering Biblical Equality*, ed. Ronald W. Pierce and Rebecca Merrill Groothuis (Downers Grove, Ill.: InterVarsity, 2004), 152, 155. Yet Fee gives no examples where the person called "head" is not the one in authority; he cites no lexicons in support of the meaning "source"; and he shows no awareness of my 2001 article (see footnote 4 above) interacting with a number of the articles he cites.

In another section of the book I. Howard Marshall favors the meaning "possessing 'preeminence' or functioning as 'ground of being'," but also shows appreciation for Fee's understanding that *kephalē* points to "Christ as the supplier of guidance and power to the body" (I. Howard Marshall, "Mutual Love and Submission in Marriage: Colossians 3:18-19 and Ephesians 5:21-33," in Pierce and Groothuis, eds., *Discovering Biblical Equality*, 198). Neither Marshall nor Fee give any answer to the obvious difficulty that comes from using verses that refer to Christ as "head" to prove that the person called "head" is not the one who has authority!

Surely such verses prove exactly the opposite, for Christ has supreme authority over the church. The egalitarian sense, "source without authority" (in an interpersonal relationship) has never been supported by any example produced by any egalitarian writer.

his people in that verse. Should we do this when the evidence for the change has never been produced, and the evidence against it is so strong?

To nullify a key verse of Scripture by substituting a wrong meaning in this way is another way of removing the Bible, bit by bit, from God's people. It is thus another step on the path to liberalism.

STRANGE MEANINGS FOR "AUTHORITY"—ARE THEY RIGHT?

*Some evangelical feminists claim that the Greek word
authenteō ("exercise authority") could mean
"murder," or "commit violence," or
"proclaim oneself author of a man," or could even
have a vulgar sexual meaning*

This chapter discusses yet another attempt by evangelical feminists to switch the meaning of an essential verse in the Bible, this time 1 Timothy 2:12, "I do not permit a woman to teach or to *exercise authority* over a man; rather, she is to remain quiet." Some evangelical feminists give a different meaning for "exercise authority" (Greek *authenteō*), but in so doing they once again chip away at God's Word, removing what God actually said from verse after verse of the Bible.

These writers argue that 1 Timothy 2:12 does not mean simply, "I do not permit a woman to teach or *to exercise authority* over a man," but rather has *some wrongful practice, some abuse of authority,* in view.[1]

---

[1] For various nuances of this "abuse of authority" interpretation see David M. Scholer, "The Evangelical Debate over Biblical 'Headship,'" in *Women, Abuse, and the Bible,* ed. Catherine Clark Kroeger and James R. Beck (Grand Rapids, Mich.: Baker, 1996), 50; Rebecca Groothuis, *Good News for Women: A Biblical Picture of Gender Equality* (Grand Rapids, Mich.: Baker, 1997), 215; Sarah Sumner, *Men and Women in the Church* (Downers Grove, Ill.: InterVarsity Press, 2003), 253; Leland Wilshire, "1 Timothy 2:12 Revisited: A Reply to Paul W. Barnett and Timothy J. Harris," *Evangelical Quarterly* 65/1 (1993): 47-48, 52; J. Lee Grady, *Ten Lies the Church Tells Women* (Lake Mary, Fla.: Creation House, 2000), 58; Richard Clark Kroeger and Catherine Clark Kroeger, *I Suffer Not a Woman: Rethinking 1 Timothy 2:11-15 in Light*

The force of this claim, if true, would be to limit Paul's prohibition to whatever special situation he would have had in mind, whereas if *authenteō* has an ordinary, neutral meaning such as "have authority," then it is more likely that Paul is making a general statement for all churches for all times.

The most common alternative interpretation is that Paul is prohibiting some kind of *misuse* of authority. For example, David Scholer, professor of New Testament at Fuller Seminary, wrote,

> I am convinced that the evidence is in and that it clearly establishes *authentein*[2] as a negative term, indicating violence and inappropriate behavior. Thus, what Paul does not allow for women in 1 Timothy 2 is this type of behavior. . . . 1 Timothy 2 is opposing the negative behavior of women, probably the women mentioned in 1 Timothy 5:15 who follow and represent the false teachers 1 and 2 Timothy are dedicated to opposing.[3]

Similarly, Craig Keener at one point held, "Paul may here be warning against *a domineering use of authority,* rather than merely any use of authority."[4]

Rebecca Groothuis says this term includes a negative and harmful use of authority:

---

of *Ancient Evidence* (Grand Rapids, Mich.: Baker, 1992), 103 and 185-188. Note that the two page citations from the Kroeger volume reference two separate variations of this proposal.

[2] Throughout this book I normally cite Greek words with their lexical form (the form in which they occur in a Greek dictionary or lexicon) which in this case is *authenteō.* Some of the writers I quote cite this same word by using the infinitive form *authentein.* We are all referring to the same word.

[3] David M. Scholer, "The Evangelical Debate over Biblical 'Headship,'" in *Women, Abuse, and the Bible,* ed. Catherine Clark Kroeger and James R. Beck (Grand Rapids, Mich.: Baker, 1996), 50. Scholer says in his final footnote that this essay is a paper given at a conference on April 16, 1994, and his footnotes indicate interaction with literature up to 1993.

[4] Craig Keener, *Paul, Women, and Wives: Marriage and Women's Ministry in the Letters of Paul* (Peabody, Mass.: Hendrickson, 1992), 109; similarly, Gordon D. Fee, *1 and 2 Timothy, Titus,* New International Biblical Commentary (Peabody, Mass.: Hendrickson, 1984, 1988), 73. However, Keener later wrote that he found the evidence in Köstenberger et al., *Women in the Church* (Baker, 1995) to be persuasive for the view that *authenteō* has a neutral sense, referring to the exercise of authority, not a negative sense. He says in this later essay, "In contrast to my former position on this issue, however, I believe that Paul probably prohibits not simply 'teaching authoritatively,' but both teaching Scripture at all and having (or usurping) authority at all. In other words, women are forbidden to teach men—period" (Craig Keener, "Women in Ministry," in *Two Views on Women in Ministry,* ed. James Beck and Craig Blomberg [Grand Rapids, Mich.: Zondervan, 2001], 52-53).

Extensive recent research into Greek usage of this term suggests that at the time Paul wrote this letter to Timothy, *authentein* . . . "included a substantially negative element (i.e., 'dominate, take control by forceful aggression, instigate trouble')." Therefore, it seems forced and unreasonable to view 1 Timothy 2:12 as denying women the ordinary and appropriate exercise of authority. It appears far more likely that the prohibition refers to a negative and harmful use of authority—which . . . in this case probably referred specifically to the women who were teaching the heresy against which Paul had written 1 and 2 Timothy. Thus, Paul would not have intended this prohibition to exclude women from either the ministry of sound teaching or the legitimate exercise of ecclesiastical authority.[5]

And Leland Wilshire clearly advocates the meaning "instigate violence":

The preponderant number of citations . . . have to do with self willed violence, criminal action, or murder or with the person who does these actions. . . . The issue may be . . . 'instigating violence.' . . . It was a problem not of authority but of violent self-assertion in a rhetorically defined form of instruction.[6]

J. Lee Grady thinks the term has some kind of negative connotation:

Bible scholars have noted that *authentein* has a forceful and extremely negative connotation. It implies a more specific meaning than 'to have authority over' and can be translated 'to dominate,' 'to usurp,' or 'to take control.' Often when this word was used in ancient Greek literature it was associated with violence or even murder.[7]

---

[5] Groothuis, *Good News for Women,* 215. The quotation in the statement by Groothuis is from an article she refers to by Ronald Pierce, "Evangelicals and Gender Roles in the 1900's: 1 Tim. 2:8-15: A Test Case," *Journal of the Evangelical Theological Society* 36:3 (September 1993), 349. Sumner, *Men and Women in the Church,* advocates the meaning "domineer over a man" (253).

Linda Belleville recently claimed that 1 Timothy 2:12 means, "I do not, however, permit her to teach *with the intent to dominate* a man" (Belleville, "Teaching and Usurping Authority: 1 Timothy 2:11-15," in *Discovering Biblical Equality,* ed. Ronald W. Pierce and Rebecca Merrill Groothuis [Downers Grove, Ill.: InterVarsity, 2004], 223, italics added). But Belleville has misrepresented her supporting verses and simply misunderstood Greek grammar: see Wayne Grudem, *Evangelical Feminism and Biblical Truth* (Sisters, Ore.: Multnomah, 2004), 318-319.

[6] Leland Wilshire, "1 Timothy 2:12 Revisited: A Reply to Paul W. Barnett and Timothy J. Harris," *Evangelical Quarterly* 65/1 (1993): 47-48, 52.

[7] Grady, *Ten Lies the Church Tells Women,* 58. See also Andrew Perriman, *Speaking of Women* (Leicester, UK: Apollos, 1998), 171.

Another possible interpretation, related to Wilshire's idea of violence, has been proposed by Richard and Catherine Kroeger:

> *Authentēs* is applied on several occasions to those who perform rit-
> ual murder. . . . Such material does not allow us to rule out the pos-
> sibility that 1 Timothy 2:12 prohibits cultic action involving actual
> or representational murder. . . . More likely than actual murder is
> the "voluntary death" or sham murder which played a significant
> part in mystery initiations. . . . It is at least possible that some sort
> of ritual murder, probably of a simulated nature, could be
> involved.[8]

And yet a third alternative has also been proposed by Richard and
Catherine Kroeger. They argue that Paul here uses the word *authenteō*
to mean, "proclaim oneself author of a man." The Kroegers then translate 1 Timothy 2:12 as, "I do not allow a woman to teach nor to proclaim herself author of man." The Kroegers understand this to be Paul's
rejection of "a Gnostic notion of Eve as creator of Adam."[9]

So which interpretation is correct? The bottom line is that it comes
down to a matter of the evidence. The most complete study of this word
shows that its meaning is primarily neutral, "to exercise authority over."
In 1995 H. Scott Baldwin published the most thorough study of the verb
authenteō that had ever been done. Several earlier studies had looked at
a number of occurrences of this verb, but no one had ever looked at *all*
the examples that exist from ancient literature and ancient papyrus
manuscripts.[10] In addition, several earlier studies were flawed by mixing

---

[8] Kroeger and Kroeger, *I Suffer Not a Woman,* 185-188.

[9] Ibid., 103. See also Cindy Jacobs, *Women of Destiny* (Ventura, Calif.: Regal, 1998), 240-241,
who finds the Kroegers' proposal persuasive. (For analysis of the Kroegers' claims that false
teachers were promoting a Gnostic heresy about Eve being created first, see chapter 24, above;
and also Wayne Grudem, *Evangelical Feminism and Biblical Truth* [Sisters, Ore.: Multnomah,
2004], 284-287.)

[10] H. Scott Baldwin, "A Difficult Word: *Authenteō* in 1 Timothy 2:12," in *Women in the
Church: A Fresh Analysis of 1 Timothy 2:9-15,* ed. Andreas Köstenberger, Thomas Schreiner,
and H. Scott Baldwin (Grand Rapids, Mich.: Baker, 1995), 65-80 and 269-305. Baldwin
updated his analysis in light of more recent evidence in his 2005 essay, "An Important Word:
Authenteō in 1 Timothy 2:12," in *Women in the Church,* 2nd ed., ed. Andreas Köstenberger
and Thomas Schreiner (Grand Rapids, Mich.: Baker, 2005), 39-51. In that same volume,
Köstenberger updated his study of the grammatical structure of 1 Timothy 2:12, interacting
with both sympathetic and critical reviews of his earlier study (see "A Complex Sentence: The
Syntax of 1 Timothy 2:12," on pages 53-84).

with the verb examples of two different nouns with the same spelling (*authentēs*).

Baldwin correctly limited his examples to the verb that is found here in 1 Timothy 2. He found eighty-two occurrences of *authenteō* in ancient writings, and he listed them all with the Greek text and English translation in a long appendix.[11] He found that in all uses of this verb, "the one unifying concept is that of *authority.*"[12] He found only one example in which the verb seemed to take a negative sense, but because language changes and meanings of words change over time, even that one Chrysostom quotation from A.D. 390, coming more than three hundred years after Paul wrote 1 Timothy, is of limited value in understanding the meaning of what Paul wrote.

What is most striking about Baldwin's exhaustive study is the complete absence of some of the other meanings that have been proposed for *authenteō,* meanings that are unrelated to the idea of using authority. These meanings turn out to be speculation without any demonstrated basis in actual examples of this verb.

Two additional reasons also support the positive meaning ("exercise authority") of the verb *authenteō.* First, the grammatical structure of 1 Timothy 2:12 rules out any negative meaning (such as, "to misuse authority, to domineer, or to murder") and shows that the verb must have a positive meaning (such as "to exercise authority").[13] Second, a recent extensive and remarkably erudite study of cognate words now

---

[11] Baldwin, "Difficult Word," 269-305. I have listed all of these examples in English translation in Grudem, *Evangelical Feminism and Biblical Truth,* 675-702. The citations with the original Greek texts can be seen at www.efbt100.com, under "Appendix 7."

[12] Ibid., 72-73. On page 73, Baldwin summarized his findings on the range of possible meaning for *authenteō* in a table. What becomes evident from his chart is that there are no negative examples of the word *authenteō* at or around the time of the New Testament.

[13] Note especially Andreas Köstenberger's study, "A Complex Sentence Structure in 1 Timothy 2:12," in Köstenberger et al., *Women in the Church,* 81-103. His study examined one hundred parallel examples (52 in the NT, 48 from literature outside the NT, ranging from the third century B.C. to the end of the first century A.D.) to the construction found in 1 Timothy 2:12. In all of these cases, where two activities or concepts were joined according to the construction found in 1 Timothy 2:12, *both* activities were either viewed positively or negatively. No exceptions were found. (Cf. Dan Doriani's observation that when an activity that is viewed positively is joined with another viewed negatively, a different construction is used—e.g., Matt. 17:7; John 20:27; Rom. 12:14; 1 Tim. 5:16 [Dan Doriani, *Women and Ministry* (Wheaton, Ill.: Crossway, 2003), 179].) The importance of this for 1 Timothy 2:12 is that if the activity of "teaching" is viewed positively in the context of 1 Timothy, then the activity of "having authority" must also be viewed positively. Köstenberger goes on to demonstrate that, in fact, "teaching" is viewed positively by Paul in 1 and 2 Timothy (1 Tim. 4:11; 6:2; 2 Tim. 2:2). For further discussion, see Grudem, *Evangelical Feminism and Biblical Truth,* 314-316.

confirms that the meaning of *authenteō* is primarily positive or neutral.[14]

I should also mention one more egalitarian claim about the meaning of *authenteō:* Catherine Kroeger proposed in 1979 that *authenteō* really meant "to thrust oneself" (in sexually immoral practices in a pagan cult), and thus 1 Timothy 2:12 means, "I forbid a woman to teach or *engage in fertility practices* with a man."[15] This argument by Kroeger has been almost universally rejected by other writers from both complementarian and egalitarian camps.[16] So far as I am aware, she is suggesting a meaning for *authenteō* that has never been found in any lexicon, ever.

However, in spite of the fact that Kroeger's 1979 article has not withstood any scholarly scrutiny, I have been both amazed and disappointed to hear of a number of instances where this very article has been accepted as fact by several unsuspecting lay persons who have no ability to check the actual ancient texts in which Kroeger claimed to find an erotic meaning for *authenteō*. When the texts she mentions are inspected, Kroeger's article turns out to be a bizarre proposal based on flagrant misrepresentation of obscure evidence that is accessible only to scholars.[17]

Once again the question must be asked of the egalitarian claim: *where is the evidence?* Where are the actual examples of *authenteō* that show that it must take a negative meaning in 1 Timothy 2:12, when the positive or neutral sense is so well established? Should a claim without clear factual support be repeated so often as if it were proven fact?

---

[14] Al Wolters, "A Semantic Study of *authentēs* and Its Derivatives," *Journal of Greco-Roman Christianity and Judaism* 1 (2000): 145-175. Initially, this journal was available only online (http://divinity.mcmaster.ca/pages/jgrchj/index.html). However, the article has now been reprinted in *Journal for Biblical Manhood and Womanhood* 11/1 (Spring 2006): 44-65.

[15] Catherine Kroeger, "Ancient Heresies and a Strange Greek Verb," *The Reformed Journal* 29 (March 1979): 14, italics in original.

[16] See William D. Mounce, *Pastoral Epistles,* Word Biblical Commentary, vol. 46 (Nashville: Thomas Nelson, 2000), 127; and I. Howard Marshall, in collaboration with Philip H. Towner, *A Critical and Exegetical Commentary on the Pastoral Epistles* (London; New York: T & T Clark, 2004), 457; both with notes to other literature. See also Grudem, *Evangelical Feminism and Biblical Truth,* 313-314n107. The rejection of this strange argument by even egalitarian scholars is a welcome exception to the pattern of silence that I mentioned above (page 150).

[17] Full discussion of the texts can be found in Armin J. Panning, "ΑΥΘΕΝΤΕΙΝ—A Word Study," *Wisconsin Lutheran Quarterly* 78 (1981): 185-191; and Carroll D. Osburn, "ΑΥΘΕΝΤΕΩ (1 Timothy 2:12)," *Restoration Quarterly* 25/1 (1982): 1-12.

BUT AREN'T THESE JUST DIFFERENT INTERPRETATIONS?
HOW CAN A DIFFERENT INTERPRETATION BE A STEP TOWARD LIBERALISM?

At this point someone may object, "These other meanings for 'head' and 'exercise authority' are not *removing God's Word* from believers; they are just giving a *different interpretation*. What's wrong with that? How can that be a step toward liberalism?"

In response I would say, there are some kinds of "interpretations" that actually nullify the original statement. For example, let's say I am driving and I see a sign that says,

SPEED LIMIT

45

But suppose I am driving 70 miles per hour, and a policeman stops me. Can I say, "Officer, I just interpreted it differently. I thought the numbers 4 and 5 placed together meant '70.' I guess we just have a difference in interpretation"?

Or let's say I sign a contract that says I agree to "teach six classes" next year, and then I show up the first day and tell the students their assignments, and I never come back again for the whole term. When my academic dean questions me, I say, "Well, I interpreted 'teach' differently. I thought 'teach' just meant 'give students assignments for the rest of the term on the first day of class.' I didn't interpret it to mean 'give lectures in classes for a whole term.' I guess we just have a difference of interpretation."[18]

In both cases, these are not legitimate "differences of interpretation" *because my meanings are far outside the commonly accepted and recognized ranges of meanings* for the words "45" and "teach." So it is no longer a difference of interpretation. It is a nullification and denial of the statements altogether.

That is what I think is happening when evangelical feminists give key verses and key words an entirely different meaning, a meaning far outside the commonly accepted ranges of meanings for those words. That is why the question of hard facts to support those meanings is so

---

[18] Incidentally, I am not recommending or contemplating this approach. I guarantee that no professor who took that approach would last long!

important. When the proposals turn out to be *contrary* to the known evidence, we should conclude that they are untruthful. When the proposals turn out to be *unsubstantiated* by the known evidence, we should conclude that they are mere speculation, and the previously established meanings of the words should stand.

The result of this egalitarian claim is again to chip away at God's Word for believers, because it removes the sense of the verse that God intended:

> **Previous meaning:** I do not permit a woman to teach or to exercise authority over a man; rather, she is to remain quiet.
>
> **New egalitarian meaning:** I do not permit a woman to teach or to *abuse authority* over a man (or: to *commit violence* against a man, etc.); rather, she is to remain quiet.

These new meanings completely change the sense of a key word in 1 Timothy 2:12. But they do so contrary to the evidence about the word's meaning and its use in a context like this one. And so by removing from God's people the sense of what his Word actually says, they move another step down the path to liberalism.

IS THE SON NOT SUBORDINATE TO THE FATHER IN THE TRINITY?

Some evangelical feminists claim that the doctrine of the eternal subordination of the Son is contrary to historic orthodox Christian doctrine

Several egalitarians, such as Gilbert Bilezikian, have recently claimed that the doctrine of the eternal subordination of the Son to the Father (in role, not in being) is contrary to the historic Trinitarian doctrine of the church.

But first, let me repeat a bit of the background on this issue.[1] Why does Bilezikian write about the Trinity in relationship to the debate over men's and women's roles in the church? It is because many complementarians, including myself, have claimed a parallel between the Trinity and marriage. Just as the Father and Son in the Trinity are equal in deity and equal in importance but different in roles, so the husband and wife in marriage are equal in human personhood and equal in importance but different in roles. This is based in part on 1 Corinthians 11:3:

> But I want you to understand that the head of every man is Christ, *the head of a wife is her husband*, and *the head of Christ is God.*

---

[1] The following two paragraphs are essentially repeated from chapter 12 above, where the doctrine of the Trinity came up in relation to Kevin Giles.

Here Paul says that, just as in the Trinity the Father is the leader and has authority over the Son, so in marriage the husband is the leader and has authority over his wife. The remarkable thing is that the parallel with the Trinity proves that it is possible to have *equality in being but differences in roles.* This then disproves the evangelical feminist argument that "if you have different roles in marriage, then men and women are not equal in value." It also disproves the corresponding argument, "If men and women are equal in value, then you can't have different roles in marriage." In response to those arguments, the doctrine of the Trinity proves that you can have both equality and differences.

Evangelical feminists have responded to that argument by saying that there have not been different roles in the Trinity for all eternity, but that the Son's subordination to the Father's authority was only a voluntary submission for a limited time (his time on earth) and for a specific purpose (his work of redemption). They have argued that there is no eternal subordination of the Son to the Father in the Trinity. This is what Bilezikian tries to argue in his book *Community 101.*[2]

Bilezikian first denies any subordination of the Son to the Father prior to the incarnation:

> Because there was no order of subordination within the Trinity prior to the Second Person's incarnation, there will remain no such thing after its completion. If we must talk of subordination it is only a functional or economic subordination that pertains exclusively to Christ's role in relation to human history.

Then he says,

> Except for occasional and predictable deviations, *this is the historical Biblical trinitarian doctrine* that has been defined in the creeds and generally defended by the Church, at least the western Church, throughout the centuries.[3]

But when Bilezikian denies the eternal subordination of the Son to

---

[2] Gilbert Bilezikian, *Community 101: Reclaiming the Church as a Community of Oneness* (Grand Rapids, Mich.: Zondervan, 1997).
[3] Ibid., 191-192.

the Father in their *relationship* (which exists along with equality in essence or *being*), he is denying the teaching of the church throughout history, and it is significant that he gives no quotations, no evidence, to support his claim that his view "is the historical Biblical trinitarian doctrine." This statement is simply not true.

The vast majority of the church has affirmed equality in being *and* subordination in role among the persons in the Trinity, not simply during the time of incarnation but in the eternal relationships between the Father and the Son. The great historic creeds affirm that there is an *eternal difference* between the Father and the Son (and the Spirit), not in their being (for they are equal in all attributes and the three persons are just one "being" or "substance"), but in the way they relate to one another. There is an ordering of their relationships such that the Father eternally is first, the Son second, and the Holy Spirit third.

The doctrine of the "eternal generation of the Son" or the "eternal begetting of the Son" found expression in the Nicene Creed (A.D. 325) in the phrase "begotten of the Father before all worlds," and in the Chalcedonian Creed (451) in the phrase "begotten before all ages of the Father according to the Godhead." In the Athanasian Creed (fourth–fifth century A.D.) we read the expressions "The Son is of the Father alone: not made, nor created: but begotten" and "God, of the Substance of the Father; begotten before the worlds."[4]

It is open to discussion whether these were the most helpful expressions of this doctrine,[5] but it is not open to discussion whether the entire church throughout history has in these creeds affirmed that there was an *eternal* difference between the way the Son related to the Father and the way the Father related to the Son; that in their relationships the Father's role was primary and had priority, and the Son's role was secondary and was responsive to the Father; and that the Father was eternally Father and the Son was eternally Son.

---

[4] Other creeds with similar affirmations include the *Thirty-nine Articles* (Church of England, 1571): "The Son, which is the Word of the Father, *begotten from everlasting of the Father*, the very and eternal God, and of one substance with the Father"; and the *Westminster Confession of Faith* (1643–1646): "the Father is of none, neither begotten, nor proceeding; *the Son is eternally begotten of the Father* (chapter 2, paragraph 3).

[5] For further discussion of the phrase "only begotten" and the Greek term *monogenēs* on which it is based, see Wayne Grudem, "The *Monogenēs* Controversy: 'Only' or 'Only Begotten'?" appendix 6 in *Systematic Theology* (Grand Rapids, Mich.: Zondervan, 1994), 1233-1234. (This appendix is in the revised printing only, from 2000 onward.)

We may describe this difference in relationship in other terms, as later theologians did (such as speaking of the eternal subordination of the Son with respect to role or relationship, not with respect to substance), and still say we are holding to the historic Trinitarian doctrine of the church. But we may not deny that there is *any* eternal difference in relationship between the Father and the Son, as Bilezikian and others do, and still claim to hold to the historic Trinitarian doctrine of the church.

Bilezikian gives no explanation of how he understands "begotten of the Father before all worlds" or "eternal generation" or "eternal begetting." It is remarkable that Bilezikian, in denying *any* eternal difference in relationship between the Father and the Son, gives no explanation for why he thinks he has not placed himself outside the bounds of the great Trinitarian confessions through history. And it is simply irresponsible scholarship to accuse all those who hold to the historic doctrine of the eternal subordination of the Son to the Father (in role, not in being) of "tampering with the doctrine of the Trinity" and coming close to Arianism and engaging in "hermeneutical bungee jumping."[6] It is Bilezikian, not complementarians, who is tampering with the doctrine of the Trinity. Bilezikian is certainly free to deny any eternal differences in the Father-Son relationship if he wishes, but he may not truthfully say that a denial of these eternal differences has been the historic doctrine of the church.

Bilezikian quotes no church historians, no creeds, no other recognized theologians when he affirms that his view is the historic doctrine of the church. But it is not difficult to find many theologians and historians of doctrine who differ with Bilezikian's unsubstantiated affirmation.

For example, concerning this inter-Trinitarian relationship between the Father and the Son, Charles Hodge (1797–1878), the great Princeton theologian whose *Systematic Theology* has now been in print for 140 years, wrote about the Nicene Creed:

---

[6] For these accusations see Gilbert Bilezikian, "Hermeneutical Bungee-Jumping: Subordination in the Godhead," *Journal of the Evangelical Theological Society* 40/1 (March 1997): 57-68. The same article is found in Bilezikian, *Community 101*, 187-202.

The Nicene doctrine includes . . . the principle of the subordination of the Son to the Father, and of the Spirit to the Father and the Son. But this subordination does not imply inferiority. . . . The subordination intended is only that which concerns the mode of subsistence and operation. . . . The creeds are nothing more than a well-ordered arrangement of the facts of Scripture which concern the doctrine of the Trinity. They assert the distinct personality of the Father, Son, and Spirit . . . *and their consequent perfect equality;* and *the subordination of the Son to the Father, and of the Spirit to the Father and the Son, as to the mode of subsistence and operation.* These are scriptural facts, to which the creeds in question add nothing; and it is *in this sense they have been accepted by the Church universal.*[7]

Professor John Frame of Reformed Theological Seminary–Orlando also affirms an eternal subordination of the Son to the Father, along with an eternal equality of being:

So we may summarize by saying that biblical Trinitarianism denies ontological subordination, but affirms economic subordination of various kinds [here Frame is referring to activities of Father, Son, and Holy Spirit with respect to the creation]. But there is a third kind of subordination that has been debated for many centuries and has been much discussed in recent literature. That might be called *eternal subordination of role.*

Both Eastern and Western thinkers have regularly affirmed that God the Father has some sort of primacy over the other two persons. . . . Furthermore, if, as I have claimed, the economic activities of the persons are analogous to their eternal relationships, then the forms of economic subordination mentioned above suggest a pattern. The Son and the Spirit are voluntarily subordinate to the commands of the Father, because that kind of subordination is appropriate to their eternal nature as persons. . . .

This kind of subordination is not the ontological subordination of Arius. Nor is it merely economic, for it has to do with the eternal

---

[7] Charles Hodge, *Systematic Theology,* 3 vols. (Grand Rapids, Mich.: Eerdmans, 1970 [reprint]), 1:460-462, italics added. A survey of historical evidence showing affirmation of the eternal subordination of the Son to the authority of the Father is found in Stephen D. Kovach and Peter R. Schemm, Jr., "A Defense of the Doctrine of the Eternal Subordination of the Son," *Journal of the Evangelical Theological Society* 42/3 (September 1999): 461-476. See also Grudem, *Systematic Theology,* 248-252.

nature of the persons, the personal properties that distinguish each one from the others. . . . it is right to describe this difference of role as eternal. We may put it this way: There is no subordination within the divine nature that is shared among the persons: the three are equally God. However, there is a subordination of role among the persons, which constitutes part of the distinctiveness of each.

But how can one person be subordinate to another in his eternal role while being equal to the other in his divine nature? Or, to put it differently, how can subordination of role be compatible with divinity? Does not the very idea of divinity exclude this sort of subordination? The biblical answer, I think, is no.[8]

John Frame here is reflecting the historic doctrine of the church. Several other great historians of Christian doctrine have affirmed the same thing.

Louis Berkhof (1873–1957) writes:

The only subordination of which we can speak, is *a subordination in respect to order and relationship.*
d. The subsistence and operation of the three persons in the divine Being is marked by a certain definite order. There is a certain order in the ontological Trinity. In personal subsistence the Father is first, the Son second, and the Holy Spirit third. It need hardly be said that this order does not pertain to any priority of time or of essential dignity, but only to the logical order of derivation. The Father is neither begotten by, nor proceeds from any other person; the Son is eternally begotten of the Father, and the Spirit proceeds from the Father and the Son from all eternity. *Generation and procession take place within the Divine Being, and imply a certain subordination as to the manner of personal subsistence, but not subordination as far as the possession of the divine essence is concerned. This ontological Trinity and its inherent order is the metaphysical basis of the economical Trinity.*[9]

Church historian Philip Schaff (1819–1893) writes:

---

[8] John Frame, *The Doctrine of God* (Phillipsburg, N.J.: Presbyterian & Reformed, 2002), 719-720.
[9] Louis Berkhof, *Systematic Theology* (original 1939; Grand Rapids, Mich.: Eerdmans, 1969 [reprint]), 88-89, italics added.

The Nicene fathers still teach, like their predecessors, a certain *sub-ordinationism*, which seems to conflict with the doctrine of consubstantiality. But we must distinguish between a subordinationism of essence (*ousia*) and a *subordinationism of hypostasis, of order and dignity*. The former was denied, the latter affirmed.[10]

And historian J. N. D. Kelly similarly says,

[speaking of the Cappadocian father Gregory of Nyssa] *It is clearly Gregory's doctrine that the Son acts as an agent, no doubt in subordination to the Father* Who is the fountainhead of the Trinity, *in the production of the Spirit.* . . . As stated by the Cappadocians, however, the idea of the twofold procession from Father through Son *lacks all trace of subordinationism,* for its setting is a wholehearted recognition of the *homoousion* of the Spirit.[11]

Finally, church historian Geoffrey Bromiley writes,

Eternal generation. . . . is the phrase used to denote the inter-Trinitarian relationship between the Father and the Son as is taught by the Bible. "Generation" makes it plain that there is a divine sonship prior to the incarnation (cf. John 1:18; 1 John 4:9), that there is thus a distinction of persons within the one Godhead (John 5:26), and that between these persons there is a superiority and subordination of order (cf. John 5:19; 8:28). "Eternal" reinforces the fact that the generation is not merely economic (i.e., for the purpose of human salvation as in the incarnation, cf. Luke 1:35), but essential, and that as such it cannot be construed in the categories of natural or human generation. Thus it does not imply a time when the Son was not, as Arianism argued. . . . Nor does his subordination imply inferiority. . . . the phrase. . . . corresponds to what God has shown us of himself in his own eternal being. . . . It finds creedal expression in the phrases "begotten of his Father before all worlds" (Nicene) and "begotten before the worlds" (Athanasian).[12]

[10] Philip Schaff, *History of the Christian Church*, 8 vols. (original 1910; Grand Rapids, Mich.: Eerdmans, 1971 [reprint]), 3:681, italics added.

[11] J. N. D. Kelly, *Early Christian Doctrines*, 2nd ed. (New York: Harper & Row, 1960), 263, italics added.

[12] Geoffrey W. Bromiley, "Eternal Generation," in *Evangelical Dictionary of Theology*, ed. Walter Elwell (Grand Rapids, Mich.: Baker, 1984), 368.

This, then, has been the historic doctrine of the church. Egalitarians may differ with this doctrine today if they wish, and they may attempt to persuade us that they are right if they wish, but they must do this on the basis of arguments from Scripture, and they should also have the honesty and courtesy to explain to readers why they now feel it necessary to differ with the historic doctrine of the church as expressed in its major creeds.

The historic creeds affirm that there is an eternal difference between the Father and the Son, not in their being (for they are equal in all attributes, and the three persons are just one "being" or "substance"), but in the way they relate to one another. There is an ordering of their relationships such that the Father eternally is first, the Son second, and the Holy Spirit third.[13] The egalitarian claim that this is not the historic doctrine of the church is simply not true.

Why do I list Bilezikian's claim in this book? I do so because he is claiming that complementarians are straying from the historic doctrine of the Trinity. But in fact it is Bilezikian who is straying from the historic doctrine of the Trinity in his denial of any eternal difference in roles between the Father and the Son.

Is this another step on the path toward liberalism? Not directly. But in repeating claims about the historic doctrine of the Trinity that are not accurate, Bilezikian "moves the boundary lines" and confuses readers about which side is really straying from sound doctrine. In that way, his argument constitutes another step on the path toward liberalism.

---

[13] For further documentation of the history of this doctrine see Wayne Grudem, *Evangelical Feminism and Biblical Truth* (Sisters, Ore.: Multnomah, 2004), 415–422. Among the theologians affirming an eternal difference in role between the Father and the Son are Augustine (354–430), Thomas Aquinas (1224–1274), John Calvin (1509–1564), Charles Hodge (1797–1878), Augustus H. Strong (1836–1921), and Louis Berkhof (1873–1957). Specialists in the history of Christian doctrine who see this as the historic Nicene doctrine include Philip Schaff (1819–1893), J. N. D. Kelly, and Geoffrey Bromiley.

WOMEN BISHOPS IN THE EARLY CHURCH?

*One evangelical feminist claims that
a catacomb painting shows
an early woman bishop in Rome*

In a 1988 issue of the journal *Christian History*, Catherine Kroeger claims that a fresco on a Christian catacomb in Rome, dating from the late third century, shows a woman in "an amazingly authoritative stance, like that of a bishop." She adds, "the shepherds on either side may represent pastors, in which case the woman may be in the role of a bishop, blessing pastors in her charge."[1]

But is this what the fresco shows? What this article does not reveal is that no expert in the study of ancient Christian art supports Kroeger's interpretation, nor does the literature on such art even mention her interpretation as a possibility.

In addition, this idea is contrary to what we know of the role of women in the early church. Such "orant" paintings, with different individuals portrayed on them, are very common in early Christian art. If Kroeger's theory is correct, it would mean that women bishops were also very common in the early centuries of the church. But that is highly unlikely. As far as I know, there is no historical record of any woman

---

[1] Comments by Catherine Kroeger in *Christian History* 17 (1988), 2. The fresco is said to come from the Coemeterium Majus arcosolium in Rome.

serving even as a pastor or an elder, to say nothing of serving as a bishop, anywhere in the entire history of the early church.[2]

The fresco in question is one example of a common kind of early painting called an *orant* or an *orans* (from Latin for "one who prays"). The entry for "Orant" in the *Encyclopedia of Early Christianity* says,

> The posture symbolizing prayer, from Latin *orans* ("one who prays"). Typically, in early Christian art, the orant is represented by a standing female facing front, arms raised and extended outward from the body. . . . The figure is widely attested in the very earliest Christian art . . . but there has been a long history of controversy surrounding its interpretation. . . . Because this image is often attested in funerary contexts, many interpreters have sought an eschatological-symbolic explanation: the orant is a symbol of the soul in paradise, or of the church (feminine) at prayer anticipating the next life.[3]

Other interpretations are that these paintings are testimonies to the piety and faithfulness of the deceased, or portrayals of prayer for those still on earth.[4]

Nothing in any of these studies even hints that the person praying in these paintings is in "an especially authoritative stance," or might be a woman "bishop," or that the shepherds represent "pastors" in the care of a bishop, as Kroeger claims. These statements are pure speculation on Kroeger's part. A sense of fairness to one's readers should require that any author who makes such statements would at the very least include

---

[2] Probably the first woman to have such a recognized public role was Margaret Fell in the sectarian Quaker movement in 1667. If there ever had been a woman bishop in Rome in the late third century, as Kroeger supposes, it would have prompted widespread comment, and even opposition and conflict. In fact, the Roman Catholic Church has a high interest in the historical succession of bishops in Rome! But there is no record of a woman bishop anywhere, to say nothing of dozens of women bishops, all of which also makes Kroeger's speculation highly unlikely. Someone might answer that the Catholic church has suppressed the evidence of these female bishops, but to say that is to admit that one has decided to believe something based on *no available historical facts* instead of something based on *many established historical facts*. People may decide to believe such things if they wish, but such a decision cannot be said to be rational.
[3] Paul Corby Finney, "Orant," in *Encyclopedia of Early Christianity*, 2nd ed., ed. Everett Ferguson (New York and London: Garland, 1997), 831.
[4] In addition to Finney's article (see previous footnote), see J. Beaudry, "Orans," in *New Catholic Encyclopedia*, ed. Berard L. Marthaler (Washington, D.C.: Catholic University of America, 2002), 621; A. M. Giuntella, "Orans," in *Encyclopedia of the Early Church*, ed. Angelo DiBerardino, trans. Adrian Walford, 2 vols. (New York: Oxford University Press, 1992), 2:615. All three articles include bibliographies of additional studies.

some kind of disclaimer, such as, "This type of figure is common in early Christian art, and there are several competing theories about what these praying figures mean. My proposal is unusual, since no scholar who specializes in the study of ancient Christian art has ever proposed the interpretation I am giving, but it still seems right to me." Then the author could give reasons and arguments for his or her interpretation. Such a procedure would be honest and fair to readers who have no opportunity to check the relevant sources for themselves. But Kroeger has not given any such disclaimer.

We might also expect that the editors of a journal such as *Christian History* either would have enough knowledge of the field themselves to know that Kroeger's statement was unprecedented in the history of scholarship concerning early Christian art, or would have access to reviewers who would have sufficient knowledge to tell them that,[5] so that at least readers would not automatically take Kroeger's interpretation as a reliable testimony from an expert in the field. If Kroeger is unaware of this other scholarly work, then one wonders how she can be considered competent to write about it herself. If she is aware of this other scholarly work but fails to mention it to her readers, then she has not met fundamental demands of honesty in an article such as this.

The procedure followed in this egalitarian claim troubles me more than most of the other claims that I consider in this book. When no explanations or disclaimers are made alerting readers to the uniform lack of support from scholarly specialists for such an interpretation, this wild speculation (or so it seems to me, after reading these other articles) is taken as truth by unsuspecting readers.

Cindy Jacobs, for example, simply trusts Kroeger's interpretation of this fresco as truthful, and counts it as evidence for women's participation in high positions of governing authority in the early church.[6] Thousands of readers of Jacobs's book will also take it as true, thinking that since it has a footnote to a journal on church history, there must be scholarly support for the idea. And so something that is a figment of

---

[5] It is not clear to me that complementarian scholars had any opportunity for input in this issue of *Christian History*. The entire issue was devoted to the history of women in the church, and five of the six "contributing editors" were women who have been authors and leaders in the egalitarian movement: Patricia Gundry, Nancy Hardesty, Catherine Kroeger, Aida Spencer, and Karen Torjesen (page 3).

[6] Cindy Jacobs, *Women of Destiny* (Ventura, Calif.: Regal, 1998), 189.

Catherine Kroeger's imagination, something that no scholar in the field has ever advocated, is widely accepted as fact. The requirements of truthfulness should hold us to higher standards than this.

Kroeger's article therefore uses apparently untruthful claims based on obscure material outside the Bible in order to turn people away from being obedient to the Bible in what it says about restricting the office of pastor and elder to men. And turning people away from obeying the Bible is another step on the path toward liberalism.

THESE TEN UNTRUTHFUL OR UNSUBSTANTIATED CLAIMS ALSO UNDERMINE THE AUTHORITY OF SCRIPTURE

The ten egalitarian claims in this section are frequently promoted as fact, but upon investigation they turn out to be only unsubstantiated speculation, and in many cases they are contrary to an abundant amount of factual evidence that we do have. Therefore, I believe there are not only fifteen egalitarian claims that *directly* deny the authority of Scripture (Part 2 above), but also at least ten others that in another way *effectively* undercut the authority of Scripture because they lead people to misunderstand what it teaches by promoting untruthful or at best unsubstantiated claims as established fact (Part 3 of this book, including the previous ten chapters).

When we put these ten claims together with the fifteen in Part 2, we see that, within the short space of about thirty years since Paul Jewett's book was published in 1975, evangelical feminism has generated, published, and promoted at least twenty-five different ways of effectively nullifying the authority of Scripture in the lives of Christians today.

Something should strike us as deeply troubling about such a movement. Is the authority of the Bible really primary for egalitarians? Or is there a deep-seated mentality that actually puts feminism first and the Bible second? The more I have read these egalitarian arguments, the more I have found myself wondering this: Are these writers actually operating from a deep conviction that says, "I know that egalitarianism is right, now let me see if I can find *any* ways to support it from the Bible. If one approach does not work, I'll try another, and if twenty-five approaches do not work, I will look for a twenty-sixth, because the one thing I cannot accept is that egalitarianism is wrong"?

I cannot say for sure. But I can think of no other viewpoint or movement within the whole history of the Christian church (except theological liberalism itself) that has generated so many novel and ultimately incorrect ways of interpreting the Bible.

PART IV
WHERE IS EVANGELICAL FEMINISM TAKING US?

THE NEXT STEP: DENIAL OF ANYTHING UNIQUELY MASCULINE

The egalitarian agenda will not stop simply with the rejection of male headship in marriage and the establishment of women as pastors and elders in churches. There is something much deeper at stake. At the foundation of egalitarianism is a dislike and a rejection of anything uniquely masculine.[1] It is a dislike of manhood itself.

This tendency is seen, for example, in Sarah Sumner's claim that even asking "What is biblical manhood?" is asking the wrong question. It is also seen in her attempts to deny every one of the characteristics that complementarians say distinguish men from women (such as a primary responsibility to lead, provide for, and protect within marriage), and in her limiting "masculinity" and "femininity" only to differences in our physical bodies.[2]

This dislike of anything uniquely masculine is also seen in Rebecca Groothuis's suggestion that Adam was a sexually undifferentiated being when he was first created.[3] But why is it objectionable that God created Adam as a *man*? It makes one wonder if this idea doesn't reflect some

---

[1] For further discussion of this trend, see Daniel R. Heimbach, "The Unchangeable Difference: Eternally Fixed Sexual Identity for an Age of Plastic Sexuality," in *Biblical Foundations for Manhood and Womanhood*, ed. Wayne Grudem (Wheaton, Ill.: Crossway, 2002), 275-289; and Peter R. Jones, "Sexual Perversion: The Necessary Fruit of Neo-Pagan Spirituality in the Culture at Large," in ibid., 257-274.

[2] See, for example, Sarah Sumner, *Men and Women in the Church* (Downers Grove, Ill.: InterVarsity Press, 2003), 86, 98. For a detailed response, see Wayne Grudem, *Evangelical Feminism and Biblical Truth* (Sisters, Ore.: Multnomah, 2004), 484-488, and more generally, 25-101.

[3] Rebecca Groothuis, *Good News for Women: A Biblical Picture of Gender Equality* (Grand Rapids, Mich.: Baker, 1997), 124.

deeper dislike of human sexuality in general, some hostility toward the very *idea* of manhood and womanhood.

A similar tendency is also seen in the emphasis, advocated by Stanley Grenz, that Jesus' *humanity* is what was really important for his incarnation, not his maleness.[4] One wonders again if this does not represent an underlying desire to reject anything uniquely male. Why should we object that the Son of God came to earth as a *man?*[5]

Another trend related to this (though not promoted only by egalitarians) is found in "gender-neutral" Bibles such as the NRSV, NLT, and TNIV that remove thousands of examples of the male-oriented words "man," "father," "son," "brother," and "he/him/his," changing them to "person," "parent," "child," "friend," and "they," in places where the original Hebrew or Greek referred specifically to a male human being or used a masculine singular pronoun (equivalent to English "he") to state a general truth. These versions have "muted the masculinity" of many passages of Scripture and, in doing so, have contributed to the feminist goal of denying anything uniquely masculine.[6]

Yet another related trend is the removal of masculine language from familiar hymns. The most recent example (though only one of many) is the new hymnal approved by the Evangelical Lutheran Church in America. It changes

> Praise to the Lord, the Almighty, the King of Creation!
> O my soul praise Him, for He is thy health and salvation!

to

> Praise to the Lord, the Almighty, the God of Creation!
> My heart is longing to offer up sweet adoration!

---

[4] Stanley Grenz, *Women in the Church: A Biblical Theology of Women in Ministry* (Downers Grove, Ill.: InterVarsity Press, 1995), 207-209.

[5] For specific responses to the claims of Sumner, Groothuis, and Grenz, see Wayne Grudem, *Evangelical Feminism and Biblical Truth* (Sisters, Ore.: Multnomah, 2004), 166-167.

[6] I have written extensively about this elsewhere: see Vern Poythress and Wayne Grudem, *The TNIV and the Gender-Neutral Bible Controversy* (Nashville: Broadman & Holman, 2004); and Wayne Grudem with Jerry Thacker, *Why Is My Choice of a Bible Translation So Important?* (Louisville, Ky.: CBMW, 2005). The second book includes an appendix with a categorized list of 3,686 "inaccurate translations" in the TNIV, nearly all of them relating to gender language. This list is also available at www.genderneutralbibles.com.

The male-oriented words "King," "Him," and "He" are removed. The new hymnal also eliminates references to God as "Father" and changes this word to expressions like "Holy Eternal Majesty." God the "Son" is now called the "Incarnate Word."[7]

A writer in the egalitarian publication *Mutuality* suggested (humorously) that a better title for John Gray's book *Men Are from Mars, Women Are from Venus* would be

> *Men Are from Mars, Women Are from Venus, But Some Men Are from Venus and Some Women Are from Mars, and All of God's Children Have Both Mars and Venus Qualities Within Them So Why Not Just Say that Men and Women Are from the Earth, and Let's Get about the Business of Developing the Unique God-Given Mars/Venus Qualities that God Has Given All of Us for the Sake of the Kingdom*[8]

When I read that, I realized that egalitarians seem to feel compelled to oppose any kinds of differences between men and women other than those that are purely physical. Even when egalitarian author Rebecca Groothuis tried to answer the charge that egalitarians think that men and women are the same, the only clear differences she could point to were the sexually based physical differences between men and women and abilities that flow directly from those physical differences.[9]

Once evangelical feminism gains control of a church or a denomination, the teaching will tend increasingly toward a denial of anything that is uniquely masculine other than obvious physical differences. The church will be embarrassed by any emphasis on strong and true "manhood," and will suppress it. This is predictable. It is the next stage on the path toward liberalism.

---

[7] Jim Brown, "ELCA Pastor: 'Gender-Neutral Hymnal Concession to Culture,'" at the online Christian news site Crosswalk.com (www.crosswalk.com/news/religiontoday/1347915.html, accessed 8-30-05).
[8] Jim Banks, untitled article, *Mutuality*, May 1998, 3.
[9] Groothuis, *Good News for Women*, 47-49.

ANOTHER TROUBLING STEP: GOD OUR MOTHER

Following the denial of male headship in marriage, and the denial of any restriction of leadership roles in the church to men, and the denial of "manhood" and anything uniquely masculine other than the physical differences among human beings, it is to be expected that egalitarians would begin to blur and then deny God's identity as our Father. This is exactly what has recently happened in egalitarian writings.

Ruth Tucker, in her book *Women in the Maze,* says,

> We sing the words of John W. Petersen in worshipful praise, "Shepherd of love, you knew I had lost my way. . . ." Would it be worse, or blasphemous, to sing something like "Mother of love . . ."? Both are figures of speech. But because of our fear of taking on the trappings of radical feminism or goddess worship, we dare not sing those words—except perhaps in our closets of prayer.[1]

We see a similar trend in literature sold by Christians for Biblical Equality through their website (www.cbeinternational.org). This is the primary website for evangelical feminists today, and it says that their bookstore contains books that further their mission: "Each resource we carry has first been evaluated by our team of reviewers to ensure that it furthers CBE's mission and vision."[2] Yet at least two books openly advocate praying to God as our Mother in heaven.

---

[1] Ruth A. Tucker, *Women in the Maze* (Downers Grove, Ill.: InterVarsity Press, 1992), 20-21.
[2] See the "About CBE's Bookstore" section at www.cbeinternational.org. These books were still being sold on February 20, 2006.

The bookstore carries a book by Paul R. Smith called *Is It Okay to Call God "Mother"? Considering the Feminine Face of God.* In this book Smith says, "In one sense I wrote this book so that our congregation could have a fuller explanation of why I believe it is important to call God 'Mother' as well as 'Father' in public worship."[3]

Smith introduces chapter 3 with a cartoon of Moses arriving in heaven, Ten Commandments under his arm, saying to God, "Gee, I didn't expect you to be a soprano!" Later in the book, Smith asks the question, "Will the next thing be to say that Jesus should have been a woman?" and though he affirms that Jesus did come as a man, he says, "Something is wrong when we cannot conceive of the Messiah coming from a different cultural setting or being of a different race or gender." He says he personally owns a sculpture of "a female Jesus hanging on the cross" and he admits that some people "have violent reactions" to it.[4] Smith concludes this section by saying, "I personally try to avoid using masculine pronouns for the risen, transcendent Christ except when I am speaking of him during his time here on earth before his ascension."[5]

Smith does not explain how he reads the dozens or perhaps hundreds of passages in the New Testament epistles that refer to Jesus as "he" and "him" after he ascended to heaven, using masculine singular pronouns in Greek, such as this passage from Colossians 1:

> *He* is the image of the invisible God, the firstborn of all creation. For by *him* all things were created, in heaven and on earth . . . all things were created through *him* and for *him*. And *he* is before all things, and in *him* all things hold together. And *he* is the head of the body, the church. *He* is the beginning, the firstborn from the dead, that in everything *he* might be preeminent (Col. 1:15-18).

Or this statement from Philippians, talking about Christ after his ascension into heaven:

---

[3] Paul R. Smith, *Is It Okay to Call God "Mother"? Considering the Feminine Face of God* (Peabody, Mass.: Hendrickson, 1993), 1.
[4] Ibid., 134, 137, 140, 141. Page 142 suggests that this sculpture, like another picture he has, is hanging on his office wall.
[5] Ibid., 143.

Therefore God has highly exalted *him* and bestowed on *him* the name that is above every name, so that at the name of Jesus every knee should bow, in heaven and on earth and under the earth. . . . (Phil. 2:9-10).

How can Smith even read these passages if he tries to "avoid using masculine pronouns for the risen, transcendent Christ"? So eager is Smith to deny the masculinity of Jesus that he has come to the point where he avoids using language like the New Testament itself.[6]

Another book sold on the CBE website is *God, A Word for Girls and Boys,* by Jann Aldredge-Clanton.[7] This book teaches us to pray prayers like, "God, our Mother, we thank you that you love us so much to want the best for us. Thank you for trusting us enough to let us do things on our own. . . . Stay near us and help us to become all that we can be. Amen."[8]

In the introduction to the book, Aldredge-Clanton says,

Masculine God-language hinders many children from establishing relationships of trust with God. In addition, calling God "he" causes boys to commit the sin of arrogance. . . . Calling the supreme power of the universe "he" causes girls to commit the sin of devaluing themselves. For the sake of "these little ones" we must change the way we talk about God and about human beings.[9]

This is a book promoted by Christians for Biblical Equality.

Catherine Kroeger, one of the founders of Christians for Biblical Equality, has also advocated calling God "Mother." In an article, "Women Elders . . . Sinners or Servants?" Richard Kroeger and Catherine Kroeger write:

So far we have referred to God as "He" and "Him" because most of us are used to employing these terms when we think of the Holy One.

---

[6] Randy Stinson ("Our Mother Who Art in Heaven: A Brief Overview and Critique of Evangelical Feminists and the Use of Feminine God-Language," *Journal for Biblical Manhood and Womanhood* 8/2 [Fall, 2003], 20-34) notes that Smith is an openly professing homosexual pastor, and cites Smith's writings on homosexuality (25-26).
[7] Jann Aldredge-Clanton, *God, A Word for Girls and Boys* (Louisville, Ky.: Glad River, 1993).
[8] Ibid., 23.
[9] Ibid., 11.

Indeed, it is sometimes asserted that those in holy office should be male to represent the Deity who is male. This is to ignore what the Bible has to say, for *God is pictured as both male and female*. Let us be clear that God does not possess sexuality—neither distinctive maleness nor femaleness; but to explain the love and work of God, both male and female imagery is used.

Consider these scriptures carefully: Psalm 131:2-3; Deut. 32:18; Isa. 49:15; 66:9-13; 42:13-14; and Matthew 23:37. Among other passages is James 1:17-18, which first speaks of God as Father and then says God brought us forth as Mother. Job 38:28-29, Isa. 63:15 and Jer. 31:20 speak of the womb of God, surely a valuable image when we think of new birth. God's likeness to a mother is an important aspect of the divine nature. Can Christians neglect any aspect of God's being as it is revealed in Scripture? *There is good biblical reason, then, to speak of God as both Father and Mother, both "she" and "he."* This is particularly important for evangelicals to remember when they seek to witness to people turning to goddess worship in their desire for a deity with feminine attributes. It is also essential to remember when ministering to those with bad father images, who may have positive feelings about their mothers. Women as well as men are made in God's image! (Gen. 1:26-27, 5:1-2).[10]

The current president of Christians for Biblical Equality, Mimi Hadad, also says "we may speak of God as father or mother."[11]

What is wrong with calling God "Mother"? Randy Stinson has a very helpful short article, "Seven Reasons Why We Cannot Call God 'Mother.'"[12] He points out, among other things, (1) that God's own Word never calls him "Mother" or "She" but regularly uses masculine terms such as "Father" and "He" and "King" (never "Queen") and "Husband" (never "Wife"); and (2) that God's self-revelation in Scripture is his own chosen way of revealing his identity to us, and we should not tamper with that or add to it by calling God names the Bible never uses and carefully avoids using.

---

[10] Richard Kroeger and Catherine Kroeger, "Women Elders . . . Sinners or Servants?" available online at http://firstpresby.org/womenelders.htm, italics added.

[11] Mimi Haddad, "What Language Shall We Use?" available online at the CBE website (www.cbeinternational.org/new/free_articles/what_language.shtml, accessed 5-1-06).

[12] Randy Stinson, "Seven Reasons Why We Cannot Call God 'Mother,'" available online at the CBMW website (http://www.cbmw.org/article.php?id=99).

Stinson recognizes (3) that the Bible sometimes refers to God with literary devices like metaphors and similes that include feminine figures of speech. For example, it refers to God in this way:

Deuteronomy 32:18: You were unmindful of the Rock that bore you, and you forgot *the God who gave you birth.*

Job 38:29: From *whose womb* did the ice come forth, and *who has given birth* to the frost of heaven?

Isaiah 42:13-14: The LORD goes out like a mighty man, like a man of war he stirs up his zeal; he cries out, he shouts aloud, he shows himself mighty against his foes. For a long time I have held my peace; I have kept still and restrained myself; now *I will cry out like a woman in labor;* I will gasp and pant.

Isaiah 66:13: *As one whom his mother comforts, so I will comfort you;* you shall be comforted in Jerusalem.

Hosea 13:8: I will fall upon them like a bear robbed of *her* cubs.

But Stinson points out that while these feminine metaphors use *verbs* to describe God's activities in vivid ways (to give birth, to cry out, to comfort), *they never use feminine nouns when they describe who God is.* And even when feminine activities occur in metaphors describing God, the gender markers in the Hebrew text use masculine verb forms when they refer to God (for example, in Deut. 32:18, "gave you birth" is a masculine participle, not a feminine one).[13]

Stinson points out that the Bible uses language in a similar way with some human beings who are men. For example, Hushai the Archite, counselor to Absalom, says that David and his mighty men are "enraged,

---

[13] See the longer analysis in Stinson, "Our Mother Who Art in Heaven." Stinson writes, "There are . . . figures of speech: similes, metaphors, analogies, or personifications. There are no cases in which feminine terms are used as names, titles, or invocations of God. There are no instances where God is identified by a feminine term" (28). He quotes with approval John Cooper's statement, "God is never directly said to be a mother, mistress, or female bird in the way he is said to be a father, king, judge, or shepherd" (28). (See John Cooper, *Our Father in Heaven: Christian Faith and Inclusive Language for God* [Grand Rapids, Mich.: Baker, 1998], 89.) In short, we should not name God with names that the Bible never uses and actually avoids using. God's name is valued and highly protected in Scripture.

like a bear robbed of her cubs in the field" (2 Sam. 17:8). Paul could write to the Galatians and say, "my little children, for whom I am again *in the anguish of childbirth* until Christ is formed in you!" (Gal. 4:19). Paul can say to the Thessalonians, "But we were gentle among you, *like a nursing mother* taking care of her own children" (1 Thess. 2:7).[14]

Does this mean that we should think that David and his mighty men and Paul *were* women? Certainly not. Does it mean that we can refer to David as "she"? Or can we call David "the Queen of Israel"? Certainly not. Can we call Paul, "Mother Paul, the founder of many churches"? No, because the similes saying that David *acted like* a she-bear or that Paul *acted like* a nursing mother do not imply at all that David *was* a woman or that Paul *was* a woman. They are just figures of speech. But if we *call* these men "she" or "mother" then we are implying that they *are* women!

And if we call God "Mother" then we are implying that he *is* a female person. That is contrary to the Bible's descriptions of him as Father and King and Lord and "he."[15] The Bible gives no justification for calling God "Mother," and in fact it is contrary to the consistent description of God as "Our Father in heaven" (Matt. 6:9). The names that God assigns to people in the Bible are very important (think of changing Abram's name to Abraham, Sarai's name to Sarah, or Jacob's name to Israel). So the names that God assigns *to himself* must be supremely important: his name affects how we think of who he is. Calling God "Mother" is *changing God's own description of himself in the Bible. It is calling God by a name that he has not taken for himself.* Therefore it is changing the way the Bible teaches us to think of God. It is thus changing our doctrine of God.

Calling God "Mother" is the next step on the path to liberalism, and Christians for Biblical Equality and several evangelical feminist leaders are now promoting that step toward liberalism.

---

[14] Here is another example: Jesus cries out to Jerusalem, "How often would I have gathered your children together *as a hen gathers her brood under her wings . . . !*" (Matt. 23:37). Does that mean that Jesus is a mother hen, or that we can pray to Jesus as "Our mother hen in heaven"? Certainly not! It is just a figure of speech, saying that his longing was like something commonly known to an agricultural community. It described a certain longing of Jesus the man. But he is still a man.

[15] I am not saying that God *is* a man (for God is not a human being at all, though God the Son did become a human being in the person of Jesus). But I am saying that the pattern of the Bible's naming of God is masculine, not feminine.

Liberal Protestants have traveled this route before, during the 1970s. Mary Kassian, in her book *The Feminist Mistake*,[16] points out how the three stages on the road traveled by secular feminists were (1) renaming themselves, (2) renaming the world, and (3) renaming God. The last stage includes "The Feminization of God," and that took place in liberal Protestant thinking and writing in the 1970s.[17]

That transformation has found its way into liberal Protestant hymnbooks. In 2002 the United Methodist Church published a supplement to its hymnal called *The Faith We Sing*, which included some new hymns such as "Bring Many Names," in which Methodists are to sing praise to "Strong Mother God, working night and day." The author of the lyrics, Brian Wren, professor of worship at Columbia Theological Seminary in Decatur, Georgia, supports these lyrics with an argument that sounds very much like the arguments egalitarians have used on other subjects. According to reporter Maura Jane Farrelly,

> Professor Wren says the Bible uses the word "Father" because it was written in a place and time when only men were in positions of authority. And because this isn't the case anymore in many Christian nations, Dr. Wren says there is no need to cling so literally to the "Father" image.[18]

A similar trend has been seen among disillusioned Southern Baptists who left the denomination in protest over the conservative control of the SBC and formed the Cooperative Baptist Fellowship.[19] At the CBF annual meeting that began June 28, 1991, in Atlanta, songs of praise to God as Mother were prominent:

---

[16] Mary Kassian, *The Feminist Mistake*, rev. ed. (Wheaton, Ill.: Crossway, 2005).

[17] Ibid., chapter 12, 159-174. Kassian points out that in 1972 feminist leader Betty Friedan uttered the question, "Is God He?" and it was prophetic because that question was "destined to become the debate of the decade" (160). During that decade the National Council of Churches, the World Council of Churches, the United Presbyterian Church, the Lutheran Church in America, and several feminist writers such as Letty Russell began promoting "inclusive language" to refer to God (ibid.).

[18] Maura Jane Farrelly, "Controversial Hymns Challenge U.S. Methodists' View of God," *Voice of America News*, July 5, 2002 (www.voanews.com).

[19] The Cooperative Baptist Fellowship was accepted into full membership as an independent denomination by the Baptist World Alliance in July of 2003, according to *World*, August 2, 2003, 23.

With songs and prayers to "Mother God," an auxiliary organization of the Cooperative Baptist Fellowship opened its annual meeting at the CBF General Assembly Thursday with a clear message—the current controversy is about more than women pastors. The annual Baptist Women in Ministry breakfast was rife with stridently feminist God language, culminating in a litany read by BWIM members about their discomfort at calling God "Father," "Lord," and "King". . . . The group sang a hymn to "strong mother God". . . . Feminist language for God continued throughout the two-hour long business session and worship service. BWIM treasurer Sally Burgess told the crowd . . . "I believe God is good, and She knows what She's doing". . . . The CBF exhibit hall bookstore displayed a new Methodist "gender inclusive" hymnal . . . with a hymn written from the point of view of the earth entitled, "I am your Mother". . . . Preacher Elizabeth Clements read a sermon about her spiritual experiences in the presence of starry skies, winding rivers, and "trees older than Jesus."[20]

Christians for Biblical Equality, the central advocacy group for evangelical feminism and the focal point for egalitarians within the evangelical world, promotes most of the evangelical feminist books that I have critiqued within this book including those mentioned in this chapter and the previous one. Therefore CBE is promoting most of the steps toward liberalism that I have outlined above. They may not think they are eroding the very foundations of evangelical Christianity, but in the methods of interpretation that they allow and in the standards of evidence that they accept, they are indeed contributing far more than they can imagine toward a movement of their churches to liberalism within a few short years.

What, then, is the doctrinal direction to which egalitarianism leads? To an abolition of anything distinctively masculine. An androgynous Adam. A Jesus whose manhood is not important—just his "humanity." A God who is both Father and Mother, and then a God who is Mother but cannot be called Father.

This is the next stage in the advance of evangelical feminist ideas. Evangelical feminists are revising our understanding of God our Father

---

[20] "'Mother God' Worshipped at Group's Gathering for CBF Annual Meeting," *Baptist Press News*, June 29, 2001 (www.bpnews.net).

as revealed to us in the Bible. They are thus changing the doctrine of God as revealed in Scripture to make people think of God as "Our Mother in heaven." They are undermining the authority of the Bible in its very description of God himself.

Changing our idea of God is nearly the final step on the path toward liberalism.

THE FINAL STEP:
APPROVAL OF HOMOSEXUALITY

Very few evangelical egalitarians up to this time have advocated the moral validity of homosexual conduct, as far as I know. And I am thankful that the leading egalitarian organization Christians for Biblical Equality has steadfastly refused pressures to allow for the moral rightness of homosexual conduct.

However, we would be foolish to ignore the trend set by a number of more liberal Protestant denominations, denominations that from the 1950s to the 1970s approved the ordination of women using many of the same arguments that evangelical egalitarians are using today.[1] And those few prominent evangelicals who have endorsed homosexual conduct have already set a pattern of following evangelical feminist arguments. Virginia Mollenkott and Letha Scanzoni are two examples in the United States.[2]

---

[1] The widely influential book by Krister Stendahl, *The Bible and the Role of Women* (trans. Emilie Sander [Philadelphia: Fortress, 1966]), contained many of the arguments that persuaded liberals to ordain women, and it is amazing to see how closely these arguments parallel the arguments being made by egalitarians today (see above, pages 59-60).

[2] However, Mary Kassian notes that Virginia Ramey Mollenkott's 1977 book *Women, Men, and the Bible* (Nashville: Abingdon, 1977) was one of the four most influential early books in promoting evangelical feminism (Kassian, *The Feminist Mistake*, rev. ed. [Wheaton, Ill.: Crossway, 2005], 248). Then, a year later, Mollenkott's book with Letha Scanzoni, *Is the Homosexual My Neighbor?* (San Francisco: Harper & Row, 1978) argued for a more tolerant view of committed homosexual relationships. Today Mollenkott's personal website identifies her as a lesbian who has won several awards for promoting lesbian causes (http://www.geocities.com/vrmollenkott). And now in 2005 Letha Scanzoni, one of the first evangelical feminist authors, has publicly endorsed committed homosexual marriage: see David G. Myers and Letha Scanzoni, *What God Has Joined Together? A Christian Case for Gay Marriage* (San Francisco: HarperSanFrancisco, 2005). (See also the tragic information about professed lesbian Judy Brown, who was previously an influential egalitarian author, in chapter 13, pages 122-123, above.)

In the United Kingdom, an even more prominent example of an evangelical leader following feminist methods of biblical interpretation in his endorsement of homosexuality is Roy Clements. Until his homosexuality was made known in 1999, Roy Clements was the well-known pastor of Eden Baptist Church in Cambridge, England. He was one of the most prominent evangelical pastors in England and had a wide conference speaking ministry in the United Kingdom and in the United States. He was often compared to John Stott, and many thought he would take Stott's place as the leading evangelical preacher in the country. Then when he made it known that he was leaving his family for a homosexual relationship with another man in 1999, it sent shock waves through the evangelical community in England. Today his website promotes a homosexual agenda and he explicitly connects the reasoning of evangelical feminism to the reasoning of homosexual activists, as he makes clear the following statement:

> Christian homosexuals, who formerly would have remained "in the closet" protected by a conspiracy of sympathetic silence, have little choice but to "come out". . . . For most this has been a profoundly liberating experience, in spite of the bullying hostility to which they have often been subjected. In many ways their experience has run parallel, if a little behind, that of Christian women in the last few decades. *In the wake of the secular feminist movement, women have found a new confidence to claim a role for themselves within the church. They have developed a hermeneutic to deal with the biblical texts which had been used to deny them that role in the past.* Of course, this was not achieved without resistance from a conservative rump mainly within the older ecclesiastical establishment, but the majority of evangelicals have now moved very substantially in the direction of welcoming women into Christian leadership. *Gay Christians are using exactly the same kind of hermeneutic tools to challenge tradition in regard to homosexuality.* If it is taking them rather longer to succeed than the Christian feminists did, this has more to do with the inferiority of their numerical strength than of the justice of their cause.[3]

In the rest of this chapter I consider the recent decisions of some lib-

---

[3] From www.royclements.co.uk/essays08.htm, accessed July 18, 2006, italics added.

eral denominations regarding homosexuality, then at the end I look at two more conservative groups.

1. EPISCOPAL CHURCH

The Episcopal Church in the United States has now approved the appointment of V. Gene Robinson as its first openly homosexual bishop, by a vote of 62 to 45 in their House of Bishops.[4] As recently as 1998, this same denomination had approved a resolution calling homosexual activity "incompatible with Scripture."

Even secular newspapers noted the parallels between the homosexual ordination controversy and the earlier controversy over the ordination of women. The *New York Times* reported:

> Bishop-elect Robinson's opponents said he would bring to the broader church schism, pain and confusion. . . . Other people called the warnings overblown. Look, they said, at other controversies that were also predicted to split the church *like the ordination of women in 1976* and *the ratifying of a woman, Barbara Harris, as Bishop, in 1989.* This evening, Ms. Harris . . . said the church had survived and would once more. "I remember well the dire predictions made at the time of my election consent process," she said. "The communion, such as it is, a loose federation of autonomous provinces, has held."[5]

Conservatives who did not leave when a woman was ordained as an Episcopal priest, and who did not leave when a woman was selected as a bishop, would probably not leave at the approval of a homosexual bishop either, or so the supporters of Bishop Robinson claimed.

A day after the House of Bishops approved Robinson's appointment, the leaders of the Episcopal Church approved a "compromise" resolution at the insistence of conservatives within the denomination. The compromise allowed local dioceses the option of whether or not to bless same-sex unions in their churches.[6] But what this meant was that

---

[4] "Episcopal Church Elects First Openly Gay Bishop" (www.foxnews.com, Tuesday, August 5, 2003, accessed 8-5-03).
[5] *New York Times*, August 6, 2003, A12.
[6] "Episcopal Vote Allows Blessings of Gay Unions," www.washingtonpost.com, August 7, 2003, A-1.

the denomination as a whole was allowing any local church to give a blessing to homosexual unions (they stopped short of officially calling it homosexual "marriage").

Then in June 2006, the Episcopal Church elected Bishop Katharine Schori as the first woman presiding bishop in the history of the worldwide Anglican Communion (of which the Episcopal Church in the U.S. is a part). She said in an interview that it was not a sin to be homosexual and that "some people come into this world with affections ordered toward other people of the same gender."[7] Bishop Schori preached a sermon in praise of "Mother Jesus" shortly after she was elected.[8] The same convention refused the demands of the worldwide Anglican Communion that it "repent" of the ordination of a homosexual bishop, saying instead that it would "exercise restraint" in appointing any more gay bishops. The *Times* of London reported, "The Episcopal Church in America descended into chaos last night after leading bishops on both the liberal and conservative wings disassociated themselves from a last-gasp effort to avert a schism with the worldwide Anglican Communion."[9] It looks increasingly likely that the worldwide Anglican Communion will divide over this issue (it has already excluded the church in the U.S. from some committees and functions), and also likely that the conservative churches in the Episcopal Church in the U.S.—numbering perhaps as many as 2,000 of the 7,000 congregations in the denomination—will separate from the more liberal group and constitute a new denomination. This fracturing of the Episcopal Church is the culmination of a trend to reject the Bible's teachings on manhood and womanhood that began a few decades ago. The final end of the slippery slope is the destruction of a denomination.

2. PRESBYTERIAN CHURCH–USA

At least 113 PCUSA congregations in 30 states have designated themselves "More Light Presbyterians" (MLP). Membership in the group, which seeks "full participation of lesbian, gay, bisexual, and transgender people of faith in the life, ministry, and witness of the Presbyterian

---

[7] From a CNN interview Monday, June 19, 2006, reported at www.newsmax.com/archives/ic/2006/6/19/214551.shtml?s=ic, accessed 6/23/06.

[8] www.timesonline.co.uk/article/0,,11069-2237322.html, accessed 6.22.06.

[9] Ibid.

Church (U.S.A.)," is up 20 percent from three years ago, according to retired MLP board member Gene Ruff.[10]

In June 2006 the General Assembly of the PCUSA voted 298-221 "to let local bodies that wish to have homosexuals serve as clergy and lay officers do so, despite a denominational ban on homosexual ministers."[11] The denomination may fracture over this issue, as Richard Ostling reports that "Thirteen evangelical caucuses issued a joint statement that the assembly's actions 'throw our denomination into crisis. . . . we cannot accept, support, or tolerate it. We will take the steps necessary to be faithful to God.'"[12]

In the same national assembly, Ostling reported, the denomination voted to "receive" a policy paper that allows congregations to use gender-inclusive language for the Trinity in worship services, so that "Father, Son and Holy Spirit" "could also be known as 'Mother, Child and Womb,' or 'Rock, Redeemer and Friend.'"[13]

3. EVANGELICAL LUTHERAN CHURCH OF AMERICA

Within the Evangelical Lutheran Church of America and other denominations, similar groups are growing:

> Meanwhile, 280 churches and 21 synods in the Evangelical Lutheran Church in America (ELCA) participate in a similar program called "Reconciling in Christ" (RIC). During RIC's first 18 years, 250 congregations across North America joined, but 30 new churches have joined this year alone. Other denominations have gay-affirming programs such as the Rainbow Baptists, the Association of Welcoming

[10] "Go Forth and Sin: A Growing Mainline Movement Seeks to Affirm Homosexuality as Biblical," *World*, August 2, 2003, 20. The same issue of *World* reports the results of a similar trend in Australia: "By a large margin, the 267 delegates to the national assembly of the 1.4 million-member Uniting Church of Australia (UCA) July 17 formally approved the ordination of homosexual men and women on a local-option basis by presbyteries and congregations. Evangelical clergy and congregations immediately began heading for the exits. . . . The UCA was formed by a merger of Presbyterian, Methodist, and Congregational churches in 1977, making it the country's third-largest denomination at the time" (*World*, August 2, 2003, 23).
[11] Richard Ostling, "Presbyterian Church Lets Locals Decide on Gay Clergy," Associated Press dispatch June 21, 2006, as accessed at www.washingtontimes.com, 6-21-06.
[12] Ibid.
[13] Richard Ostling, "Presbyterians Revisit the Trinity," Associated Press dispatch June 20, 2006, as reported at www.chicagotribune.com.

and Affirming Baptists, and the United Methodist Reconciling Congregation Program.[14]

The ELCA has established a task force to formulate a recommendation regarding homosexuality, but some observers think the membership of the task force almost guarantees a liberalization of its current policy opposing homosexual activity:

> In April, the ELCA Task Force on Human Sexuality met in Chicago for its second conference. The denomination commissioned the task force "to guide" the ELCA's decision making on gay clergy and the blessing of same-sex relationships. But its expert panels may actually be a series of stacked decks. For example, task force science panelists included a pair of Lutheran clinical psychologists who offered as fact the opinion of the gay-friendly American Psychological Association: "[Sexual] orientation is not a choice, it cannot be changed, [and] efforts to attempt to modify it may even be harmful." Another science panelist cited the discredited Kinsey Report as support for legitimizing homosexuality.
>
> Roanoke College religion professor Robert Benne, a biblical conservative and task force panelist, told *World* the ELCA task force "certainly is weighted toward those who are open to revising basic teaching on homosexual relations." In addition, he said the presence of open homosexuals at every discussion "makes it difficult for folks who are uncertain or just plain nice to voice objections or even reservations about the revisionist agenda. Most church people like to be polite and accepting, so they often accept that agenda out of the desire to 'keep the peace in love.'"[15]

In August, 2005, the quadrennial Assembly of the ELCA passed an ambiguous statement that opened the door for regional bishops to endorse same-sex unions and ordinations. One proposed recommendation urged "that this church welcome gay and lesbian persons into its life, and trust pastors and congregations to discern ways to provide faithful pastoral care to same-sex couples." It was amended to replace the words "same-sex couples" with "all to whom they minister," a

---

[14] Edward E. Plowman, "Gathering Storm," *World*, May 6, 2006, 20.
[15] Ibid., 21.

retreat into ambiguity that still allows local churches and regions to make their own decisions about what it means. The resolution passed 670-323. Reporting on the decision, Edward Plowman wrote, "In effect, same-sex blessings will now be a matter of local option, depending on each bishop's ideology."[16]

The ELCA constitution still defines marriage as a relationship between a man and a woman and prohibits ordination of clergy in same-sex relationships, but it has not been uniformly enforced, and this resolution essentially guarantees it will not be enforced. A separate resolution that would have explicitly allowed for ordination of gay or lesbian clergy "in life-long, committed and faithful same-sex relationships" was defeated 490-503 (proposed as a constitutional change, it would have required a 2/3 majority to pass).[17]

4. UNITED METHODIST CHURCH

As I noted in a footnote in chapter 2, in April, 2004,

> a clergy jury in the [United Methodist Church's] Pacific Northwest regional unit voted to retain the ministerial credentials of Karen Dammann, a self-avowed lesbian who recently 'married' her partner. . . . Church members looking to their bishops for a decisive response in defense of church discipline didn't get one. In a wobbly statement, the 15-member executive committee of the UMC Council of Bishops in effect said that the bishops are committed to upholding the church's laws but what regional conferences do is their own business.[18]

The denomination's General Conference (the nationwide meeting of the denomination) does not have authority to overturn this regional decision, but when they met in May 2004 they voted 579 to 376 (61 percent to 39 percent) to affirm a policy statement against homosexual practice which said, "The United Methodist Church does not condone the practice of homosexuality and considers this practice incompatible

---

[16] Edward E. Plowman, "Lutheran Retreat," *World*, August 27, 2005 (www.worldmag.com, accessed 5-1-06).
[17] Ibid.
[18] Edward E. Plowman, "None of Our Business," *World*, April 17, 2004, quoted from www.worldmag.com/world/issue/04-17-04/national_5.asp.

with Christian teaching," and they voted 674 to 262 (72 percent to 28 percent) to retain a ban on the ordination and placement of practicing homosexuals as ministers.[19] The votes show significant minorities in the General Conference (somewhere around one-third) advocating the approval of homosexuality, but these vote margins suggest that they are unlikely to win majority approval in the near future.

5. AMERICAN BAPTIST CHURCHES

Religion writer Edward Plowman reported that the 1.5 million member American Baptist Churches (U.S.A.) "has a strong position on homosexual practice as incompatible with Scripture. But its liberal-dominated governing board has blocked all efforts to enforce the policy on member churches on grounds Baptist churches are autonomous, don't have creeds, and have the right to interpret the Bible as they wish."[20] Plowman predicted that the denomination "will fracture" over this issue in the summer of 2006.[21]

In fact, Plowman's prediction proved correct in May 2006, when "The governing board of one of its largest and most thriving regional units, the American Baptist Churches of the Pacific Southwest, voted unanimously to withdraw from the ABCUSA."[22] This action removed some 300 churches in Southern California, Arizona, northern Nevada, and Hawaii. The article added that "The American Baptist Evangelicals renewal group, reportedly representing some 500 churches, recently announced that there is no hope left for Bible-based renewal of the ABCUSA; leaders disbanded it . . ."[23] Other regions are considering withdrawing as well, and it appears the denomination may soon be only a shell of its former self. The end of the slippery slope is the destruction of a denomination.

6. CHRISTIAN REFORMED CHURCH

Nor is this movement confined to liberal denominations. The Christian Reformed Church (CRC) is still thought to be largely evangelical, and it was only in 1995 that the CRC approved the ordination of women.

---

[19] Edward E. Plowman, "Four More Years," *World*, May 22, 2004, quoted from www.world mag.com/world/issue/05-22-04/national_5.asp.
[20] Edward E. Plowman, "Mainline Mess," *World*, January 14, 2006, 28.
[21] Ibid.
[22] "Cracked Foundation," *World*, June 10, 2006, 72.
[23] Ibid.

But now the First Christian Reformed Church in Toronto has "opened church leadership to practicing homosexual members 'living in committed relationships,' a move that the denomination expressly prohibits."[24]

In addition, Calvin College in Grand Rapids, Michigan, the college of the Christian Reformed Church, has increasingly allowed expressions of support for homosexuals to be evident on its campus. *World* magazine reports:

> Calvin has since 2002 observed something called "Ribbon Week," during which heterosexual students wear ribbons to show their support for those who desire to sleep with people of the same sex. Calvin President Gaylen Byker . . . [said], ". . . homosexuality is qualitatively different from other sexual sin. It is a disorder," not chosen by the person. Having Ribbon Week, he said, "is like having cerebral palsy week."
>
> Pro-homosexuality material has crept into Calvin's curriculum. . . . At least some Calvin students have internalized the school's thinking on homosexuality. . . . In January, campus newspaper editor Christian Bell crossed swords with Gary Glenn, president of the American Family Association's Michigan chapter, and an ardent foe of legislation that gives special rights to homosexuals. . . . In an e-mail exchange with Mr. Glenn before his visit, Mr. Bell called him "a hate-mongering, homophobic bigot . . . from a documented hate group." Mr. Bell later issued a public apology.[25]

This article on Calvin College in *World* generated a barrage of pro and con letters to the editor in the following weeks, all of which can still be read online.[26] Many writers expressed appreciation for a college like Calvin that is open to the expression of different viewpoints but still

---

[24] "Reformed Congregation OKs Gay Leaders," *Christianity Today*, December 9, 2002, 19.
[25] Lynn Vincent, "Shifting Sand?" *World*, May 10, 2003, 41-42.
[26] See www.worldmag.com. A search for the phrase "Calvin College" turned up letters in the "Mailbag" section of *World* for June 7, June 14, June 21, June 28, and July 3, 2003. Calvin's president, Gaylen Byker, posted a response to the *World* article on the Calvin website under "Calvin News" for May 2003; see www.calvin.edu/news/releases/2002_03/calvin_letter.htm. He defends the diversity of the campus as well as its steadfast Christian orientation and academic excellence. He also says that the *World* article failed to give a balanced representation of the entirety of the college campus, which is excellent in many ways. Regarding homosexuality, he says, "Despite what *World*'s story might lead people to believe, homosexuality is not a preoccupation on Calvin's campus. We are working as a college to follow the call of our denomi-

maintains a clear Christian commitment. No one claimed the quotes in the article were inaccurate, but some claimed they did not give a balanced view. Some letters from current and recent students confirmed the essential accuracy of the *World* article, such as this one:

> I commend Lynn Vincent for writing "Shifting sand?" (May 10). As a sophomore at Calvin, I have been exposed firsthand to the changing of Calvin's foundation. Being a transfer student, I was not fully aware of the special events like "Ribbon Week." I asked a classmate what her purple ribbon meant and she said it's a sign of acceptance of all people. I later found out that "all people" meant gays, lesbians, and bisexuals. I have been appalled by posters advertising a support group for GLBs (as they are called) around campus. God condemned the practice, so why cannot God's judgment against GLB be proclaimed at Calvin? I am glad Calvin's lack of the morals it was founded on is being made known to the Christian community outside of Calvin. Much prayer and action is needed if a change is to take place.—Katie Wagenmaker, Coopersville, Mich.[27]

Then in June 2004, the Christian Reformed Church named as the editor of *Banner,* its denominational magazine, the Rev. Robert De

---

nation's Synod (the Christian Reformed Church's highest ruling body) which in 1999 said the entire denomination is 'called as a Church to repent for our failures' in this area. 'Ribbon Week' is one way of reaching out with love and compassion to Calvin students who are gay. . . ." He goes on to affirm that homosexual conduct is wrong. Interested persons may read the letter themselves and notice both what he says and what he does not say about the positions that are advocated on the campus. In another letter responding to the *World* article, professor Quentin Schultze says, "The fact is that the Christian Reformed Church, which 'owns and operates' Calvin College, has encouraged the entire denomination to love gays and lesbians even while not accepting the sinful practices of some of them" (quoted from http://www.calvin.edu/news/releases/2002_03/schultze_letter.htm, accessed 10-24-03).

His expression "the sinful practices of some of them" seems consistent with the picture of Calvin College indicated by the other quotations in the article: The repeated theme is that there are some people who just "are" gays and lesbians, and if they refrain from putting their same-sex inclinations into practice, our attitude toward them should be one of love and acceptance. Hence, the campus-wide week-long emphasis on raising student awareness of gays' and lesbians' need for acceptance and support.

At one level, who can object to showing love and support for any other human being? However, at another level, one suspects a larger agenda here on the part of homosexual rights advocates, an agenda of gaining acceptance by degrees. What would we think of a Christian campus, for example, that sponsored a week-long campaign to show acceptance and support of people who had lustful and adulterous desires, or were alcoholics, or were addicted to gambling, or were always tempted to lie or curse, or who struggled with constant greed or envy? It seems from reading these comments from Calvin faculty, administrators, and students, that homosexuality is being made into a special cause at Calvin.

[27] "Mailbag," *World,* June 7, 2003 (www.worldmag.com, accessed 10-23-03).

Moor, who had earlier written an editorial supporting legal recognition for homosexuals as "domestic partners." The CRC's position paper on homosexuality states, "Christian homosexuals, like all Christians, are called to discipleship, to holy obedience, and to the use of their gifts in the cause of the kingdom. Opportunities to serve within the offices and the life of the congregation should be afforded to them as they are to heterosexual Christians."[28]

This does not indicate that the Christian Reformed Church has approved of homosexual activity (it has not), but it does indicate the existence of a significant struggle within the denomination, and the likelihood of more to come.

7. FULLER SEMINARY

In 1999 InterVarsity Press (USA) published *Authentic Human Sexuality* by Fuller Theological Seminary professors Judith K. Balswick and Jack O. Balswick.[29] In the chapter on homosexuality the Balswicks say that "it is not surprising that vastly different positions are taken by Christians within and between denominations,"[30] and then the two "centralist" positions they report are "Accept homosexuality in committed relationships" and "Homosexual is responsible to change."[31]

The Balswicks say that chapter 5 will "focus on the specific biblical references relevant to homosexuality,"[32] but in chapter 5 when they consider the key biblical passages on homosexuality (Genesis 19; Lev. 18:22 and 20:13; 1 Cor. 6:9-10; 1 Tim. 1:10; and Rom. 1:26-27), in each case they summarize only the standard pro-homosexual interpretation of those passages without giving any response or any alternative interpretation that would support the view that all homosexual conduct is wrong. The Balswicks tell us the following things about those passages: The sin of Sodom in Genesis 19 was "despicable gang rape . . . rather than homosexual behavior per se" (90-91). Leviticus forbids homosexual behavior but "there are other parts of the Holiness Codes that are

[28] Jeff Robinson, "Christian Reformed Church Approves Editor Despite Sympathies for Gay Unions," accessed on 3-5-06, at www.gender-news.com/article.php?id=24.

[29] Judith K. Balswick and Jack O. Balswick, *Authentic Human Sexuality: An Integrated Christian Approach* (Downers Grove, Ill.: InterVarsity, 1999).

[30] Ibid., 89.

[31] Ibid., 93.

[32] Ibid., 89.

no longer observed in today's world, because of Paul's teachings about our newfound freedom in Christ" (91). Moreover, 1 Corinthians 6:9-10 "refers specifically to sexual relationships between men and boys, which would be a coercive and perverted relationship" (91), and 1 Timothy 1:10 shows "that it is the power differential of these sexual acts that make them despicable" and "taking a power advantage over another is the perversion that is rightly condemned here" (92). And concerning Romans 1:26-27, "For some theologians, unnatural refers to perverse and hedonistic sexual practices, *not* the mutually loving interaction that occurs between same-sex consenting adults. Therefore it is argued that the persons with a homosexual orientation are *not* going against *natural* tendencies" (92, italics in original).

They go on to mention "the high view of scriptural authority held by many of the founders of the gay church" (94) and they give an extended and sympathetic summary of the decision of Mel White, former Fuller professor, to leave his family and pursue a homosexual lifestyle. They quote his former wife as saying, "Mel had no choice about being a homosexual" (95). They say, "No one is to blame, Mel asserts; he believes homosexual orientation is part of God's plan" (95). The Balswicks do not give one word of disagreement with any of this positive assessment.

While at the end of the chapter they say that they personally find the Genesis account of God's creation of male and female "persuades us to uphold the male and female union as God's intended design for authentic sexual union" (101), they follow that by saying that because of the fall "none of us achieves sexual wholeness in accordance with God's highest ideals" and that some people "have natural attraction for a same-sex partner" (101). They conclude,

> We acknowledge that some gay Christians may choose to commit themselves to a lifelong, monogamous homosexual union, believing this is God's best for them. They believe that this reflects an authentic sexuality that is congruent for them and their view of Scripture. Even though we hold to the model of a heterosexual, lifelong, monogamous union, our compassion brings us to support all persons as they move in the direction of God's ideal for their lives.[33]

---

[33] Ibid., 102.

While not personally endorsing lifelong homosexual relationships as morally legitimate, the Balswicks also carefully avoid saying that committed homosexual relationships are wrong. While they say they hold to a heterosexual "model," this is simply stated as their personal preference, and the chapter as a whole gives much greater argument and support for the view that committed homosexual relationships can be legitimately defended from Scripture and may be God's will for people who naturally have a homosexual "orientation." In response to that same quotation from the Balswicks' book, *World* magazine founder Joel Belz wrote, "If that isn't an explicit example of relativism at work, I'm not sure I'd ever know one."[34]

A Fuller student who took a gender/sexuality class from the Balswicks in the spring of 2006 reported that on the day that the class was scheduled to discuss the morality of homosexuality the Balswicks brought in a pro-homosexual guest lecturer for the entire class period. This student wrote to me,

> If there was any doubt about the agenda of the class it was made clear today. I sat through the most liberal, leftist, sad, theologically bankrupt lecture on homosexuality this morning. . . . According to the schedule this was the last class time devoted to the issue. . . . pray that God will change the hearts and minds of those in authority at Fuller Theological Seminary."[35]

This does not indicate that everyone at Fuller Seminary is now advocating the moral legitimacy of homosexuality in committed lifelong relationships. But this class clearly promoted that view. And it does indicate that the seminary is allowing steps to be taken in that direction, and it suggests further movement in that direction yet to come.

The approval of homosexuality is the final step along the path to liberalism.

---

[34] Joel Belz, "Relativism at Fuller," *World*, July 1, 2006, 8.
[35] Private e-mail from Kim Livesay to the author April 18, 2006, quoted by permission.

SOME COMPLEMENTARIANS HELP EVANGELICAL FEMINISTS BY BEING HARSH, MEAN, OR ABUSIVE

At this point many readers may be deeply troubled by what they see going on in the evangelical feminist movement. And that deep concern may lead some to respond to evangelical feminists with harshness or meanness of spirit, or even in some situations there may be some kind of abuse.

This is never right.

Paul tells Timothy,

> And the Lord's servant must not be quarrelsome but kind to everyone, able to teach, patiently enduring evil, *correcting his opponents with gentleness.* God may perhaps grant them repentance leading to a knowledge of the truth . . . (2 Tim. 2:24-25).

No matter how seriously we differ with other brothers and sisters in Christ, we must continue to treat them with kindness and love. We must continue to report their positions truthfully, without distortion or misrepresentation.

A number of egalitarian leaders today grew up in some extremely strict, harsh, even oppressive environments that taught "male headship" from the Bible but did so without love or without respect and honor for the equal value of women in our churches and before God, and without promoting and honoring the valuable ministries of women in their church. If you support what I say in this book, I ask you, please be careful not to make the same mistake as others have made and thereby drive other gifted women into the egalitarian camp.[1]

---

[1] See further the section "A Strategy for Complementarians" and the section following it in Wayne Grudem, *Evangelical Feminism and Biblical Truth* (Sisters, Ore.: Multnomah, 2004), 532-536.

SOME COMPLEMENTARIANS HELP EVANGELICAL FEMINISTS BY BEING COWARDLY OR SILENT

Another ally of egalitarianism is a large group of Christian leaders who believe that the Bible teaches a complementarian position but who lack courage to teach about it or take a stand in favor of it. They are silent, "passive complementarians" who, in the face of relentless egalitarian pressure to change their organizations, simply give in more and more to appease a viewpoint they privately believe the Bible does not teach.

This is similar to the situation conservatives in liberal denominations face regarding homosexuality, where too many people who think it is wrong will not take a stand. As mentioned above, Robert Benne, member of the task force on homosexuality in the Evangelical Lutheran Church in America said, the presence of open homosexuals at every discussion

> makes it difficult for folks who are uncertain or just plain nice to voice objections or even reservations about the revisionist agenda. Most church people like to be polite and accepting, so they often accept that agenda out of the desire to "keep the peace in love."[1]

One of the leaders who helped conservatives retake control of the Southern Baptist Convention after a struggle of many years told me pri-

---

[1] *World*, August 2, 2003, 21.

vately, "Our biggest problem in this struggle was not the 'moderates' who opposed us. Our biggest problem was conservatives who agreed with us and refused to say anything or take a stand to support us."

How different was the ministry of the apostle Paul! He did not lack courage to stand up for unpopular teachings of God's Word. When he met with the elders of the church at Ephesus and recounted his three-year ministry among them, he was able to say with a clear conscience, "Therefore I testify to you this day that I am innocent of the blood of all of you, for I did not shrink from declaring to you the whole counsel of God" (Acts 20:26-27).

The word "for" indicates that Paul was giving the reason why he was "innocent of the blood of all of you." He said he would not be accountable before God for any failures in the church at Ephesus because he "did not shrink from declaring" to them *the whole counsel of God."* He did not hold back from teaching something just because it was unpopular. He did not hold back from teaching something because it would have created opposition and struggle and conflict. In good conscience he proclaimed everything that God's Word taught on every topic, whether popular or not. He proclaimed "the whole counsel of God." And he stood before God blameless for his stewardship of the ministry to the Ephesian church.

If the apostle Paul were alive today, planting churches and overseeing leaders in those churches, would he counsel them to shrink back from speaking and teaching clearly about biblical roles for men and women? Would he counsel them to shrink back from giving a clear testimony of God's will concerning one of the most disputed and yet most urgent topics in our entire society? Would he tell pastors simply to be silent about this topic so that there could be "peace in our time" in our churches, and so that the resolution of the controversy would be left for others at another time and another place?

When Paul began to preach that people did not have to be circumcised in order to follow Christ, great persecution resulted, and his Jewish opponents pursued him from city to city, at one point even stoning him and leaving him for dead (Acts 14:19-23). But Paul did not compromise on the gospel of *salvation by faith alone in Christ alone*, rather than *salvation by faith plus circumcision*. And when Paul later wrote to some of those very churches where he had been persecuted and even stoned and left for dead, he insisted on the purity of the gospel that he had proclaimed and said, "For am I now seeking the approval of man, or of God? Or am I trying to please man? If I were still trying to please man, I would not be a servant of Christ" (Gal. 1:10).

It is important for church leaders—in fact for all Christians—to ask themselves this same question.

35

PLACES WHERE EVANGELICAL FEMINISM ALREADY HAS MUCH INFLUENCE

As I look at the churches and parachurch organizations in the evangelical world in the United States today I see several organizations where an evangelical feminist position is the dominant position and in some cases the only position allowed to be advocated in the organization.[1] It is those institutions that I hope will turn back from the direction in which they are headed.

Among colleges, the evangelical feminist position is the dominant position at Wheaton College, Azusa Pacific University, and several other Christian colleges.

Among seminaries, evangelical feminism is the only position allowed at Fuller Seminary, and it is strongly represented on the faculty at Denver Seminary, Gordon-Conwell Seminary, Bethel Seminary, Asbury Seminary, and Regent College–Vancouver. Even among seminaries that are committed to a complementarian position, some have begun hiring women to teach Bible and theology classes to men, arguing that "we are not a church" (see discussion in chapter 11 above).[2] But

---

[1] For more information on these organizations, see Grudem, *Evangelical Feminism and Biblical Truth* (Sisters, Ore.: Multnomah, 2004), 521-524.

[2] For example, Dallas Theological Seminary has one woman faculty member, Dorian Coover-Cox, who teaches Old Testament. Reformed Theological Seminary–Orlando in the spring of 2006 had a woman, Carolyn Custis James (wife of seminary president Frank James) teach an Old Testament class on the book of Ruth for both men and women (see www2.rts.edu/new-sevents/newsdetails.aspx?news_id=790, accessed Feb. 20, 2006). I am thankful for the excellent ministries of these seminaries over many years, and they are still predominantly complementarian, and I still recommend them to students. However, I differ with this policy, for the reasons I explain in chapter 11 above.

it seems to me that having a woman teach the Bible to men is doing just what Paul said not to do in 1 Timothy 2:12. And I don't think such a position will remain stable for very long, but will lead to further movement in an egalitarian direction. This is because it will be very difficult to explain why a woman can teach the Bible to men in a seminary on Monday but cannot teach the same passage to the same men in a church on Sunday—on the surface it seems inconsistent. And it will be difficult to answer the argument, "If a woman can train hundreds of pastors to preach, surely she herself should be able to preach!" I think most Christians will reason that, if we allow the one, surely we can allow the other. So I personally expect that seminaries who hire women as Bible professors will move in a more egalitarian direction in a few years. I hope I am wrong.[3]

Among book publishers, the largest number of evangelical feminist books are being published by InterVarsity Press[4] and Baker Books.

Among popular journals, both *Charisma* magazine under the editorship of J. Lee Grady and *Christianity Today* under the leadership of David Neff clearly favor an evangelical feminist position (though *Christianity Today* has made some attempts to represent both sides fairly).

Among parachurch ministries, InterVarsity Christian Fellowship is strongly committed to an evangelical feminist position, as is Youth With A Mission. The Lausanne Committee on World Evangelization is apparently now dominated by a thoroughgoing evangelical feminist

---

[3] As I explained more fully elsewhere, I think it is consistent to distinguish between teaching *skills* and teaching *Bible*. I can agree that teaching beginning language courses (such as Greek or Hebrew) is more teaching a skill than teaching Bible, and I think it is possible to understand the teaching of missions or counseling in this way as well (it is primarily teaching a skill, not primarily teaching Bible in the sense that Paul had in mind in 1 Tim. 2:12). See Wayne Grudem, *Evangelical Feminism and Biblical Truth*, 84-101, 384-392.

[4] Sadly, InterVarsity Press (USA, not UK) has published other books that move in a more liberal direction, such as *Authentic Human Sexuality*, by Judith and Jack Balswick, which says that "Accept homosexuality in committed relationships" is a "centrist" position, and it is the position they give much more support for in their discussion (see pages 247-249 above). IVP-USA has also published *Recovering the Scandal of the Cross*, by Joel Green (Downers Grove, Ill.: InterVarsity Press, 2000), which argues against the penal substitutionary view of the atonement (see pages 30-32, 91-97, and 132-133), a doctrine at the heart of the gospel. And it has published books advocating "open theism," the view that God does not know the future choices of human beings: see *The Openness of God*, edited by Clark Pinnock *et al.* (Downers Grove, Ill.: InterVarsity Press, 1994), and *The God Who Risks*, by John Sanders (Downers Grove, Ill.: InterVarsity Press, 1998).

viewpoint, at least according to their 2004 "Lausanne Occasional Paper No. 53: Empowering Women and Men to Use Their Gifts Together in Advancing the Gospel."[5] The paper was edited by Alvera Mickelsen, founding chair of the board of Christians for Biblical Equality, and includes significant contributions from egalitarian author Kevin Giles and CBE executive director Mimi Haddad, but no input from complementarian writers. Sadly, the authors did not deem it necessary even to give readers access to an alternative position: the bibliography given "for further reading" (106-107) lists over twenty evangelical feminist books, but not one complementarian book, and only the CBE website is given for more information (108, 112). When the complementarian position is summarized in eight points (92-93), the paper makes such absurd statements as the claim that the complementarian view of men and women is "completely novel" (92) and that "Never before in the history of the church has anyone suggested that this is what the Bible teaches" (93).

Among denominations that are not already egalitarian, there are strong egalitarian components in the Baptist General Conference and the Association of Vineyard Churches,[6] and among large numbers of independent charismatic churches. In addition, evangelical feminism is the only position allowed at Willow Creek Community Church, and it is strongly promoted through the Willow Creek Association.

But the fountainhead of all evangelical feminist influence is the organization Christians for Biblical Equality, based in Minneapolis.

One telltale sign that a church or organization is moving in an egalitarian direction is often the use of a gender-neutral Bible (such as the

---

[5] Accessed June 23, 2006 at www.lausanne.org/lcwe/assets/LOP53_IG24.pdf.

[6] More specifically, about five years ago the Board of Directors of the Association of Vineyard Churches agreed that the question of the ordination of women "should be settled in each local church as they endeavor to live under the Lordship of Jesus Christ" (see www.vineyardusa.org/publications/positionpapers.aspx, accessed 6-23-06). But then in early 2006 the board adopted guidelines that will likely begin to force complementarian pastors out of the denomination. The guidelines say, "Those who do not believe women should be senior pastors should not show disrespect to women speakers or women pastors in any of the gatherings. They should bless these women . . ." (quoted in Jeff Robinson, "Vineyard Ministries Moves Toward Accepting Both Views of Female Pastors," May 16, 2006, at www.gender-news.com/article.php?id=121, accessed 6/23/06). It will be difficult for people who think women pastors are disobeying God by serving as pastors to "bless" them in that activity. How can I in good conscience bless someone who I think is directly disobeying God's Word? This is the most recent example of a pattern in which the evangelical feminist view first seeks acceptance as a permitted option but soon moves to exclude all other views.

TNIV or NRSV). Such translations water down several verses that teach male leadership in the church. The TNIV, for example, in updating the NIV, consistently makes questionable changes that favor an egalitarian position: it changes the "men" who will arise from the elders at Ephesus to "some will arise" (Acts 20:30); makes Phoebe a "deacon" (Rom. 16:1); makes Junia to be "outstanding among the apostles," with no marginal note of any alternative translations (Rom. 16:7); disconnects the phrase "As in all the congregations of the Lord's people" from the statement, "women should remain silent in the churches" (1 Cor. 14:33-34); and changes the requirements for an elder from "husband of but one wife" to "faithful to his wife" (Titus 1:6), thus changing the noun "husband" for the verb "faithful" and making it easier to argue that it is the quality of "faithfulness," not actually being a husband (or a man), that Paul thinks important.

In 1 Timothy 2:12 the TNIV adopts a highly suspect and novel translation that gives the egalitarian side everything they have wanted for years in a Bible translation. It reads, "I do not permit a woman to teach or to *assume authority* over a man" (italics added). If churches adopt this translation, the debate over women's roles in the church will be over, because women pastors and elders can just say, "I'm not *assuming* authority on my own initiative; it was given to me by the other pastors and elders." Therefore any woman could be a pastor or elder so long as she does not take it upon herself to "assume authority." In the footnotes to this verse the TNIV introduces so many alternative translations that the verse will just seem confusing and impossible to understand. It is no surprise that egalitarian churches are eager to adopt the TNIV (see also page 224, above).

I hope I am wrong in my prediction that the pressures and arguments of evangelical feminism will push these organizations in a more liberal direction in the coming years. But if I am right, and if the historical pattern continues, then we will see these organizations moving more and more in a liberal direction in the coming years as they increasingly adopt methods of interpretation that undermine or deny the authority of the Bible. I encourage readers to pray that that would not happen in any of these institutions.

36

WHAT IS ULTIMATELY AT STAKE: THE BIBLE

As I have spent more and more time analyzing egalitarian arguments, I have become more firmly convinced that egalitarianism is becoming a new path to liberalism for evangelicals in our generation.

The pioneers of evangelical feminism are liberal denominations. A number of the arguments now being used by evangelical egalitarians were used by these liberal denominations when they were approving the ordination of women. Many of the current leaders of the egalitarian movement either advocate positions that undermine the authority of Scripture or at least advertise and promote books that undermine the authority of Scripture and lead believers toward liberalism. The hints we now have of the doctrinal direction in which evangelical feminism is moving predict an increasing emphasis on an abolition of anything that is distinctly masculine. Egalitarianism is heading toward an androgynous Adam and a Jesus whose manhood is not important. It is heading toward a God who is both Father and Mother, and then only Mother. And soon the same methods of evading the teachings of Scripture on manhood and womanhood will be used, once again, by those who advocate the moral legitimacy of homosexuality.

The common denominator in all of this is a persistent undermining of the authority of Scripture in our lives. And thus my conclusion at the end of this study is that evangelical feminism is relentlessly leading Christians down the path to liberalism.

At this point someone may object, "But aren't there evangelical feminists who don't adopt any of these arguments you have listed? At the beginning of every chapter you have said, '*Some* evangelical feminists . . .' Doesn't this imply that there are *other* evangelical feminists who don't adopt any of these arguments?"

My response is that I do not know of any.

Of course nobody adopts *all* of the arguments I have listed, because a number of them are mutually exclusive.[1] But every evangelical feminist author I know of adopts at least some of the arguments I have listed in this book, and most of them adopt a number of these arguments.

Moreover, these arguments are widely promoted by the egalitarian advocacy group Christians for Biblical Equality,[2] and they are widely represented in the most recent and most comprehensive statement of the egalitarian position, the book *Discovering Biblical Equality.*[3]

As explained at the beginning of this book, I am not saying that all egalitarians are liberals, or are moving toward liberalism. But I am saying that the *arguments* used by egalitarians actually undermine the authority of Scripture again and again, and in so doing they are leading the church step by step toward liberalism. Today some egalitarians have only taken one step in that direction and have gone no further. But a number of younger egalitarian leaders have gone further (as in calling God our Mother), and the next generation will go further, for that is the direction toward which evangelical feminism inevitably leads. Those who adopt an evangelical feminist position "buy into" an interlocking system of interpretation that will relentlessly erode the authority of Scripture in our churches.

Which will we choose? Will we follow faithfully in the path of life-

[1] For example, the "trajectory hermeneutics" advocates argue that Paul taught male headship for his day, but that should not be our standard today. But those who argue that "head" in Ephesians 5:23 means "source" or that "exercise authority" in 1 Timothy 2:12 means "misuse authority" think that Paul did not even require male elders in his day. In general, if egalitarians think the New Testament commands *are* binding on us today, they hold that the New Testament did not require male headship even for that time. But if they think the New Testament commands *are not* binding on us today, then they tend to admit that the New Testament taught male headship in the home and the church for its time.
[2] See www.cbeinternational.org.
[3] Ronald W. Pierce and Rebecca Merrill Groothuis, eds., *Discovering Biblical Equality* (Downers Grove, Ill.: InterVarsity Press, 2004), which I have cited frequently in this book.

long obedience to all the teachings of the Word of God, believing that that is the only path to true blessing?

Or will we turn aside to evangelical feminism and be led step by step down the path to liberalism and to an ever-increasing denial of the authority of the Word of God?

GENERAL INDEX

SCRIPTURE INDEX

SCRIPTURE INDEX